Conversations on Communication Ethics

COMMUNICATION AND INFORMATION SCIENCE

Edited by
Brenda Dervin
The Ohio State University

Recent Titles

Laurien Alexandre • The Voice of America: From Detente to the Reagan Doctrine
Bruce Austin • Current Research in Film, Volume 5
Barbara Bate & Anita Taylor • Women Communicating: Studies of Women's Talk
Donal Carbaugh • Talking American: Cultural Discourses on Donahue
Kathryn Carter & Carole Spitzack • Doing Research on Women's Communication: Perspectives on Theory and Method
Fred L. Casmir • Communication in Development
Gladys Ganley & Oswald Ganley • To Inform or to Control Revised Editon
Robert Goldman & Arvind Rajagopal • Mapping Hegemony: Television News Coverage of Industrial Conflict
Enrique Gonzalez-Manet • The Hidden War of Information
Karen Joy Greenberg • Conversations on Communications Ethics
Gary Gumpert & Sandra Fish • Talking to Strangers: Mediated Therapeutic Communication
Robert Jacobson • An "Open" Approach to Information Policymaking
Manfred Kochen • The Small World
John Lawrence and Bernard Timberg • Fair Use and Free Inquiry Second Edition
Sven B. Lundstedt • Telecommunications, Values, and the Public Interest
Thomas Mandeville • Understanding Novelty: Information Technological Changes and the Patent System
Richard Morris & Peter Ehrenhaus • Cultural Legacies of Vietnam: Uses of the Past in the Present
Susan B. Neuman • Literacy in the Television Age
Eli M. Noam & Joel C. Millonzi • The International Market in Film and Television Programs
Eli M. Noam & Gerald Pogorel • Asymmetric Deregulation: The Dynamics of Telecommunication Policy
Gerald M. Phillips • Teaching How to Work in Groups
Carl Erik Rosengren & Sven Windahl • Media Matter: TV Use in Childhood and Adolescence
Michael Rogers Rubin • Private Rights, Public Wrongs: The Computer and Personal Privacy
Ramona R. Rush & Donna Allen • Communications at the Crossroads: The Gender Gap Connection
Majid Tehranian • Technologies of Power: Information Machines and Democratic Processes
Sari Thomas • Studies in Mass Media and Technology, Volumes 1–4
J. M. Wober • Fission and Diffusion: The Possibility of Public Power Over and Through the Machine

Conversations on Communication Ethics

edited by

Karen Joy Greenberg

ABLEX PUBLISHING CORPORATION
NORWOOD, NEW JERSEY

Library of Congress Cataloging-in-Publication Data

Conversations on communication ethics / Karen Joy Greenberg, editor.
p. cm.
Includes bibliographical references and index.
ISBN 0-89391-656-0
1. Communication—Moral and ethical aspects. I. Greenberg, Karen Joy.
P64.C59 1990
170—dc20 90-49965
CIP

Ablex Publishing Corporation
355 Chestnut Street
Norwood, New Jersey 07648

Conversations on Communication Ethics is dedicated to Michael Greenberg, without whose support it would not have been possible.

Table of Contents

Acknowledgments

I wish to thank Barbara Bernstein and Brenda Dervin for their direction; Richard L. Johannesen for his encouragement; Kenneth E. Andersen, Vernon E. Cronen, and Ray E. McKerrow for their support; Stephen W. Littlejohn and J. Michael Sproule for their candor; J. Vernon Jensen, Kenneth E. Andersen, Vernon E. Cronen, Ronald C. Arnett, Frederick J. Antczak, Josina M. Makau, J. Michael Sproule, Robert A. White, and Samuel M. Edelman for their scholarship; and Michael Greenberg for his hugs.

Foreword

It is said that during World War II, Prime Minister Winston Churchill presided at British Cabinet sessions by giving stirring orations, lengthy monologues, with little being heard from the others. But when he was absent and the Deputy Prime Minister, Clement Attlee, presided, the latter viewed a cabinet session as a process of "collecting voices," and while considerably less enthralling, the sessions saw more participation and more efficient decision making.

This volume is a collection of voices, not a coherent pronouncement of dogma. While lectures, discussions, and writings on the subject of ethics sometimes become stirring monologues, with an explicit or subtle bias, this book brings a wider and less doctrinaire message. What holds it together is the premise that indeed the subject of ethics in communication is extremely important and needs to be studied and discussed.

Like any stimulating conversation, this volume roams over a broad terrain, showing us various scenes and the same scene from various places of view. Like most conversations, it is part advocacy, part exposition, and part inquiry. The chapters are fed by insights and information not only from communication, but also from history, philosophy, religion, literature, and psychology. We are transported from the ancient to the contemporary, from Aristotle to Bok. An historical survey of communication ethics shows the length and magnitude of the subject, and a bibliographical survey of 20th-century scholarship on communication ethics shows the breadth and depth of the work to date. Abundant footnotes and helpful bibliographies throughout show us the multiple avenues open for further exploration. The volume is at once theoretical and practical. This wide landscape, then, lays before us ethical concerns for the communication researcher, teacher, student, practitioner, and critic. All will find some fresh insight, new information, and considerable challenge and guidance.

This is a timely book. The general public in recent years has been stirred to worry about ethics as a result of scandals in government, influence peddling, Pentagon waste, insider trading, exposes by whistleblowers, life and death issues in health care, raping of the environment, televangelist escapades, and media manipulations. Partially in response to these happenings and motivated by a desire to explore the place of values in the educational enterprise, colleges and universities across the country have generated a host of applied ethics courses in the last decade in professional schools of medicine, law, business, journalism, and engineering, and in liberal arts areas, such as philosophy, political science, and communication. Research increasingly reports that moral development is not confined to early youth as some earlier research had contended, that moral values indeed *can* be taught successfully at the college and university level, and that moral sensitivity can be transferred into application outside the classroom.

Interdisciplinary ethics seminars are developing. Academic conventions have seen an increasing number of papers and panels on ethics. Journal articles on communication ethics have been increasing, and journals devoted to ethics have been created, such as the *Journal of Mass Communication Ethics*, and in 1988, the newly formed Josephson Institute's *Ethics: Easier Said Than Done*. A number of journals and magazines devoted to business ethics have appeared since 1982. Funded in large part by generous alumni, programs in business ethics are being created, for example, at the Harvard Business School and at the University of Minnesota's Carlson School of Management, where a new prestigious Chair in Corporate Responsibility has just been filled. Corporations are increasingly arranging off-site ethics seminars, which permit concentrated reflection on the subject. Centers for the study of ethics in business, medicine, and mass media have been springing up around the country, usually aided by generous benefactors. Codes of ethics are mushrooming, as are ombudsmen and ethics committees (especially in hospitals). Public programs on ethics are increasingly appearing in local committees and in national media, including Fred Friendly's landmark PBS 10-part television series, "Ethics in America," aired early in 1989. An increasing number of newsletters are being sent to enlarging mailing lists of interested people.

Bibliographies on ethics are increasingly becoming available. Books dealing with ethics centrally or in large part are increasingly being published, and the recent provocative volume, *The Company We Keep: An Ethics of Fiction*, by the distinguished rhetorical and literary scholar, Wayne C. Booth, adds glitter to the list. Thus, *Conversations on Communication Ethics* comes at an opportune moment, adding another pioneering effort toward greater ethical sensitivity.

This volume converses with us on a host of ethical concerns in communication. We grapple with the tension between relativistic and absolute ethics, between ends and means, between the "is" and the "ought," and between private and public goals. How do we balance reason and emotion? What are the sources for our ethical standards? What is the place for value propositions in collegiate debate, and how can we best employ ethical guidelines in rhetorical criticism? What of the presence of two-valued orientation—"God" terms and "devil" terms? What are the effects of a given communicative act, both immediate and long range, on whom and with what significance? Specifically, what is the effect of the entertainment component of our culture, especially the movie industry and television? Cable television, computers, and satellite technology come into our conversation. Not only are we concerned here with ethics for individual rhetors, but also with communicating in small groups or in larger organizational frameworks. We are given glimpses of the pervasiveness and power of modern institutional communication, special interest groups, public relations, and advertising. We are led to worry about the access to the mass media. Who has the power to generate, house, and disseminate information? How responsibly do they use that power? Are the power-full increasingly strengthened and the power-less inevitably weakened? How does freedom of the press and fairness in reporting fare in today's world? Is the credibility gap between government and the governed dangerously wide? We are reminded of the need for intercultural sensitivity and the need for tolerance—crucial ingredients in today's compressed world. We view intolerance in action as we become better informed of Arab-Israeli rhetoric. We are reminded that ethical responsibility rests with the receiver as well as with the rhetor as the circular transaction which is communication unfolds.

It is relatively easy to discuss ethics and hurl accusations in the third or second person: "They . . ." or "You . . ." But the real struggle and the real significant discourse is in the first person: "*I* . . . (have fallen short). . . ." Self-examination is the beginning of meaningful growth, and a large part of that introspection is knowing how multiple motives lead us to decision making. We need to agonize along with the late Dag Hammarskjöld, former Secretary General of the United Nations, when he sensitively ruminated: "In any crucial decision, every side of our character plays an important part, the base as well as the noble. Which side cheats the other when they stand united behind us in an action?"[1] Mixed motives reside in and direct us all. *Conversations on Communication Ethics* should strengthen our more noble inclinations.

This thoughtful collection of voices leaves us with heightened ethical sensitivities and an enlarged storehouse of information. It raises more questions than it answers and leaves us with the tasks of synthesizing, reconciling, deciding, and acting. But that is what a good conversation should do.

Professor J. Vernon Jensen
Department of Speech-Communication
University of Minnesota
Minneapolis

NOTES

[1]*Markings*, trans. by Leif Sjoberg & W. H. Auden (New York: Alfred A. Knopf, 1964), p. 65.

Part I

A History of Systems of Account Making

1

A History of Communication Ethics

Kenneth E. Andersen

Department of Speech Communication
University of Illinois at Urbana-Champaign

> Who does not know that words carry greater conviction when spoken by men of good repute than when spoken by men who live under a cloud, and that the argument which is made by a man's life is of more weight than that which is furnished by words? Therefore the stronger a man's desire to persuade his hearers, the more zealously will he strive to be honorable and to have the esteem of his fellow citizens.[1] (Isocrates)

> The character (*ethos*) of the speaker is a cause of persuasion when the speech is so uttered as to make him worthy of belief; for as a rule we trust men of probity more, and more quickly, about things in general, while on points outside the realm of exact knowledge, where opinion is divided, we trust them absolutely. This trust, however, should be created by the speech itself, and not left to depend upon an antecedent impression that the speaker is this or that kind of man. It is not true, as some writers on the art maintain, that the probity of the speaker contributes nothing to his persuasiveness; on the contrary, we might almost affirm that his character (*ethos*) is the most potent of all the means to persuasion.[2] (Aristotle)

The uses of history, the systematic written account and explanation of past events, are many. The various discussions of communication ethics which constitute this book are grounded in and informed by various authors' knowledge of the history of the field of communication generally, various specialties within the field, and the standards for, and treatment of, communication ethics. A brief overview of the history of communication ethics will provide the reader with a framework for the "conversations" which follow.

A complete history of the ethics of communication has yet to be written. Indeed, such an overview of communication ethics, even as limited to the rhetorical tradition from ancient Greece to contemporary American, English, and European communication theorists, does not exist. Hence, some preliminary observations prior to offering a highly selective history are helpful.

To this writer, the existence of an inexorable relationship between communication theory and practice is incontestable, although the nature of that relationship is often disputed. While most writers agree that ethical issues arise in actual communication, some do not concede that communication theory and ethics have any necessary relationship. Many communication theorists offer advice on ethical communication practice that ranges from prescribed dos and don'ts to describing a variety of philosophical positions which a practitioner is to draw upon to determine what constitutes acceptable ethical practice in communication. Still other theorists believe that only an individual or particular group, culture, or society can determine what constitutes ethical practice; hence there is no ultimate basis for resolving ethical issues.[3]

Given these constraints, any list of generalizations, including those that follow, must confront exceptions which have persisted over time as well as in individual cases. Nevertheless, a framework within which to interpret this account of the history of communication ethics is needed. To some degree, evidence will be adduced for each generalization, although a demonstration of their validity and heuristic power is not attempted.

Briefly stated, this writer believes formulating a history of communication ethics necessitates taking into account: the relationship between communication theories and the culture in which they are formed; the relationship between communication theory and politics; the relationship between ontological positions on *human nature* and communication theories; the relationship between the manageability of information and communication theory; the relationship between credibility as an attribute of a source, a communication, and communication ethics; the relationship between the rationale for examining communication ethics and the outcome of such examinations; and the relationship between epistemology and communication ethics.

Communication theories reflect the culture in which they are produced. The theorists of ancient Greece lived at a time in which communication was essentially oral, the practitioners were free men in a culture dependent upon slavery, decisions were made by relatively few men who essentially knew and interacted with each other over extended periods of time, city-states were relatively small and self-contained, and communication was thought to serve the needs of the polis (the community) and more incidentally, although powerfully, the individual. In contrast, individuals in the eighteenth century, such as Hugh Blair, as exemplified in his *Lectures on Rhetoric and Belles Lettres*, wrote in an era in which written communication was commonly used for many purposes, the printing press had revolutionized communication, literacy was growing, individual influence extended over great distances, readers were increasingly unknown by writers, and increasing specialization and a growing middle class were a mark of the society. Contemporary theorists exist at a time in which instantaneous worldwide communication is a reality; computers store, retrieve and analyze an incredible amount of information; tremendous fortunes are made in managing the transmission of information and providing entertainment; and communication technology plays an increasingly powerful, even dominant role.

The political system is a powerful conditioner of communication theory and, particularly, of practice. For example, a totalitarian state will both conduce to certain communication theories and practices and prohibit others as contrasted to a democratic society. A book on persuasion in the Soviet Union in 1989 will not only differ from one published in the United States but also will likely differ significantly from one published some years ago in the Soviet Union. The role of ethics, and of the particular ethical issues seen as relevant to communication, are altered by the political assumptions of the theorist and the society in which he or she anticipates the practical application of any theory.

Responses to the question of what it is or means to be human often profoundly affect the implicit or explicit ethical stance of communication theorists. As suggested above, if the individual is seen as serving the state, a different rhetoric with different ethical components will evolve than if the state is seen as serving the individual. Aristotle argued one cannot lead a good life in a bad state; hence, good men must be concerned with politics for reasons of self interest if no others. Richard Weaver emphasized the importance of the goal being sought both in terms of the specific purpose of the speech and the ethical substance of the underlying warrant which implicitly or explicitly justified the particular goal. Weaver's approach was tied to a concept that each individual is an ethical agent and the bases for belief have profound practical as well as ethical consequences.[4] The conception that humans are choice makers with an ethical dimension at least potentially relevant in every choice yields a different rhetoric than, for instance, a mechanistic view of humans as incapable of choice, and a different rhetoric than the view that actions are prudential matters linked solely to some presumed *ultimate good* such as wealth, power, or pleasure and not to be judged by other values in whole or in part. (Ultimate good is used here in the sense of some object, goal, or state which is valued for its own sake, not as a means or instrumentality to some other end. Further, things valued as *good* exist in a hierarchy, and the ultimate good may be conceived as the first on the list of *goods* individuals seek.)

Writers on communication theory differ markedly in the degree to which they provide a relatively complete exposition of their ontology. Classical communication theorists such as Aristotle and Plato wrote extensively on ethics, politics, rhetoric, logic, cosmology, epistemology, etc. Even though many classical writers failed to provide clear statements on ethical issues in treating communication, their statements on ethical practice are often directly accessible. In contrast, the explosion of knowledge and growing disciplinary specialization over the centuries, most notably in modern times, have led to limited treatments of particular areas. Even within the field of communication, theorists may deal with only one aspect of a message in one medium being used for one purpose. There may be no basis for inferring any aspect of that theorist's view of communication ethics.

Individual theorists, whether classical or contemporary, rarely address ethical issues directly in terms of the role and function of communication in a society and for individuals. However, many theorists give attention to the impact of receiver's judgments of the source, whether called *ethos*, *credibility, reputation, authority*, or *expertise*. The emphasis is more typically on the impact of the credibility of the source in terms of outcomes rather than the impact or ethical quality of a particular choice or practice. Thus, there is often a tension between Quintilian's dictum of actually being a good man speaking well and offering the appearance of a good man, whatever the reality may be. Pragmatic questions of effect, rather than ethical quality, are the usual concern.

Historically, most communication theorists have focused upon the practice of communication and equipping individuals to be more effective communicators, whether in the service of God, the state, truth, knowledge, the group or the individual. Hence, treatments of ethical responsibility and ethical injunctions have tended to center largely upon the source and secondarily on message elements rather than focusing upon the ethical responsibilities of the society, group, or individual responding. Ethical issues are generally treated in relation only to the source or message, without consideration of interaction with situation, medium, or audience.

This tendency to treat ethical issues in a limited context is further intensified when theorists focus narrowly on aspects of the communication process. Rather than focusing upon a relatively complete treatment of the elements of the communication process, or even of the elements of the communication message, some communication theorists focus upon issues of logical proof (demonstration via reasoning and evidence), style, delivery elements, or performance rather than the full interaction of all the elements in communication. In such limited treatments of the process, even implicit treatment of ethics normally vanishes. For example, John Bulwer's *Chirologica* and *Chironomia*, which focuses upon bodily action in delivery, offers 64 descriptive analyses of the gestures of the hand, 35 analyses of gestures of the fingers,[5] and nothing on communication ethics. In a different sense, the 150-year "persuasion–conviction" controversy that raged well into this century about the feasibility of separating conviction (a mental result of logical demonstration) from persuasion (which included emotional proofs and presumably the effect of various other communication variables as well) raised a somewhat different issue about the treatment of communication ethics. Many writers assumed that logical proof which resulted in conviction was inherently ethical, whereas persuasion, which stemmed from emotion or various other appeals, including ethical appeals, was necessarily unethical.[6] This dispute (largely resolved or ignored since the 1930s) still lingers in the tendency of some textbook authors to treat ethical issues only in the context of persuasion, and in courses on persuasion, and not to deal with communication ethics in relation to expository speeches, argumentation, introductory courses, listening, or interpersonal and group communication settings.

These preliminary generalizations provide a basis for exploring the history of communication ethics in terms of three topics briefly traced from classical origins to contemporary treatment: the nature of the relationship between ethics and communication, some ethical tensions between individual and societal goals and functions of communication, and some of the ethical issues in actual communication activities.

THE RELATIONSHIP BETWEEN ETHICS AND COMMUNICATION

Classical sources on rhetoric define rhetoric in relationship to the "art of persuasion." Classical writers on communication treat it in terms of persuasion. They link ethics to communication and usually stress the role of the moral character of the source as important, even essential for successful communication. Nonetheless, the tension between the appearance of being moral and actually being ethical is evident in classical sources. William Sattler in summarizing various pre-Aristotelian sources, notes: "while the persuasive effect of good character is recognized . . . an 'appearance of honesty' is the usual recommendation given."[7]

Perhaps the strongest attack on a "false" rhetoric of appearances rather than reality is by Plato. Particularly in the *Gorgias*, Plato derides rhetoric as a false art, as a base form of flattery.

> Above all else, a man must study, not how to seem good, but to be so, both in public and in private life. . . . Flattery of every kind, whether of oneself or of others, whether of the few or of the many, is to be avoided; and so rhetoric, like every other practice, is always to be used to serve the ends of justice, and for that alone.[8]

He condemns those who teach rhetoric for a fee, as well as those who utilize rhetoric. Rhetoric does not assure individuals possess full, true understanding of the subjects on which they speak. For Plato, the rhetorician is superficial, necessarily deluding and misleading people, whether intentionally or unintentionally. In contrast to the rhetorician, the philosopher can truly know the good and hence promulgate it effectively. In a more balanced view, Plato's *Phaedrus* argues for a rhetoric in which the speaker "know(s) the truth of the matter about which he is going to speak."[9] Plato's true speaker must be a philosopher/logician and a psychologist "able to discern the nature of the soul and discover the different modes of discourse which are adapted to different natures."[10]

One of Plato's students was to offer the most realistic balance of the ideal and practical application. Aristotle provides the most complete treatment of the relationship between ethics and persuasion of writers in the classical tradition. In his unprecedented systematization of rhetorical theory, Aristotle stresses the importance of ethos, the perceived moral character, wisdom, and good will of the speaker. Aristotle utilizes the doctrine of choices explicated in his *Nicomachean Ethics* to explain how an ethos is created. "Character is manifested in choices."[11] Since the choices available to speakers include all aspects of discovering arguments and choosing content, since organization, style, and delivery are not fixed, the choices the speaker makes consciously or unconsciously provide a basis for judgments of character by the audience. In judging the choices made by the speaker in every dimension of the communication process, the listener unconsciously or consciously forms a judgment of the nature of the speaker. Such judgments are powerful factors in determining audience response. For further understanding of ethics and ethical choices, Aristotle explicitly refers his students to the *Ethics* and its analysis of the virtues, as well as to the Politics.[12]

Later writers in the classical period did not give the comprehensive treatment to ethical issues that Aristotle provides. Cicero sought to emphasize the point of view of the actual speaker. While continuing the stress on rhetoric as demanding great learning and skill, he seems less concerned with ethical issues. However, Quintilian in his *Institutes of Oratory* seeks to develop a complete educational program for the perfect orator "cannot exist unless as a good man."

> Since an orator, then, is a good man, and a good man cannot be conceived to exist without virtuous inclinations, and virtue, though it receives certain impulses from nature, requires notwithstanding to be brought to maturity by instruction, the orator must above all things study *morality*, and must obtain a thorough knowledge of all that is just and honourable, without which no one can either be a good man or an able speaker.[13]

During the medieval period and into the renaissance such rhetorical theory as existed was largely preserved and presented by the clergy with special adaptation to homiletics. Writers on homiletics assumed, not only a moral character, but also a knowledge of the good by the preacher. Hence, ethical knowledge and practice were assumed for the most part. Speaking in the name of, and inspired by, God removed many of the burdens of developing an extended treatment of ethical communication. By the eighteenth and nineteenth centuries the classical tradition of rhetoric flowered again in the works of such authors as Blair, Whately, and Campbell. While Whately, for example, could challenge Quintilian's dictum that the good speaker must be a good man,[14] writers usually emphasized the moral and virtuous individual as the basis for sound speaking. Blair urged young speakers not to speak on both sides of an issue, even for practice, for this might harm their reputation and thus their future.[15] In the context of a discussion of ethos, Whately devoted 30 pages to an analysis of items of character and the problem of dealing with emotional opposition to the speaker as an individual.

Contemporary writers are dealing with a far larger range of communication settings, media, and purposes. Whereas earlier writers largely thought in terms of direct communication among individuals within a community with almost daily interaction, modern communication theorists often think in terms of a mass audience which transcends, not just a political community, but almost any kind of community tie. Further, the focus moves from communication serving a limited role of ritual and decision-making functions to the full range of communication activities between and among persons, groups, and nations. While contemporary writers on persuasion usually give overt attention to ethical issues, writers on such areas as small groups, exposition, written communication, drama, and entertainment, rarely mention ethical issues. Such treatment as they accord arises out of specific message elements or in association with advice about enhancing source credibility.

The field of journalism, however, traditionally maintains a lively interest in ethical issues confronting the individual reporter, editor, and publisher, particularly in terms of reporting the news. Journalists are highly sensitive to ethical issues which involve the role and function of the reporter and the journalistic enterprise in society. In part this may be the result of numerous legal and governmental constraints as well as the perception of the central role of the journalist in providing accurate information both as to the facts and the opinions and judgments of others.

In summary, while the surviving ancient writings on communication stress that ethical concerns are relevant to the persuasive process and essential for effective persuasion, that view lost dominance as the emphasis in writings on communication moved from its role in the governance of the polis to communication by the clergy or other learned professions or to a limited treatment of one or a few of the elements in communication. Contemporary theorists treat communication much more broadly in terms of functions, settings, and media. Modern authors in most communication fields give less attention to the relationship of ethics to the communication process than was true in the classical period, and the treatment is likely to be prudential in its focus. The prudential focus as well may explain the greater sensitivity to ethical issues in journalism.

SOCIETAL AND INDIVIDUAL GOALS

A key determinant of a communication theory is the degree to which it is designed to serve the goals of the society, the state, or humanity as a whole, versus the degree to which it is designed to serve the goals of the individual. To the degree the goals of the individual and the larger entity are the same or can be harmonized, there is no necessary conflict. To the degree that the goals can, or inevitably do, conflict, there will be a choice to be made in the theory of communication to be developed. Similarly, the necessity for treatment of communication ethics and the communication ethic implicitly or explicitly recommended will vary with the emphasis of the theory.

The initial systematization of rhetoric by Corax and Tisias presumably resulted from the need to return property previously taken from rightful owners by an ousted dictator. Rhetoric functioned to provide the individual citizen with a means of gaining redress through a public judicial process. Rhetoric served an individual and a community (state) function. Later, Isocrates articulated the power of rhetoric in serving individuals but stressed its power in a civic role in building communities, making good laws, inventing the arts. His *Antidosis* stressed the importance of giving directions on good morals and good government in speeches. Rhetorical training was seen as the best preparation for active service as a good citizen.[16]

Plato, as noted previously, stressed the importance of serving the goals of the society and, in the *Gorgias*, savaged those who mislead, who make the poorer appear the better. True knowledge must be the guide, and the orator is to bring the listener to true understanding. Aristotle similarly focused upon the role of communication in the life of the polis in treating three rhetorical settings: the deliberative, concerned with political and advisory situations; the forensic, dealing with trials and the courtroom; and the epideictic, ceremonial settings typically concerned with praise and blame which provided clear opportunities for instruction in what is and is not true virtue.

In contrast, for other writers and in the practice of communication itself, there was often a focus upon individual rather than collective goals. Plato was assuredly correct that many used persuasion for individual gain rather than to serve truth and the community. Indeed, in both Plato's time and again in Rome's "Second Sophistic," a rhetoric of display often dominated with little concern about positively influencing the community or affecting individual decisions.

Classical theorists did not offer a complete communication theory: the entire focus was on public speaking. There was no attention to communication in the ordinary lives of individuals, in trade or business, to interaction in the family or in ordinary social interchange. There was no recognition of the communication between and among the vast majority of the individuals in the society: women, slaves, those excluded from public decision making. Classical writers developed theories which tied communication ethics to communication activity designed to serve maximally the interests of the community (state), taking account only of the shared public functions of communication.

While only coming to full realization in modern times, the democratization of theories of communication has been a key evolution. Communication has been made accessible to ever-growing numbers of individuals. This involves recognition of functions of communication for individuals of all economic and social classes. The movement toward expanded, inclusive communication theories surged with the emergence of a literate, economically and socially powerful middle class. In recent years, communication theorists have extended consideration to the poor, the oppressed, and minority groups as well as to new settings such as interpersonal communication, therapeutic communication, and new media such as television and computers. Numerous new, dramatically different emphases developed and are developing which evoke new ethical problems for which there are significantly more alternative bases to draw upon in forming a communication ethic.

One aspect of this move toward more inclusive theories of communication is identification of the role communication plays in balancing individual and collective interests. George Campbell, for example, broadens communication's focus beyond the classical norm, claiming "there is always some end proposed, or some effect which the speaker intends to produce in the hearer. . . . the ends of speaking are reducible to four: . . . to enlighten the understanding, to please the imagination, to move the passions, or to influence the will."[17] Campbell may be credited with developing a clearer conception of audience analysis and of giving greater emphasis to it than earlier writers. Campbell saw each audience as unique both collectively and in terms of individuals within it. "The hearers must be considered in a twofold view, as men in general, and as such men in particular."[18] "Now the difference between one audience and another is very great, not only in intellectual but in moral attainments."[19]

Contemporary sources focus quite specifically upon the source and the intended audience as determining the purpose and means to be employed. In many situations the larger interests of society are either seen as irrelevant or are untreated. One can argue that the future value of the communication process to the individual, to those immediately impacted, and to the whole of society is being determined, at least potentially, by every act of communication. An abuse of the process may mean people are less likely to use it, to trust it, or to refrain from more and greater abuses. Such a lively sense of acting within a moral frame with a responsibility to protect the value of the communication process for both individual and society is absent from most instructional textbooks on communication. That is not to say it does not exist in contemporary sources; it is particularly likely to emerge in books that focus upon communication criticism, upon public policy issues relevant to communication, and in theoretical analyses of the societal role of communication.

The historical tension between serving the individual's goal and the shared larger societal interests is seen in many specific contexts in our society. One example was the extensive criticism of the 1988 Presidential campaign, in which negative advertising and an apparent unwillingness of candidates to explore significant issues resulted in intense critical comment from the media, political commentators, and individual citizens. The history of the evolution of Supreme Court decisions in the area of free speech illustrates the difficulty of balancing individual rights against the needs of the community and the state. Over time, the decisions have expanded protections for individuals, constricting the power of the state to control individual actions. The right of privacy in some arenas grows, yet the ability to sue, or gain damages, for libel and slander is sharply restricted.[20]

In summary, the focus of classical sources on a restricted public speaking role in a particular culture and setting lead to a focus upon collective interests and an ethical vision of the individual serving the interests of the state and community. The changes in society and technological resources have markedly reshaped communication theory and practice. Individual rather than societal goals are now a far more dominant focus of communication. This evolution makes the task of developing a consensus on appropriate ethical standards exceedingly complex and difficult. This may be one reason that explicit treatment of the ethical dimensions of communication has been relatively rare in most modern works on communication, although there is increasing current interest in ethics of communication.

ETHICAL ISSUES IN COMMUNICATION ACTIVITIES

Given the variety and scope of current communication theories, as well as the complexity of the historical evolution of those theories, it is unrealistic to attempt a history of ethical stances and their justifications. Later chapters by various authors explore various ethical approaches. For now, it is realistic to list some of the major issues treated by theorists over the centuries which continue to be discussed by current writers. These issues include such questions as sources of ethical standards; appropriate adaptation to an audience; the comparative ethical worth of different types of proof; the relationship between ethos, ethics, and ethical proof; ethical responsibility of receivers; and the relationship between ethics and communication criticism.

Sources of Ethical Standards. A useful departure point is to ask, "What is the basis for ethical standards to be applied to communication?" (Ethical standards are used here in terms of the norms which either direct the participants in the communication activity or which a critic may use in judging the ethical quality of a communication.) Few communication theorists address this question. When they do, the responses vary widely. For some writers, ethical standards are presumed to be self-evident. Those writing on communication for specific professions such as the ministry or law often assume ethical issues need not be treated or that they will be treated as part of the professional training. Some authors argue that individuals will simply bring their ethical standards to communication. Such approaches as these do not point to the junctures at which significant ethical issues arise in the communication process. Nor do they suggest the possibility of certain ethical norms being derived from the nature and functions of the communication process itself. Effectiveness or success in attaining the goal set by the speaker or writer implicitly becomes the test of "good communication." The failure to apply a test of the ethical worth of that goal implies that the ethical dimension has no role to play in determining what constitutes "good communication." Some writers briefly stress the necessity of justifying the particular end or goal sought, but this focus is rarely maintained throughout the entirety of the work. Finally, one popular approach is to provide specific lists of proscribed practice and to prescribe certain approaches such as adequate research and adherence to specific guidelines.

Obviously, few authors can follow Aristotle in explicitly referring readers to a comparatively complete treatment of ethics in his other writings. Even so, several chapters in his *Rhetoric* treat ethical issues, and he carefully explains the interaction of ethical choices with a number of elements in selecting and implementing a strategy. His doctrine of choices describes how an individual's ethics necessarily influence communication activity. Whenever an individual makes a choice—particularly a conscious choice, but including in some very profound senses unconscious choices as well—to the degree the choice has an ethical component, the communicator's choice draws upon his or her virtues or vices. In referencing the discussion of ethics in the *Nicomachean Ethics*, Aristotle provides a practical resource to develop a base for ethical communication actions.[21] While Aristotle recognized various goods, he ultimately argued for the good of happiness which resulted from being active in terms of intellectual activity per se and in using practical reason to govern appetites, desires, and feeling. The good life demands one learn how to be a fully functioning, flourishing human being.

Aristotle's conception of the relationship between politics, ethics, and rhetoric builds a powerful fusion implied by Isocrates and Plato and reflected in many succeeding works. No other communication theorist has provided, within her or his own work, as complete a basis for understanding ethics and the practical role ethical choices play in determining the results of communication acts. Most contemporary basic textbooks on communication are likely to turn to a list of proscribed behaviors. Such categories of unethical behavior include: failing to prepare adequately, whether through insufficient research or not meeting logical standards of truth; sacrificing convictions in adapting to an audience; insincerity, i.e., appearing to be what one is not; withholding or suppressing evidence about self, purposes, sources, evidence, opposing arguments; relaying false information by lying, unintentional misrepresentation, deliberate distortion and slanting, or fallacious reasoning to misrepresent truth; using motivational appeals to hinder truth by substituting emotion for the lack of sound reasoning and evidence and failing to use balanced appeals; and failing to employ critical and evaluative listening.[22]

Communication theorists usually stress the necessity for adequate preparation to increase effectiveness and, presumably, for ethical reasons as well. Writers stress the need for adequate preparation in terms of general educational background, specific knowledge relative to communication theory and guided practice in its application in practical settings and research or specific knowledge relative to the specific topic. For many authors instruction in rhetoric became equivalent to a liberal arts education. Cicero indicates the necessity of studying the poets, history, all the liberal arts and sciences, civil law, all antiquity, usages of the senate, nature of the government, and all the interests of the state.[23] Quintilian undertook in his *Institutes of Oratory* to provide a complete system of education for the orator, one who as a result would be preferable to the philosopher.

Appropriate Adaptation to the Audience. A variety of ethical considerations have been raised about the degree to which the communicator adapts to the audience. Most writers have admitted, some quite reluctantly, the need to adapt to the audience. Even Plato suggests that not all audiences can follow certain demonstrations of the truth. While the need for adaptation is widely acknowledged, the degree and the proper method of adaptation is disputed. Questions posed include the ethicality of concealing one's actual beliefs and purpose, using arguments which are persuasive to the audience but not to the source, changing attire, or concealing association with particular groups that would be negatively evaluated by the specific audience. As audiences have become more diverse in terms of those reached (contrast an audience assembled in one place with the audience for a network television commercial), issues of adaptation have become more complex. The difference in shared knowledge increases the difficulty of ensuring adequate comprehension, let alone acceptance with heterogeneous audiences. As the complexity of the process increases, so does the difficulty of dealing with the ethical issues involved.

Ethical Value of Various Forms of Proof. A recurring issue has been the comparative ethical value to be assigned to logical proof, as contrasted to emotional or motivational proofs and ethical appeals per se. The rhetorical tradition has typically espoused an emphasis upon logic and logical demonstration as being the ethically desired basis for inducing belief. Numerous writers justify emotional appeals only on the grounds of the imperfection of individuals. Typically, those individuals who could be reached by purely logical demonstrations were accorded a higher status and worth than those who "needed" the help of baser motivational appeals. Such an analysis rests upon an assumption of the reality of clear differentiation of bases of belief. This belief reached its zenith in the persuasion–conviction dichotomy–duality arguments of the 19th and early 20th centuries.[25] In experimental studies in which individuals were asked to rate message elements as logical or emotional, the reliability of such judgments turned out to be negligible. Contemporary theorists recognize that the same message unit may evoke a logical response in one individual, an emotional response in another. Moreover, the same message unit may be active in both dimensions, be the basis for an ethical appeal for action as well for one individual and elicit absolutely no response from another. Further, the report of the individual often is not an accurate reflection of what is actually transpiring.

The tradition of stressing the ethical worth of logical argumentation as the basis for belief antedates Plato and continues to the present. Arguments building upon reasonable amounts and sources of evidence serve many positive functions in gaining acceptance, in maintaining a belief in the face of counterpersuasion, in providing a basis for spread of influence. Many theorists, ancient and modern, have recognized that the hard work of assessing an argument and probing an issue must be motivated, and that various other elements may provide the motivation for such logical analysis and contribute both to acceptance and retention of the claims made. While modern theorists and authors call for more acceptance of varied sources of belief, the implied or stated superior ethical value gaining belief and action through logical reasoning, sound argument, and good evidence continues. Simultaneously, this valuing of logical proof as the "most ethical" approach is balanced by injunctions never to underestimate the intelligence of the public and its indifference to reasoned argument. The emphasis upon logic and evidence is not as strong in many non-Western traditions. In fact, other elements may be seen as more desirable or more important concerns.

Relationship of Ethos, Ethics, and Ethical Proof. As previously noted, ethical issues are discussed by many authors only in the context of creating a favorable image (a good ethos) or in terms of ethical proof, the offering of the character of the speaker or certain message elements that will be evaluated as ethical. Indeed, for some authors the only suggestion of the need or desirability of ethical practice of communication is in the pragmatic context of enhancing effectiveness. The implication is, one is ethical when it pays, but ethics can be ignored when failing to act ethically has no impact on the immediate outcome. While most theorists stress that an audience can be misled, the implication is generally that the truth will out. Also, theorists vary in the degree to which they perceive ethical actions as necessarily producing a favorable image. Whately, for example, warns:

> It is requisite to consider who and what the hearers are; for when it is said that good Sense, good Principle, and Good-will, constitute the character which the speaker ought to establish of himself, it is to be remembered that every one of these is to be considered in reference to the opinions and habits of the audience. To think very differently from his hearers, may often be a sign of the Orator's wisdom and worth, but *they* are not likely to consider it so.[26]

Aristotle and later writers gave emphasis to the idea that a communication should demonstrate or develop a favorable image without depending upon a prior favorable reputation even if one existed. Practical advice, typically, covers means to overcome a negative image through various techniques. In *Speech Criticism* Thonssen and Baird provided an extended summary of methods for developing a favorable ethos:

Good character:

1. associates either self or message with what is virtuous and elevated;
2. bestows, with propriety, tempered praise upon self, client, and cause;
3. links the opponent or the opponent's cause with what is not virtuous;
4. removes or minimizes unfavorable impressions of self or cause;
5. relies upon authority derived from personal experience; and
6. creates the impression of being completely sincere.

Sagacity:

1. uses what is popularly called *common sense*;
2. acts with tact and moderation;
3. displays a sense of good taste;
4. reveals a broad familiarity with the interests of the day; and
5. shows intellectual integrity and wisdom through the way in which speech materials are handled.

Good will:

1. captures the proper balance between too much and too little praise of the audience;
2. identifies with the hearers and their problems;
3. proceeds with candor and straightforwardness;
4. offers necessary rebukes with tact and consideration;
5. offsets any personal reasons for giving the speech; and
6. reveals, without guile or exhibitionism, personal qualities as a messenger of the truth.[27]

Recent advice on the creation of a favorable image has been far more influenced by social and behavioral science research and stresses the interactive nature and variability of the processes involved. Relatively little research, empirical or otherwise, has sought to assess the actual effects of ethical and unethical behaviors per se in communication. Thus, the focus has been on the perceived ethics of the communicator, either in his or her her own eyes, those of the audience, or those of the critic, rather than on actual ethical quality.

Ethical Responsibility of the Audience. Classical sources did not accord an active role in the speech process to the listener unless the person responded overtly with another speech, a vote or other action. Although writers such as

Aristotle described the audience as having various characteristics associated with particular demographic traits, the writer's emphasis was usually upon preparation of the discourse. There has been essentially no treatment of the ethical responsibility of the audience in any theoretical or applied communication textbooks. The emphasis from classical to contemporary theorists is upon the source acting ethically. Audience responsibilities of an ethical nature must be inferred. One could infer from Plato's attack in the *Gorgias*, for instance, that people should not allow themselves to be misled. Even minimal attention was not accorded the ethical responsibilities of the audience by communication theorists until well into the twentieth century. The focus was on the preparation and training of the speaker and the particular speech rather than understanding the communication process as a whole.

Ethics and Communication Criticism. In contrast to those writers who sought to provide direct advice to improve the effectiveness of individual communications, authors who engaged in criticism of, and commentary about, communication have given extended attention to ethical issues in judging communicators and their messages. Ethical considerations often are prominent in criticism. Plato's *Gorgias* provides a criticism of current oratory. In the *Brutus* Cicero argued speakers should be appraised by the standards of their time and culture, as well as holding them to an absolute standard such as he established in the *De Oratore*. These dual standards have persisted in criticism through the ages. In evaluating ethics, critics considered both the quality of the ideas and the character of the individual speaker.

Chauncey Goodrich's *Select British Eloquence* established a system of criticism that lasted well into this century.[28] Goodrich placed the speech and the speaker in an historical context and analyzed a full range of message elements. Unlike many critics he was concerned with communication criticism viewed broadly rather than a limited focus upon literary and stylistic characteristics. Goodrich gave attention to the "decision" and often commented upon the merit of that decision from an ethical point of view.

Thonssen and Baird's seminal work, *Speech Criticism*, cited above, gives attention to such topics as the integrity of ideas and espouses a philosophy of rhetoric that provides ethical considerations a prominent place.

> The techniques of an art are superficial means of achieving ends; their use must always be assessed with regard to the terminal values they help to realize. A speech is effective therefore, if it achieves an end or response consistent with the speaker's purpose—provided that the purpose is in turn, consistent with the dictates of responsible judgment and solicitous regard for the positive good of an enlightened society.[29]

Many critics do not focus significantly upon ethical issues, but, in discussing the quality of proof, the nature and character of the speaker, or the positive or negative impact of the presentation in various long-term measures, critics accord ethical considerations a clearer role than authors of textbooks designed to improve the quality of individual communication. But even in modern times, scholars engaged in communication criticism have given far less attention to ethical issues in communication and to evaluating the result of the communication process than commentators and pundits who analyze our institutional life in terms of political and social issues.

CONCLUSION

As this chapter demonstrates, there is a tradition of concern with ethical issues in the long history of communication theory, especially in terms of the definition of the role and function of communication, the study of pragmatic aspects of the communication process such as the effort to create a favorable ethos, and in the evaluation of the impact of communication.

The attention given to ethical issues in communication relates quite directly to the particular conception of communication being posited. For many theorists, ethical concerns are at best implicit and secondary. Some theorists overtly set ethical considerations aside, viewing the communication process as amoral.

In general, however, those who, in writing on communication, are concerned with its role in the life of the individual and the society, accord ethical considerations a place in the communication enterprise. But the complexity of the relationship between ethics and many aspects of the communication process is such that most theorists require the reader of their works to incorporate the shared ethics of the society and the individual's own ethic into the theory being developed, if a guide to ethical communication activity is to be derived.

ENDNOTES

[1]Isocrates, "Antidosis," Trans. George Norlin. *Isocrates* (London: Heinemann, 1929) 2: 239.

[2]Lane Cooper, Trans. *The Rhetoric of Aristotle* (New York: Appleton, 1932) 8-9.

[3]This material is a reworking of ideas contained in Kenneth E. Andersen, *Persuasion Theory and Practice, 2nd ed.* (Boston: American, 1983) 341.

[4]See Richard L. Johannesen, "Richard M. Weaver on Standards for Ethical Rhetoric," *Central States Speech Journal*, 29 (1978): 127-137; Charles K. Follette, "A Weaverian Interpretation of Richard Weaver," diss., U of Illinois, 1981.

[5]Lester Thonssen, *Selected Readings in Rhetoric and Public Speaking* (New York: Wilson, 1942) 189.

[6]See Melvin W. Donaho, "A Critical Analysis of Variations Among Concepts of Persuasion and Conviction," diss., U of Michigan, 1966.

[7]William M. Sattler, ''Conceptions of *Ethos* in Ancient Rhetoric,'' *Speech Monographs*, 14 (1947): 56.

[8]Plato, *Gorgias*, Trans. W. C. Helmbold (New York: Liberal Arts, 1952) 106-107.

[9]Plato, ''Phaedrus,'' Trans. Benjamin Jowett, *The Works of Plato*, ed. Irwin Edman (New York: Modern Library, 1928) 303.

[10]Plato, ''Phaedrus,'' 326.

[11]Cooper, *Aristotle*, 46.

[12]Cooper, *Aristotle*, 20.

[13]Lester Thonssen and A. Craig Baird, *Speech Criticism* (New York: Ronald, 1948) 92. The passage referenced by them is footnoted as from the *Institutes of Oratory*, Trans. J. S. Watson, 1856. XII, ii, 1.

[14]Richard Whately, *Elements of Rhetoric, New Ed.* (New York: 18[46]) 21.

[15]Hugh Blair, *Lectures on Rhetoric and Belles Lettres* (Philadelphia: James Kay, 1829) 287.

[16]Isocrates, ''Antidosis.''

[17]George Campbell, *The Philosophy of Rhetoric, New Ed.* (New York: 1851) 23

[18]George Campbell, *The Philosophy of Rhetoric, New Ed.* (London: 1850) 71.

[19]Campbell, *Philosophy of Rhetoric*, (1850) 95.

[20]For a particularly interesting view on these issues, plus a history of their evolution, see Franklyn S. Haiman, *Speech and Law in a Free Society* (Chicago: U Chicago, 1981).

[21]Aristotle, ''Nicomachaen Ethics,'' W. D. Ross, trans. in *Introduction to Aristotle*, ed. by Richard McKeon (New York: Modern Library, 1947), 340.

[22]Aristotle, ''Nicomachaen Ethics.''

[23]Mary Klaaren Andersen, ''An Analysis of The Treatment of Ethics in Selected Speech Communication Textbooks,'' diss., U of Michigan, 1979, 245-247.

[24]Thonssen, *Selected Readings*, 70.

[25]Donaho, ''Persuasion and Conviction.''

[26]Whately, *Rhetoric*, 244.

[27]Thonssen and Baird, *Speech Criticism*, 387. Material is edited and reworded by this author.

[28]Chauncey Goodrich, *Select British Eloquence* (New York: Harper & Row, 1852).

[29]Thonssen and Baird, *Speech Criticism*, 461.

2

Coordinated Management of Meaning Theory and Postenlightenment Ethics*

Vernon E. Cronen

Department of Communication
University of Massachusetts

Sometimes important features of a moral order are vividly displayed in a few moments of discourse. Several years ago I observed therapists working with a family that included an anorectic daughter. Although the anorectic daughter was the identified patient, all members of the family repeatedly pointed to the father's behavior as a focal point of conflict among family members.[1] During one interview the therapist asked father, "Why do you think your family is like this, the daughters always fighting with each other, your wife acting the way she does?" The father answered, "Well, Jeanie (pseudonym for the identified patient) is sick. She has this disease, anorexia, so she can't help what she does. When she acts that way, I am obligated, as a father, to say what's right. So, when I have to say the things I do, I can see why other members of the family could think it's right to act like they do."

Case studies of families in therapy are particularly valuable for those interested in the study of morals and ethics. This is so because the families in therapy are often engaged in negotiation over who is mad and who is bad.[2] In father's brief statement, he denies Jeanie bears any moral responsibility for her own

*The author wishes to thank his colleague Assistant Professor Catherine Swichtenberg for her helpful comments on an earlier draft of this chapter.

actions or for the family's pattern of activity. Her *disease* is said to *cause* her behavior. In the Western tradition, one is responsible for what one chooses, not for what is produced by nature. Yet, in denying Jeanie's responsibility, father denies her the role of a moral agent. He denies that she is one who behaves intentionally, defining or redefining affordances and prohibitions for others as they participate in social activity.[3] In contrast to his description of Jeanie, father sees his own behavior as obligatory[4] for his role. He is a moral agent, but a critique of his action must be addressed either to the cultural rules for a father's role, or to the extent of his compliance with those rules. Father's actions are intentional in the most basic sense; they point beyond themselves. Family members other than father and Jeanie are, by implication, fair game for criticism. Their actions are neither caused by forces beyond them, nor prescribed by their roles. However, the other members of the family are engaged in actions that are at least legitimated by the fulfillment of father's obligations.

This father and his family are engaged in a process fundamental to human communication wherever we find it. They are working out which activities deserve praise or blame, and which are outside the purview of moral judgement. Father describes action in terms of obligation, legitimation, and by implication, prohibition. He relegates some behavior, in this case Jeanie's, to the realm of motion, not action, saving her from responsibility at the price of losing her place as a moral agent in the family. This is the stuff of which the moral dimension of human activity is made. Ethics is the study that aims to give an account of this moral dimension of human activity.[5]

Traditionally, the study of ethics takes us beyond the domain of description. In the forgoing case, the therapist had decided that it was appropriate to intervene in the family's pattern of activity, and thereby alter the moral order they had created. By what right does a therapist or theorist undertake to change a moral order? In the aforementioned case we may be satisfied with the answer that the family has asked for intervention. Members of the family expressed great discomfort, and there was a threat to the life of the identified patient. However, therapists in some cases refuse treatment to a family that requests it. The therapist may judge that the family may be experiencing discomfort in working through a problem, but that the problem is one the family should deal with on its own. Therapists often discuss the problem of "clientizing" persons or families, that is, making them unnecessarily dependent on outside professionals. Not many years ago, a member of our research group studied a family that experienced a recurrent conflict.[6] After a number of sessions the family said to the researcher that, while they understood this was research and not therapy, they hoped the researcher would tell them how to avoid these arguments. The researcher, however, believed the conflict functioned as an essential proof of commitment, and that to tamper with the conflict outside a clinical connection in which other aspects of the relationship could be explored might be disastrous for the relationship.

Just as therapists may decline to provide services when requested, they may be required to do therapy in a family when no member of the family has asked for intervention. In Massachusetts, for instance, courts may require therapy for families in which there is incest, even when the members of the family do not seem to consider it a problem. The question of whether therapy may be imposed is compounded if the family lives in a town where incest is considered normal behavior by many residents, including many of the women victims. By what rational standards can the norms of one community be imposed on another?

The theory "coordinated management of meaning" takes the position that all human communities are organized as moral orders. This claim rests on the observation that coordinated human activity always entails questions like the following: " What must we do?" "What can we do?" " What are we prohibited from doing?" "What do we do because of forces beyond our control?" On what grounds can one offer a rational critique of social and cultural conditions? Our uncertainty regarding the possibility of a rational critique of moral orders is a consequence of the dualistic conception of individual and society inherited from 17th- through early 19th-century thinkers. In this judgment I align myself with the general thrust of ethicist Alasdair MacIntyre's evaluation of the enlightenment project, though not with his prescription for the problem.[7] The dualism of individual mind (that which is *inner* and subjective) and material world (that which is *outer* and objective) seems to yield a characteristic but unhelpful way of developing a rational critique of moral orders such as those created by the family with an anorectic daughter, or by an incestuous family in a Massachusetts town.

Recent work in the systemic tradition has shown the limitations of attempting to understand the actions of individuals outside the patterns of coordinated activity they create and reconstitute.[8] Particularly fruitless has been the unending discussion of whether the actions of individuals should be attributed to something about the individuals themselves (their inner thoughts, egos, personalities, etc.), or to the social conditions outside them (their schedules of conditioning, social norms, corrupting institutions, etc.). The struggle over whether to give a privileged place to the inner individual world or the outer social world as the locus of explanation for how moral life is organized merely reconstitutes the problematic dualism. This debate over where to locate accountability gives the illusion of being a useful question, because it seems that, once we locate responsibility one place or the other, we will have the seed of a solution. In our example of the family with an anorectic daughter, father locates responsibility for his own and one daughter's behavior on forces external to human choice, namely, disease and role obligations. He then locates responsibility for other family members' behavior in their own choices, legitimated, though not required, by the background conditions of disease and role obligations.

Attempts to locate responsibility within the confines of the inner–outer dualism are reminiscent of a story from Jewish folklore. This story is from a series set in the mythical town of Chelm, a town in which all the inhabitants are crazy or fools. It is about a debate among the wise men of Chelm over which is more important, the sun or the moon. The debate went on for many days before it was settled this way; It was decided that the moon was more important, because, without its light, farmers could not find their way home from their fields at nightfall. The sun, however, comes out during the day, when it's light anyway, so they didn't really need it.

Analyzing a moral order from the perspective of the inner–outer dualism repeats two-fold the mistake of the wise men of Chelm. The wise men failed to see that light is a product of the sun, not just the condition in which they observe the sun. The story is funny because of their obviously wrong-headed conception of agency. In my view, both behaviorists and humanists share a wrong-headed way of understanding conditions and actions. Individuals' inner thoughts do not set the conditions that produce behavior, nor do outer behaviors or conditions determine their thoughts. Rather, ways of thinking and acting emerge together as persons create and engage in practices. This interaction is what the Pragmatist philosophers meant by *experience*.[9] Bateson called it a *co-evolutionary* process.[10]

If mind and social action are mutually constitutive, then ideas and intentions must be social as well as individual, and patterns of action must have idiosyncratic as well as social dimensions. If the inner–outer distinction breaks down, we cannot locate responsibility simply in the individual or the social environment. How then, are we to understand and rationally critique practices from a moral perspective?

The remainder of this chapter will focus on the following themes: First, this chapter will provide an overview of what Alisdare MacIntyre calls the *enlightenment project*, with attention to the problems it now causes for the development of ethical theory.[11] Second, this chapter will provide a brief review of MacIntyre's proposed alternatives to the enlightenment approach, from the perspective of coordinated management of meaning theory. MacIntyre's critique and proposals will be taken as our orientation point for reasons beyond their justifiably high visibility. MacIntyre's earlier work attempted to found an ethical perspective focused on social practices, and that is precisely what the theory of the coordinated management of meaning proposes to do. Third, and finally, the chapter will sketch an approach to the development of a rational basis for the analysis and critique of moral orders; It will explicate, in a preliminary way, how a rational basis for the critique of moral orders can be developed from the perspective of communication as the primary social process.

THE WISE MEN OF THE RENAISSANCE AND ENLIGHTENMENT: SOCIAL ORIGINS OF THE ENLIGHTENMENT PROJECT

The wise men of Chelm did not comprehend the relationship between the sun and the light, but their mistake had little consequence beyond establishing the winner of their debate. The people of Chelm went on tending their sheep and plowing their fields. The question grappled with by the wise men of the Western intellectual tradition, though, led to an answer with far-reaching consequences. The question, as articulated by people like Bacon, Descartes, and Locke can be stated roughly (and simplisticly) like this: "Which should be given more importance, society or the individual?" In order to see why it is that a number of social theorists have come to believe that a new ethical perspective is needed, it is important to briefly review the case that has been made against the adequacy of the enlightenment project and its orienting problematic.

Over and above the many important differences among the wise men of the Renaissance and Enlightenment, they all set the individual against society in a variety of ways. Bacon, for example, wanted to expunge "idols of the mind" that inhibited individual efforts to understand the world as it really is. Descartes elaborated the problem of individual and society into the famous dichotomy of mind and body and argued that secure foundations for knowledge could be found in the clear and distinct ideas of the mind. Locke did not agree that mind provided innate ideas as Descartes thought, but he did claim that all thought was a matter of the *individual mind* forming associations from the data of the senses. For Locke, an idea was merely an individual's association of sense data. Utilitarian wisemen, like Bentham, reached a similar conclusion; each individual experienced increments of pleasure and pain. Policy could be assessed by calculating its consequences, not for society as an organic whole, but as a kind of arithmetic in which increments of pleasure and pain are calculated for each individual and then summed across individuals.

Not all of the thinkers in the Renaissance and Enlightenment tradition agreed on the privileged position of the individual over society. Kierkegaard, for example, thought "pure dread" was individual freedom looking down upon its own possibilities. He enjoined others to find significance by becoming knights of faith. True, Kierkegaard gave a different answer to the individual versus society problem, but he was addressing the same question and thereby accepting the idea that there were two possible and mutually exclusive answers.

The folk literature does not tell us why the wise men of Chelm became involved in the sun versus moon debate, but we do know some of the reasons why the wise men of the Renaissance and Enlightenment became involved in the question of individual versus social dominance. We know that there were important socioeconomic developments contributing to the new sense of individuality, too. Probably these developments started with the reopening of commerce in the 12th century and the later rise of the bourgeoisie; a new class was not defined by its relationship to a place on the land or to a place in the socioreligious hierarchy.[12]

The reinvigoration of Western intellectual life, and the rise of the new class, placed the wise men of the Renaissance and Enlightenment in a very different position than the one experienced by their predecessors in the Classical period.

The wise men of the Enlightenment needed to change the patterns of practice which had characterized European life for centuries. Developments in science seemed to be characterized by the struggle of independent minds such as Galileo's against the received traditions of Aristotle and Aquinas. Similarly, new styles of art, informed by the new science of optics and by the rediscovery of classical texts, struggled against traditional forms. Concurrently, economic changes seemed to require liberating the "new" persons, giving them the power to come and go and do business, powers not granted by the feudal political system.[13]

INDIVIDUALISM AND WESTERN ETHICS

Developments in government and religion seemed to require a rationale for the tolerance of individual differences when intolerance and rule by the monarch's decree were the norms. Locke was especially important in providing an epistemologically based justification for religious toleration and for Parliamentary government. Thus, in their efforts to liberate individual conscience, the wise men of the Renaissance and Enlightenment helped to form a new kind of individualism and, concomitantly, new ethical foci. However, as MacIntyre has observed, this liberation of individual conscience was purchased at a price. First, this liberation created an *is–ought* gap.[14] Facts about the world seemed to be the stuff of which rational debate could be made. Independent observations through proper instruments, particularly when aided by experimental methods provided a way by which people could rationally dispute what was really *out there*. But what *ought* to be is not observable. "Ought" questions seemed to be the stuff of individual judgment. Judgments about what was *good* became either matters of objectified scriptural authority, or matters of individual subjectivity that could not be rationally decided upon the basis of observed fact. To clarify, consider this example. Someone says that a policy you advocate causes pain and suffering to particular people. You could respond, however, that, although there is no doubt about the *fact* of suffering, you personally feel no moral obligation to reduce their suffering and you have heard no logical reason why you should change your mind.

Debates over matters of moral judgment were *usually*, but not always, beyond rational debate, because the Enlightenment did provide an image of human kind that united individuals via certain common interests. Those interests were in the exercise of "natural rights" derived from our common human condition as individual knowers. It was not the case that all arguments about moral matters were thought to be outside of rational argument, but it was the case that rational arguments were thought to lead only to conclusions about constraints on individual thought and action. Like Aristotle, Locke *had* identified some common essence in human life. On the basis of his associational psychology, one could make the following functional argument: All persons are by nature unique loci of knowledge. All actions, institutions, and laws inconsistent with the essence of our humanity are morally wrong. Restriction of free speech is functionally inconsistent with the essence of our humanity. Therefore, restriction of free speech is morally wrong. The contemporary "is–ought" problem may be properly conceived, not as a universal problem for all moral judgments, but as a problem that frequently arises due to an *impoverished* account of our common humanity.

A second problem, directly derived from the first, is the production of an academic split between those scholars concerned with morals and ethics and those concerned with behavior and cognition. Once united under the rubric *natural philosophy*, matters of behavior and cognition (as long as they could be treated as matters of *fact*) became the preserve of the social *sciences*. Matters of ethics and morals, though, remained the preserve of philosophers debating about unobservable *oughtness*. This split signaled complete destruction of the Aristotelian organization of the arts that united rhetoric, politics, and morals under the rubric of *praxis*. The Aristotelian system had united these arts on the grounds that human action has a moral and political dimension as well as contingent character due to its substance. In consequence of this long developing split, citizens with a specialized education in the social sciences often have little to go on when they confront questions about their moral obligations.

The foregoing problems combine to produce a third. By reducing the domain of rational judgment to the arena of restraint on individuals, and by separating the study of social systems from the problem of critique, the Enlightenment project encouraged a plurality of inconsistent moral orders to fill the void. Sociologist Robert N. Bellah and his colleagues described four moral systems operating in contemporary United States.[15] One, a *utilitarian* morality, strongly influenced by Bentham's ideas, developed originally in and for economic relationships. Another is *traditional* morality. It relies on authority and has its original focus on subjects of concern to religious commitments such as sexual practices and ritual observance. A third moral system Bellah and his colleagues termed *republican* morality. This system is that of Aristotle, and it relies on the ability to assume a community consensus regarding what a good life is. Republican morality filled the need for a rational basis for legislative action when there was sufficient agreement to invoke it. Finally, Bellah's group identified an *evocative* moral system, dependent upon the sincerity of expression, and having its original locus in the expression of values.

The incommensurability of these foregoing moral systems would not be so problematic if each remained limited to its own realm of activity. Today, however, any of these moral systems can be invoked when discussing almost any question. For example, when we hear arguments concerning funding abortion, the religious, personal, social, economic, and political matters intersect, and the discourse concerning this issue reflects the cacophony of incommensurate moral systems.

The fourth consequence of the Enlightenment project is that its focus on the individual had, and continues to have, the effect of reducing all social problems to individual ones. The solution to individual difficulties is usually sought from an outside agency operating on individuals from an objective stance. It is supposed to help them take an objective *scientific* position themselves with respect to their own minds. This objective view is that of the individual abstracted from ongoing practice. Social psychologist Edward Sampson, a critic of traditional psychology, described the situation in the following way:

> The emphasis on the individual chooser's psychology tends to mask the particular alternatives from which people can freely choose. This psychology of abstracted individualism can all too readily serve the existing structures and social interests. . . . We make it appear as though an individual could in fact act wisely, rationally, or autonomously when confronted with choices that have been cast up by a social process that disallows rationality or autonomy in any sense other than fitting one's behavior into the achievement of pregiven ends.[16]

Not long ago network television provided a graphic illustration of the process Sampson described. A special on stress began with an account of a company that monitored every moment of an employee's time via computer, keeping a running visual account of sales per minute before the employee. Although the program started with a perspective critical of such stress-inducing forms of work, it ended with a self-administered individual test for viewers and information on where one can go to obtain help for improving individual stress management techniques. By the end of the program responsibility was clearly upon the individual to objectively analyze personal capacities, and on authorities whose job is to alter individuals' mental approach to stressful conditions. The effect of such advice is, of course, to reconstitute the individualist ideology while deflecting responsibility from institutions.

Another example of the destructive force of the individualist ideology can be found in DSM III.[17] DSM III is the official listing of diagnostic categories and criteria of the American Psychiatric Association. Conditions attributable to a mental disorder include paranoid disorders, anxiety disorders, schizophrenic disorders, etc. Toward the back of the book are the so-called *V Codes*. V codes are conditions not attributable to a mental disorder and, very importantly, therefore frequently not covered by insurance. These include such matters as child abuse, problems of separation from parental control, inability to comply with medical treatment, marital conflict, and ''uncomplicated'' bereavement. Such problems are covered by some insurance policies only if attributed to the ''mental disorder'' of a particular individual and *not* to patterns of interaction.

The last problematic consequence of the social–individual dualism requiring attention in this chapter is the paradoxical situation illuminated when the positions of Bacon, Descartes, and Locke are contrasted with that of Kierkegaard. The former group had argued that, if the individual works from within a social

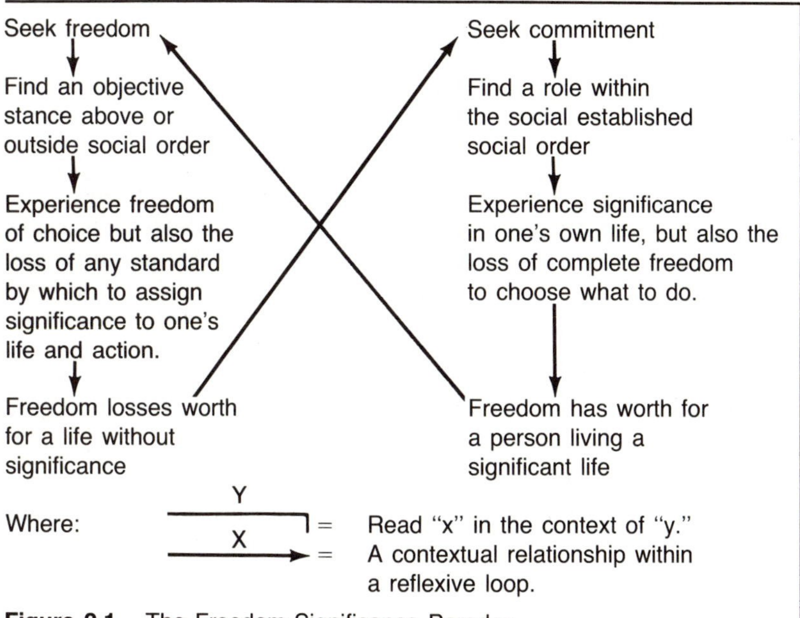

Figure 2.1. The Freedom-Significance Paradox.

context of traditions of practice, the individual is not truly free. Kierkegaard argued that, unless there is a context higher than the individual, there is no way to assess the significance of any individual's activity. The paradox is displayed in Figure 2.1. The paradox works like this: In the context of seeking to be truly free, one must find an objective position outside or above society. In the context of having this freedom, one cannot find significance, for there is no higher standard or system in light of which individual choices have importance. In the context of lost significance, freedom is not worth having. Loss of significance forms the context in which one seeks a place within a social system that assigns significance to individual acts. In the context of having such a position, one finds significance but has lost freedom. Yet freedom has worth for a significant person, so, in this context, one should seek to be truly free! The foregoing set of relationships all depend on a higher order context, a tradition of thought and action, held even by those who thought tradition was not a positive influence. That context is the dualistic cast of mind holding that the more individual an action or belief is, the less social it must be, and, conversely, the more social an action or belief is, the less individual it must be.

Although this is not the place to develop a detailed historical argument, it could be contended that the paradox in Figure 2.1 is a factor in the recurrent phases of runaway individualism and nationalist commitment that Europe and America exhibit. The "me" generation and the Eisenhower era are recent examples of this shifting in our own national life.

MACINTRYE'S ALTERNATIVES

A variety of resolutions have been proposed for the problems of Enlightenment ethical thought. These range from Marx's rejection of ethics,[18] through Dewey's reflective relativism,[19] Rawls's neo-Kantianism,[20] and Nozick's foundationalism.[21] Space does not permit a response to the many alternatives that have been offered. However, because this chapter has taken MacIntyre's critique as its point of depature, and because MacIntyre originally focused his ethical position on traditions of social practice, It is important to review his position and criticisms of it.

MacIntyre's views on the possibilities for post-Enlightenment ethics are expressed in his two books *After Virtue* and *Whose Justice? Which Rationality?* These books show a movement from the effort to construct a rational and universal basis for ethical thought to the denial that such a project is possible.

In the first book, MacIntrye attempted to develop an ethical position based on three key ideas. Those were the idea of a practice, the unity of an individual life, and the concept of virtue. According to MacIntyre, *goods* have significance for real social *practices* and are internal to them.[22] For example, courage can be developed through playing football. To play well requires developing it. In contrast, results such as fame or profit are not internal to the practice.

MacIntyre recognized that he needed some standard beyond particular practices in order to decide among *competing* goods. He introduced such a standard in the concept of "the unity of an individual life."[23] MacIntyre recognized that Aristotle framed the question of ethics in a useful way by asking, What is it for the sake of which we live a human life? However, MacIntyre could not identify a *telos* that transcends particular practices. In place of such a transcendent *telos*, MacIntyre substituted the unity of an individual life *involved in a narrative quest for the good life*. A *good* then becomes that which facilitates the unity of an individual life engaged in this quest.

Finally, in *After Virtue*, MacIntyre invoked another perspective intended to span divergent practices. He invoked the concepts of tradition, and *virtues* appropriate to a tradition. If a tradition is in good order, it indicates goods the pursuit of which gives the tradition its purpose.[24] The virtues of courage and leadership, for example, are developed in particular practices of our tradition, such as sports. The virtue of total obedience is not highly developed in our tradition, as it has no important place in what we see our tradition to be about. Even in American military practices, obedience is given a singularly temporary place. It is taught that the senior surviving private should be prepared to take command if those of higher rank are dead or incapacitated.

Virtues may be contrasted with values. Values are peculiar to the Enlightenment view. They are conceived as the preferences of autonomous individuals. One may, for example, choose to "value" material comfort. Virtues are always social. The virtues of courage and leadership, for example, must develop in the course of cultural practices such as war, sports, and community enterprises. Conversely, without those virtues, the practices would lose their distinctive character or even become impossible.

MacIntyre's position, as developed in *After Virtue*, has much to commend it. It attempts to restore the essential roles of practice and tradition, while recovering the concept of virtue. However, criticisms of this position were very powerful and eventually led MacIntyre to redirect his own project. Pragmatist philosopher Richard Bernstein provided a most insightful analysis,[25] and I shall rely on it for critique of the constructive position taken in *After Virtue*. Bernstein argued that MacIntyre's effort to identify goods by their internal relationship to practices provides no way to distinguish between the practice of an inquisiter and the practice of a democratic statesman. Insensitivity to the pain of infidels, and the capacity to revel in spilling blood for the race, meet MacIntyre's criteria for virtues that are both intrinsic to practices *and* necessary to sustain these practices.[26] This problem necessitated a standard broader than the place of a good in a practice, but, argued Bernstein, MacIntyre's resolution was not satisfactory. The unity of a human life in the quest for the good life simply turns us back toward Enlightenment-style individualism.[27] This standard reopens the questions of how the good for oneself can be decided, and how to proceed if the narrative quest of one individual conflicts with that of others. MacIntyre provided no adaquate answers to these questions. In addition to Bernstein's criticism, we might enquire about the applicability of this standard to a culture that does not view the individual life as a unity. Such a culture may mark off portions of the physical life span into radically different identities, each with its own quest.

Bernstein was also critical of MacIntyre's appeal to *traditions* of practice. He argued that MacIntyre did not give any convincing argument to show that all traditions must be good.[28] Moreover, because traditions are not objectivities but interpreted histories of practice, there is no single unambiguous understanding of a tradition. Different understandings will entail different conceptions of the virtues necessary to sustain tradition. MacIntyre's emphasis on being inside of a particular tradition in order to understand what it is to be virtuous reveals a strong conservatism in his position that is more fully realized in the second book. In *After Virtue* his conservatism is clearly revealed in the claim that Nietzsche is the antithesis of Aristotle. This argument rests on his failure to recognize virtues appropriate to conditions wherein one wishes to produce ambiguity in order to facilitate reconstruction.[29] Irony is a virtue for Nietzsche as it was for Socrates. It is not a virtue, however, if we assume that the tradition in which it is practiced needs only reaffirmation, clarification, and extension.

MacIntyre recognized that something was amiss in his effort to restore a rational basis for ethical argument. He knew that the problem was his inability to slip between the horns of a dilemma. Either he must argue for a transcultural, transhistorical, transindividual *telos* (which he came to think was impossible), or he must reject the idea that there is any form of rational argument about virtues or goods that is not limited to a particular tradtion. In *Whose Justice? Which Rationality?*, MacIntyre firmly grasped the second horn of this dilemma. He argued that rationality itself cannot be defined outside a tradition.[30] A particular tradition can have a kind of universality insofar as it can flourish in environments very different from, or even hostile to, that in which it originated. That, however, is the only kind of universality possible. MacIntyre turned from the problem of how to judge among incommensurate rationalities to a defense of the right of a tradition to develop in its own way. His second book ended with a defense of the right of universities to impose tests of doctrinal orthodoxy for admission of faculty and students.[31] This, he said, allows a tradition to develop, treating alternatives according to the logic of its own tradition, without confusion.

If rationality is a central aspect of a particular tradition, one can either work from within a coherent tradition and be rational, or work outside of a coherent tradition and be nonrational. When differing traditions are in contact, MacIntyre says that the result is conflict.[32] If the conflict is rational, it must be so by the standards of one tradition or the other. For example, one may find that another tradition offers a way to construct theories and concepts that more adequately manage an epistemological crisis within their own tradition. In such a case, the judgement that an alien tradition offers superior resources is made on the basis of standards derived from one's own tradition. What MacIntyre called the "rationality of tradition" then would require switching allegiance to the superior tradition. Thus, MacIntyre saw change in persons' commitment to traditions as a matter of allegiance switching.

Clearly, the second of the two books amounts to an argument that the constructive project of book one ought to be abandoned, because no universal basis for rational argument is possible in ethics. The argument seems to make a kind of sense until one recognizes the truncated view of tradition and rationality that is at work. First, observe the overintellectualization, almost scholasticism, of his view. There is no place for the passions in it. An alternative tradition might become attractive because it better solves a crisis. But in MacIntyre's revised view, if a new tradition provides resources to experience life in new ways, with passions one has not before experienced,[33] this only introduces confusion. Moreover, in his analysis, the crises traditions face seem to be the sort that interest traditional Western philosophers. They are *epistemological* ones having to do with the abstract problem of knowing (*episteme* as opposed to merely *doxa*). His claim that the tradition of the Catholic church has met all challenges successfully is hard to maintain if one moves from epistemology to real practice.

MacIntrye's conception of tradition was also impoverished by the fact that he explicitly limits his attention to Western traditions. The effect of this was to lose sight of the fact that Western traditions are held together by diverse and widely known set of cultural practices.[34] One could say that MacIntyre's traditions are only the relatively formalized aspects of complex and related sets of roles, forms of consciousness, speech games, aesthetic preferences, etc. By losing track of the broader conception, culture, MacIntyre failed to see the diversity of resources by which one tradition may encounter another. Had he not lost track of these resources, he would perhaps have seen that traditions are not so sharp-edged as he implies. Was Socrates outside of tradition, and thus without virtue?

The truncated view of tradition, along with MacIntrye's seeming unfamiliarity with recent work on the problem of translation in anthropology,[35] lead to a series of errors. It is not true that an alternative tradition is useful only as replacement for one in crisis. One tradition can enrich the *development* of another. Of course, such borrowings can result in confusion. What makes periods of confusion universally abhorrent? Borrowings can also result in enrichment. Eastern mathematics was taken and transformed by the Greeks from Egypt. That borrowing and transformation has profoundly influenced the course of Western intellectual life. To be sure, the Greeks profoundly reworked what they borrowed. But without that borrowing, we might not have had the influence of the mathematical ideal that appears in Plato, Aristotle, Descartes, and Frege, to name but a few. Similar cases exist in the arts. One can also cite the cross fertilization of Western harmony, African drum and chorus, and other sources that are synthesized as American jazz. It is worth noting that the introduction of new musical forms typically produces confusion in the music world, and that that confusion is usually healthy.

A root cause of MacIntyre's problem is the mistaken idea that, because one cannot obtain a purely native point of view, one must judge the value of another tradition only by one's own standards. The diverse resources of culture will not render different traditions commensurate, but will allow them to become comparable.[36] Multiple resources, including literature, art, science, and the multiplicity of everyday practices, permit one to find what Wittgenstein called *family resemblances*.[37] Extended and varied forms of interaction will increase these resources. Thus, contact with another tradition does not make one a native, but it does not leave one wholly an outsider either.[38] If we restrict our view of rationality to inference-making procedures within traditions, and treat traditions as technologies for problem solution, it certainly holds that any judgment about what is good must either be made within such a technology or be nonrational. If, however, our view of rationality encompasses the use of cultrual resources for rendering alternative traditions comparable through interaction, then it is possible to be rational in a way that draws upon traditions but is not tradition bound.

In sum, MacIntyre is not convincing in his claim that traditions have nothing to offer each other but conflict and confusion or the victory of one over another. Indeed, alternative perspectives far more culturally diverse than those MacIntyre describes seem capable of enriching one another. Neither is he convincing in his argument that rationality is wholly tradition bound. The possibilities of comparison afforded by the culture and communication give us a way to partially but usefully transcend such limits.

Perhaps the most frightening prospect in MacIntyre's proposals is his treatment of alternative traditions. The value of a minority view for a widely spread and strongly felt tradition can only be that, should the establishment tradition reach an epistemological crisis, the minority view may offer an alternative. However, that judgment must be made within the rational system of a tradition by its adherents. Thus, if the Catholic church does not value the lives of those who do not accept Christ, neither the silence of the Pope during World War Two, nor the 1948 pogrom in Poland, represent crises. The effect of MacIntyre's proposals for education are chilling. Precisely because learning an alien tradition is not exactly the same as learning one's own, authorities *within* a particular tradition are thought to have a privileged place in deciding whether other traditions have anything to offer for extending their tradition or as an alternative to it. These intellectual masters, earning their roles in part by their orthodoxy, have authority by virtue of their position in the tradition. Just what are the chances that they will see rival traditions as anything but threats to their own position? Do they have the right to destroy other traditions once *they* are sure the alien tradition cannot offer a viable alternative, as judged by their own rational standards? MacIntyre has nothing to say about genocidal efforts manifested in a tradition.

WERE THEY WISE AFTER ALL?

At first glance, the wise men of Chelm seem foolish. They did not seem to notice that the sun is the cause of daylight. However, David Hume might have observed that they wisely avoided the mistake of assuming that contingency is causation. They simply failed to apply the same good skepticism to observations of the moon. Were the Renaissance and Enlightenment wise men really so foolish? MacIntryre's ethical positions should lead us to reassess their work also.

The wise men of the Enlightenment did observe correctly that a problem exists when alternative views are not argued by their own adherents. They also knew serious problems arise when an institutional position provides a privileged place for deciding who counts as an acceptable colleague or student, what counts as an epistemological crisis, and what counts as an alternative tradition worth preserving.

The wise men of the Renaissance and Enlightenment also must be credited with reviving the possibilities of individual creativity. We may be frustrated today with the dualities produced by the form of individuality developed, but consider the historical circumstances. Few people had access to books or education. The dominant folk practices, the authority of Aristotle, the role of the church, and the power of lords and kings, all militated against unorthodox ideas. What alternatives were there but to place the individual thinker in radical distinction to society, and focus on the inner workings of the individual mind? Rather then engage in further ''modernity bashing,'' it would be better to say that the new forms of individuality, and the splintering of moral systems in the modern period, served very important political and social ends. Today, however, these achievements do not help us to cope adequately. A new vision is necessary, and it must entail a nondualistic way to think about individuality, sociality, and rationality.

THE COORDINATED MANAGEMENT OF MEANING: ITS ETHICAL PERSPECTIVE

The Enlightenment project developed a set of ethical perspectives based upon individualism. More precisely, it was based on a form of individualism which has been termed *psychologism* by its critics. Aristotle's work might be properly termed a *sociologized* ethic, as it cannot exist outside the traditions of a particular community. What follows here is a venture into the possibilities of developing an ethical perspective that is based on communication rather than psychology or sociology. Communication is a new kid on the social science block. It is a viable discipline only if it can offer a distinctive family of perspectives on the human condition. The argument developed below is based on a particular communication theory called *coordinated management of meaning*.[39]

The theory coordinated management of meaning (CMM) has its intellectual roots in some of the work that has challenged the Enlightenment project. Challenges to the Enlightenment project have occured through the last two centuries. Most notable among the 19th-century challengers were Nietzsche and Marx. Both challenged the separation of the self from its expressions in material life. In the twentieth century, new challenges have come from several perspectives, including phenomenology, philosophical pragmatism, systems theory, and the later philosophy of Wittgenstein. CMM has its philosophical roots in the latter three bodies of work.

CMM is a communication theory; it is not a theory about communication derived from another discipline. As such, CMM takes communication to be the fundamental social process. This orientation allows us to describe the primary unit of social analysis in the same way as philosopher Rom Harre does: ''persons in conversation.''[40] This is a single unit, though it has multiple dimensions. *Persons* does not refer to *minds* or to any particular form of identity. It refers to our embodiment and to the fact that persons are indexicals; they are physical locations in time and space from which acts come and to which acts are addressed. Secondary social processes are constituted through the primary one and include forms of selfhood and identity, social institutions, various emotions, social practices, kinds of relationship, forms of consciousness, and moral orders.[41]

The ethical implications of CMM will be developed in four stages. First, there are ethical implications that derive simply from taking communication to be the primary social process. Second, the basics of the CMM's analytic tools are presented, to show how this theory represents a moral order. Third, a general model is presented that describes what people do when they communicate. Further ethical implications are derived from this *elaboration-transformation* model. Lastly, a set of specific propositions are offered which illuminate the model and introduce additional ethical implications.

The Communication Perspective: Two Immediate Implications

When communication is taken to be the primary social process, two inferences are obvious to those with an interest in ethics and morals.

Borrowed ethical systems have sever limits. Because CMM takes communication as primary, CMM cannot borrow its ethical and moral content from traditions that take *individual* thought or the social group as primary. For example, Kantian ethical ideas that take the *individual* as end (not merely as means) cannot be simply grafted on to such a theory in order to evaluate the moral content of discourse. For CMM, the constitution of *individuals* as ends is itself a process that must be understood in its particular cultural and historical context. Individuality must have a social basis because it takes culturally unique forms no matter how it is developed. Conversely, social structure must be created by entities at least individualized by the unique locations of their actions and embodiments in time and space. As philosopher Hannah Arendt observed, diversity of position does not threaten the existence of a common world but instead makes it possible.[42] The tradition of relying on fundamental human sentiments from ethical grounding becomes equally problematic. If communication is the primary social process, then emotion is a secondary process that is socially constructed through interaction. How else could we account for the appearance of different kinds of emotions in different historical circumstances, or the existence of very different ones in other cultures?

Morality, social structure, and action are inextricably related. A second obvious inference from the distinction of secondary and primary social process is the interrelated character of such topics as selfhood, consciousness, relationship, action, and morality. John Dewey observed, as did Nietzsche, that the separation of selfhood from action is a particularly confusing inheritance. Dewey went on to say that all moral theory must somehow acknowledge an essential unity of self and action.[43] In CMM theory, forms of selfhood are created and sustained in the primary social process. If this is so, then selfhood is not the same in all cultures.[44] If the self is different in various historical and cultural settings, it follows that different moral orders will exist when different forms of selfhood exist.

Representing Moral Orders With CMM

A social theory with ethical implications should be able to represent patterns of practice. CMM theory provides a set of analytic tools and procedures for doing so that have been useful in a variety of studies. Several of these studies have focused on differences between moral orders. These studies of cultural differences are important because the theory contends that forms of identity, relationship, etc., are socially constructed and vary across time and place. In these studies, conversation is analyzed by applying the analytic model shown in Figure 2.2.

In Figure 2.2 persons are loci of dense structure. The structure a person holds is represented as a hierarchy of narratives. Any two levels of narrative may be organized as distinguishable higher and lower levels. For example, relationship to a husband or father is often, for the working class American woman, a higher-order context within which she assesses and develops her *autobiography*. This hierarchical arrangement is symbolized $\frac{\text{Relationship}}{\text{Autobiog.}}$. Based on our reading and preliminary research, we think middle class, and especially, professional women in North America often hold a structure in which *autobiography* and *relationship to husband* exhibit a clear higher and lower hierarchical relationship, but the levels are reversed. Autobiography is the context for assessing and developing the relationship. This suggests a different kind of moral order. We suspect part of the reason working class women in some communities are resistant to leaving even abusive relationships might be because having *an* identity requires the context of a relationship to a strong male.

The way two levels of narrative are related depends on still higher contexts. In the foregoing example, broad and deeply felt cultural patterns are important influences on the structural connection of relationships to autobiography. For working class women, the "obligation" to stay in a relationship may come from a kind of selfhood that is itself strongly connected to cultural patterns of practice.

CMM does not specify what hierarchical relationships among levels of narrative "really" are, or what the hierarchical arrangements "should" be. The kinds of narrative levels present are also empirically determined. The European nuclear family, for example, is a narrative context that has no parallel in rural India. Levels of context, and their ordering, coevolve with social action.

Hierarchically embedded levels of context may exhibit clear distinctions as to which is higher and lower, or they may be reflexively related such that, by going

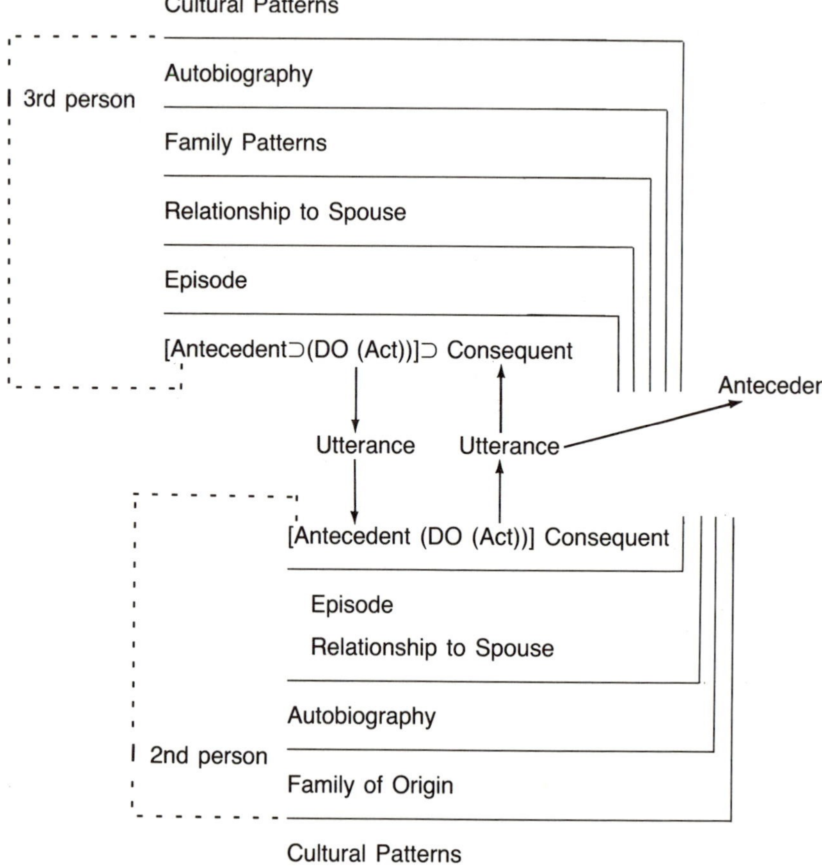

Figure 2.2. The CMM Analytic Model.

higher or lower in the system, one returns to the original level. Such a reflexive relationship is symbolized in CMM as □. Some reflexive relationships are termed *charmed loops* and symbolized □♥. Charmed loops are structural features in which each level is equally context for the other. For example, in the course of a developing relationship there is usually a time during which the episodes enacted are context for defining and developing the relationship, while the developing relationship is *equally* the context for defining and developing episodes of action.

Charmed loops are distinguished from *strange loops*. In strange loop arrangements, each hieirarchical level contains two mutually exclusive possibilities. The relationships among levels are such that all mutually exclusive alternatives are affirmed. To illustrate a strange loop $\square^{s}$ that has obvious ethical implications, let us consider Joseph Heller's novel *Catch 22*. The "catch" refers to conditions under which members of a group of American fliers may stop flying missions. The only condition under which a healthy pilot may stop flying is if he is crazy. However, continuing to fly is suicidal. Suicidal persons are crazy; rejecting suicide is, of course, sane. Sane action must begin by claiming to be crazy, since this is the only allowable reason to stop flying. To claim you are crazy thus provides the context that defines you as sane.

The cultural pattern needs illumination if we are to find out why such a strange loop exists for the flyers. Certainly, the sanity of preserving one's own life is not a cross-cultural universal. In many cultures it is both sane and honorable to die even if the cause is lost. Many Americans also knowingly gave their lives believing this a sane and honorable thing to do. The story holds together for us because it sensitizes us to a cultural concept of individualism and the preservation of the individual that is difficult to integrate with the demands of preserving the culture that gives rise to it.

Turn your attention to the lowest narrative level of the models in Figure 2.1. Here there are four important terms: *antecedent, deontic operator, act, and consequent. Antecedent* refers to a prior message and/or circomstance interpreted within the structure at a specific time. The term *deontic operator* reflects CMM's commitment to the idea that all human action is moral action. Thus the operators are not those usually found in accounts of logic, even informal social logics. The operators in CMM's models are moral terms. They describe action as *obligatory, legitimate, undetermined, and prohibited*. When the human agent's structure includes a form of consciousness in which action is *constucted and experienced* as beyond conscious choice, the operators are *caused, probable, random*, and *blocked*. This latter group of operators should not be regarded as only modal terms. They are *moral* terms in CMM in that they describe a particular kind of moral position of the actor with respect to their actions.

The term *act* refers to actors' interpretation of their own communicative activity. The relationship of act to *utterance* is not that of an abstract idea and its external representation. The movement from neurological activity to physical expression is considered to be one continuous process. CMM does not accept the Cartesian notion of ideas. All of what we know and are able to do emerges from participation in or observation of social action. Ideas thus do not have to be transformed into some kind of communicative expression.

Narrative levels such as autobiography or relationship have a past, a presence, and projection into the future. So too, the terms *antecedent, act*, and *consequent* all have a dynamic quality. In CMM theory, a human action is never to be regarded as a static moment in Aristotelian time. Each bears a history of practice without which it would have no meaning. Each also has projection into the future as well as presence, because each participates in the creation of structure.

The term *consequence* refers to the kind of responsive action an actor may desire. This term requires a special note of clarification. CMM does *not* make the assumption that actors always have a clear understanding of antecdents or of their own action. Nor is it assumed that actors necessarily know what consequence they desire. It is also important to observe that consequents can only emerge within embedded levels of narrative and in the process of social interaction. Thus, they act as transitory orientation points. This representation is in marked contrast to the Enlightenment tendency to view ends as somehow freely chosen among alternatives outside us. Consequents are aspects of structure, and structure defines identity.

CMM theory describes actors' structure as integrated by *rules*. Indeed, in the communication discipline it is often described as a rules theory. Here we must be careful, because in social theory the term *rule* is used in many ways. In CMM, the term *rule* is used in a way consistent with the thrust of Wittgenstein's later philosophy. Rules evolve in the course of social action along with all other aspects of structure. Their stability, like that of all other aspects of structure, depend upon their reconstitution through social action. Two sorts of rules are distinguished, *constitutive* and *regulative*.

Constitutive rules integrate structure vertically and integrate it with physiological processes. For example, when a World War Two Japanese officer says, "Charge!" this utterance (antecedent) is constituted as meaningful by virtue of its having a place within a soldier's higher-order narratives. Similarly, the soldier's obedient act is constituted by the place of such obedience in higher-order narratives. The deontic operator is *obligatory*. Hearing the command entails a physiological response that is deeply woven into the narrative structure via constitutive rules. Because CMM theory treats emotion as socially constructed and not distinct from thought, emotion becomes an intrinsic aspect of moral life.

For the Japanese soldier, the moral obligation to obey comes from narratives quite different from those that obligated an obedient response by an American soldier of the same era. The Japanese soldier was enacting his proper place in much more than narratives about selfhood, his place in his unit, and military forms of life. The moral force that obligates the Japanese soldier comes from his relationship to his family and the family's place in the community. Both of those narratives involve further relationships to the Emperor and country quite unlike the relationship of an American to his family, community, country, and president.

CMM theory directs the researcher to inquire how acknowledgment of obedience by the soldier's superior (consequent) counts as *reconstituting* important levels of narrative context. In this example, aspects of structure that are reconstituted include narratives of much higher-order than individual identity, without which identity *itself*, (not just a positive identity) is impossible.

The second sort of rule in CMM is regulative. Such rules integrate the structure horizontally and thus temporally. For example, they connect antecedent to the deontic operator and act, and both of these to the consequent. As in the case of the constitutive rules, these connections evolve with varying degrees of logical force.

The symbol ⬚ in Figure 2.2 locates the indexical "I," the "person position" from which one acts, and those aspects of structure that can be reported back to a location in structure as self-awareness. *Person positions* are features of language. For example, one may act and interpret from the *third-person position.* This third-person observer position is much valued by the Western scientific tradition. However, it is very clear that there are nuances of experience a first- or second-person participant has that are not available to a third-person observer. The fact that one kind of person position is valued for a particular kind of activity is evidence that we learn different forms of consciousness for different activites. The moral implications of person position have been discussed at length by developmental psychologist John Shotter.[45] The obligation to extend action and to immediately exhibit an understanding of it is, in Western culture, assigned to the second person. In various sorts of episodes and relationships we are prohibited from such actions as stepping out of our participant's position to offer a critique of the action, or from declining to answer when asked.[46] Thus, what we observe, interpret and do are importantly related to the person positions we take in moral action.

The apparatus shown in Figure 2.2 functions as a heuristic device, directing our study of a moral order. The coevolution of structure and action represented by CMM models should be thought of as constituting a logic of conversation. The relationships among logical forces acting in the structure can be revealing of a moral order. Not many years ago, the author and his colleague Linda Harris encountered a two-person system in which the mother strongly needed a particular kind of response from her son to sustain the constitution of her autobiography as that of a successful mother. The acts performed were strongly obligated by various elements of her autobiography and her relationship to her son. However, those acts obligated her son to give her just the sort of responses that she did not want. The mother readily reported that her actions could not get the responses she needed. Yet she said that she must go on as before, because that is what a good mother and a person like her "must" do. Talking to the mother, it seemed that, whether engaged in an advice-giving episode with her son, or even talking about such an episode, she assumed a second person position. She focused on her own responsibilities in terms of certain very salient narrative contexts. The third-person position, which might have given her some insight into the larger pattern, we think may have been incommensurate with various features of the structure mother held.

A CROSS-CULTURAL ILLUSTRATION OF CMM

The following illustration is meant to show, by means of actual case data, how CMM theory can represent culturally different conceptions of selfhood, relationship, and moral order. In a dissertation recently completed at the University of Massachusetts Department of Communication, Hyesook Kim observed how, in traditional Korean families, the conceptions self-as-husband and self-as-son are related, so that, in the context of being a good son, one can be a good spouse, and in the context of being a good spouse, one can be a good son.[47] Korean tradition assumes that a proper harmony in these relationships is both desirable and attainable. This loop forms a higher order context for understanding crucial aspects of selfhood. In one of the families studied by Hyesook Kim, the wife seems able to tell when a request she makes transforms the relationship into one with features commonly called paradoxical. The wife introduced a Western idea. She suggested that she and her husband get their own apartment and not live with her husband's family. So long as her request stood and was presented as important for her happiness, the husband was in the following situation: In the context of being a good husband, he would move and be a bad son. In the context of being a bad son, he cannot be a truly good husband. If he is not a good husband, he would not move, and, in that context, he would be a good son. But in the context of being a good son, he should endeavor to be a good husband, and that means moving. This whole paradox becomes the context in which the husband must try to understand who he is. The strange loop is shown in Figure 2.3. When the wife recognized the untenable nature of the husband's situation, she reported that she felt obligated to withdraw her request to reestablish harmony for her husband and the whole family.

In Western tradition, the force of the obligation to produce harmony is not derived from a structure that places selfhood clearly within the context of this type of a relationship. While the request to break up a multigenerational living arrangement might lead to strife for a Western family, it is not likely to lead to a paradox. Being a good or bad son is not culturally a determining factor in whether or not one is a good or bad spouse. In North American middle class tradition these are presumed to be separate and naturally conflicting obligations. Moreover, the location of selfhood in structure is not clearly subordinated to familial relationships in the North American middle class. Therefore, even if such a paradox should exist, it would not *necessarily* produce a crisis in identity.

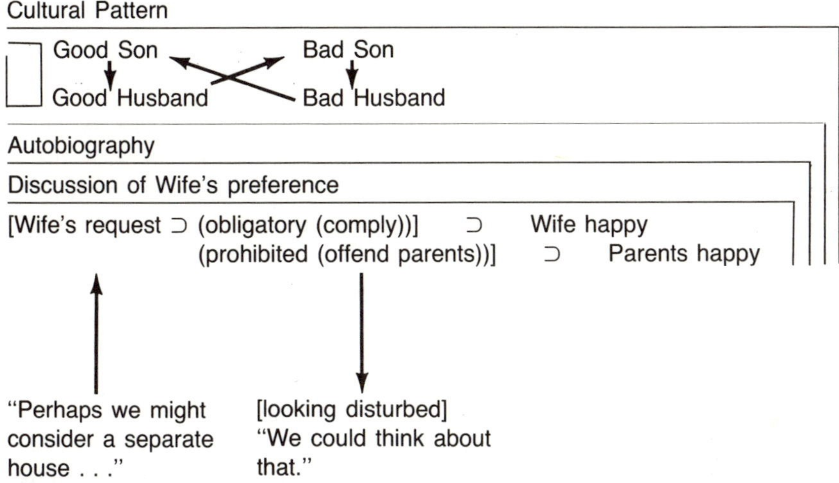

Figure 2.3. Korean Husband's Structure Forming Strange Loop.

To understand the force of the Korean wife's felt obligation to withdraw her request requires a knowledge of the social structure of which obligations, legitimations, and prohibitions are a part.

The problems that the Western idea seem to produce have another very important function for both husband and wife. The pattern of action that subsequently develops acts as the context in which Korean traditional forms of identity and relationship are reaffirmed.

A feature of the foregoing case that should not escape us is the ability of the wife to be aware of the paradoxical potential that particular requests can have. She must read this potential in very subtle behaviors of her husband. An appropriate form of consciousness is necessary for skilled performance in the maintenance of personal and familial harmony. The management of consciousness is always a vital aspect of social patterns. The fact that the management of consciousness is a socially learned phenomenon means that people's awareness of what they are doing and experience of intentionality are culturally and historically variable. In our earlier example of the family with an anorectic daughter, the father argued that his anorectic daughter's behavior is *caused* as opposed to being either obligated or chosen from a range of legitimate options. The daughter may well have come to experience her behaviors as *caused, probable*, or *blocked*. That is why in CMM the foregoing terms are treated as deontic operators, just as are the terms *obligatory, legitimate*, and *prohibited*. All make a moral statement about the responsibility of actors.[48]

CMM THEORY AND ARISTOTLE'S QUESTION

If moral concepts have their place in systems of practice, can we do more than explain the moral orders that have been created and critique these orders by their own standards? Alternatively, do we have any knowledge about communication that transcends culture and history which might give us any guidance in the development of ethical theory? CMM answers this question in the affirmative.

Aristotle organized his ethical inquiries around the right question. "What is it for the sake of which we lead a human life?"[49] He was insistent that the answer to that question must be given with reference to the quiddity of a human life. In CMM theory, the quiddity of human life is to be found in human communication. This alone, however, does not give us much guidance. What is needed is a description rich enough to be ethically informative that is not based on a single speech game, particularly not one rooted in a particular culture.[50]

According to CMM, an analysis that is ethically informative must be one based on an analysis of particular conditions. CMM provides a set of tools for the analysis of communication, and examples of CMM analyses can be found in a variety of sources.[51] Researchers involved in CMM theory have developed a set of descriptions of communication that go beyond accounts of particular patterns of communication. No ethical theories save those of a strictly authoritarian-ontological sort attempt to provide a yardstick against which each act or practice can be measured. All that is attempted here is to provide enough of an account of the distinctly human process of communication so that we can rationally argue moral issues. This is a major claim in light of MacIntryre's argument that rationality is a local matter, relevant only to particular traditions. Our argument, to the contrary, is based on two premises. The first is that, although traditions of practice may be incommensurate, they may be made comparable. Here CMM again follows Bernstein's analysis. Bernstein argues that traditions include resources rich and varied enough so that, although one may not know an alternative tradition like a native, that fact does not preclude useful and mutually enriching discourse.[52] The second premise is that our current knowledge of communication allows us to make use of a common set of ideas about that primary process.

What is Done by Communication: The Elaboration-Transformation Model

CMM's heuristic power has been questioned on the grounds that it does not posit any causal laws of behavior that predict communication *effects*. CMM researchers were likened to the wise men of Chelm who could not tell cause from effect. CMM argued that all theories, including our own, are elaborated and developed under particular material conditions. We argued that, as a theory is developed and as it encounters new social conditions, it becomes more prone to crises.[53] Unlike MacIntryre's epistemological crises, we thought of these crises as problems in action, that is, in the ability of a theory to help people get on by illuminating and critiqueing the social order. In the context of such crises, it is legitimate for scholars to search out new premises for theory building. With new premises, the old crisis is left behind. It is not a muddle solved but a muddle discarded in favor of a perspective that does not entail that muddle.

The movement from clear starting points, to elaborations, to crises, then to the ability to leave the crisis behind and find new starting places can be conceptualized, as returning not to an original position, but to new starting places, new elaborations, and, yes, new crises.

This process, in Figure 2.4, distinguishes what humans and only humans do. No other creature constitutes, elaborates, and transforms institutions, forms of identity, consciousness, emotional meaning, or institutions through communicative action. It is clear that such transformations occure through practice. The emotions we experience today are not the ones people experienced under earlier social arrangements.[54] No one today suffers from accidie[55] or has courtly love, to name two obvious cases. Our American sense of identity, even our ways of organizing volitional control over our personal lives, have changed since colonial agrarian times.[56] The movement in Figure 2.4 cannot be accounted for if the social order or the individual is taken as primary. To be engaged in the process

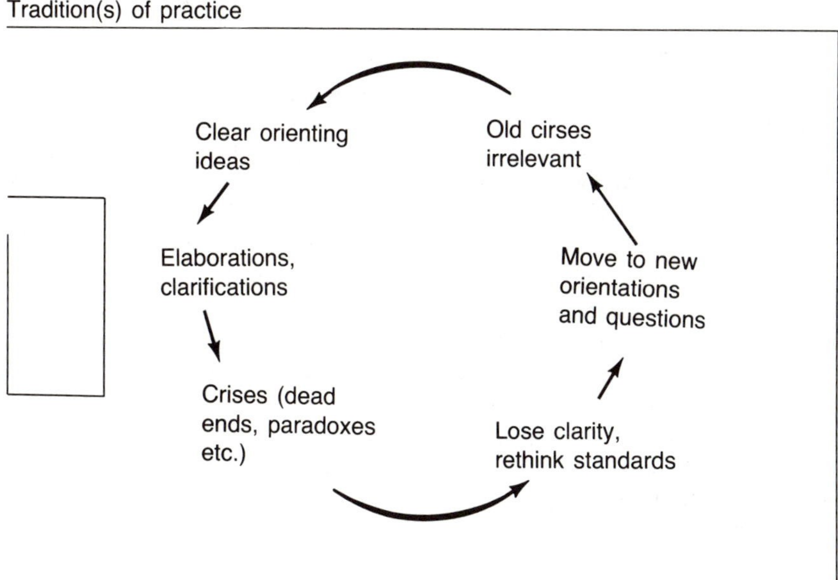

Figure 2.4. The Elaboration-Transformation Model.

that produces elaborations and tranformations is distinctive of leading a human life, and can be understood as the consequence of human communication.

Some additional observations about moral life can be made by taking Figure 2.4 as a description of the uniqueness of human life. It is similar to the Aristotellian *telos* in the sense that it is intrinsic to what we are, not as individuals, but as persons communicating. Yet it is unlike the Aristotellian view of the *telos* in its universality. The potential of any action for elaboration or transformation requires an analysis of the historical and cultural conditions of its occurrence. It is also unlike Aristotle's treatment because of its radical potential. It amplifies the range of what may be considered virtues to include the Nietzscheian virtues appropriate to those circumstances in which the possibilities of transformation need to be opened by destabilizing the existing order.

Accepting this model brings with it an additional implication that is out of step with the mainstream Western tradition. The model stresses the unfinished quality of human life. It beckons us to heed John Dewey's advice that we learn to appreciate that which is unfinished and indeterminate, as we have traditionally appreciated that which is finished, and determined.[57] Finally, the model has an important relationship to the Pragmatic conception of truth as *utility*, that is, being of service in the organization and reorganization of experience. When Pragmatists say that ideas are true to the extent that they are useful, they do not mean useful in some self-serving or narrow sense. This model is intended to give a better sense of what it means to consider the full breadth of affordances and prohibitions created by in action.

Guides For Using The Elaboration-Transformation Model

In the course of working with CMM theory, the author and his associates have developed a set of propositions that describe communication. They amplify the model and suggest further implications of it for ethical theory.[58]

1. All communication is both idiosyncratic and social. Earlier it was observed that communality requires, not identity, but distinction, and that forms of individuality are socially constituted. The reaction against the Enlightenment sense of individualism in contemporary social thought sometimes shows the tendency to equate the social with the good. However, social systems can be anything but good. They can foster a kind of individualism that masks the tyranny of institutions. They can submerge the creative possibilities of individuality through a variety of practices. In doing so, the possibilities of creative elaboration and transformation may be curtailed. What must be recognized in applications of the elaboration-transformation model is the interdependence of individuality and sociality that pervades every act.

2. Communication entails a reflexive relationship between structure and action. This proposition focuses us clearly on practice. As persons are the loci of dense structure, any attempt to disconnect their thoughts from their actions is mistaken. This does not mean persons cannot sometimes produce bad results in spite of good intentions. Rather, it commands our attention to the fact that intentions are developed in social practice.

3. Punctuated historicity is endemic to human communication. In his classic paper on the problem of induction, Nelson Goodman observed that inductive moves in science are not justified by a priori principles but by histories of practice.[59] Even radical transformations in social systems are not historic "jumps" out of context. Such transformations are captured in the German word *aufheben*, which means both to preserve and to destroy. Hegel and Marx both gave accounts of the historicity of radical change, and CMM offers an alternative to their views.[60]

Human rationality is not rooted in repeated individual reflections on static objects, but in the flow of activity that is realized and unified in communication. The ethical implications of this proposition are apparent when viewed in conjunction with Proposition 4 below.

4. Human communication is inherently imperfect. The great power of human communication depends on this. This proposition can be supported by a variety of arguments. These include Godel's demonstration of the inherent limits to formalizing,[61] the ineffability of aspects of experience,[62] the later Wittgenstein's account of language,[63] the conjoint production of communication episodes,[64] and evidence that confusion, misunderstanding, and ambiguity, can be productive.[65] Taken together, Propositions 3 and 4 remind us of Dewey's plea that we learn to appreciate the unfinished and undetermined as we have come to appreciate that which is finished and determined.

5. Technologies are unique episodes in the process of communication. Given what we know about communication, it is hardly exhausted by or best characterized as technology. A technology is a set of procedures to get from one state or condition to an end state or condition. However, this merely opens the question of where ends or goals come from. From the CMM perspective we think of "ends" as Dewey did. They are orientation points created and reconstructed in the course of the activities they temporarily guide.[66] Thus, a further implication of the view is that it is mistaken to be overly committed to the virtues of technology. Based on what has been said so far, a technology can only be a episode in the larger process of communication.

It is not, however, reasonable to reject all technological episodes. A kind of rational debate that ought to be generated by the perspective CMM offers would be over the value of further pursuing a particular technology. The practice of a technology usually reconstitutes important aspects of the moral order. For example, the practice of mediation seems to reconstitute traditional notions of individualism, objectivity and emotion.[67] Do we want to encourage further technological episodes in which emotional energies are contrasted with constructive individual bargaining, as they are in mediation? Or have these ideas exhausted their creative potential?

The foregoing questions are matters of evidence and argumentative consistency. They are *is* questions. If we conclude that the creative potential of these oppositions has been exhausted, then it is *good* to attempt destabilizing the inherited conception of selfhood with its notions of inner emotions and rational exchange-based action. Working toward its transformation would be good, because to act otherwise would deny the distinctive capacity of human actors—the ability to transform systems. This holds because the good must be that which develops our distinctive humanity. In this way we can rationally move from matters of what is to conclusions about what *ought* to be. Here we have the kind of functional argument that MacIntrye wanted in which matters of *is* and *ought* are unified, though neither is simply reduced to the other.

6. Moral orders emerge as aspects of communication. Unlike the Enlightenment project, which separated moral from factual matters, CMM uses deontic operators as central features of its analytic apparatus. This is because the creation of moral orders seems to be one of the few universal features of human societies. All peoples indicate what can be done, what must be done, what is prohibited, and what is beyond their responsibility. Any description of human social arrangements that does not recognize these distinctions and their places in social structure and action is incomplete.

7. Communication is the process by which the dual modes of liberation may be realized. The dual modes are the ability to elaborate systems and the ability to transform them. The exercise of these powers is not of course a matter of random or individual whim. The desirability of elaborating a system depends on the analysis of a social order's problem and potentials. Such an analysis must include consideration of whether a social system provides the kind of education that prepares persons to participate in both modes of liberation, and to do so in a variety of domains from personal relationships to political action. An education focused narrowly on learning technique is thereby intrinsically unacceptable. It conveys the pernicious idea that distinctive human activity, as recognized by society's most advanced educational institutions, amounts to the elaboration of technologies in place.

The analytic "machinery" of CMM directs one's attention to the hierarchical organization of social structure, with persons as the dense loci of structure. Thus, as illustrated earlier by Hyesook Kim's study, we are interested in the hierarchical relationships of selfhood, role, culture, etc. Thus, analyzing the possibilities of elaboration and transformation must be done with reference to a variety of levels of structure. However, if Proposition 1 is correct, it is hard to imagine that a society of persons who cannot elaborate and transform their sense of selfhood under appropriate conditions could produce a creative social system, or that an uncreative social system could produce creative individuals.

It might be argued that the theory does not give us any reason why some individuals' opportunities, or some communities' opportunities, could not be sacrificed for those of others. The answer is that all persons and communities deserve such opportunities by virtue of the fact that they are human, and that elaboration and transformation characterize a human life.

8. Diversity is essential to elaboration and transformation. There is no way to know a priori if, when, or how one tradition, culture, or idiosyncratic view will meet another and will produce a transformation or open a new means of elaboration. As was observed early in this chapter, such meetings are not limited to challenges. To attempt the elimination of cultural traditions is wrong, because to do so is not consistent with encouraging the very kind of life that is distinctively human. Neither the taking of individual nor cultural life can be easily reconciled with this view, except in those cases where the individuals or cultures themselves are both committed to the destruction of others and have some capacity to do so.

THE ROAD TO WISDOM OR THE ROAD TO CHELM?

Sometimes when working on a very old, important, and perplexing problem like the relationship of ethical thought to communication theory, one wonders whether one is being wise or holding debates that belong in Chelm. In this chapter I have attempted to set out the general outline of an approach to ethics that is emerging from CMM theory. The position presented above has these attributes: It seems to embrace some of the crucial insights of past thinkers. It does so by recognizing the importance of both sociality and individuality, recasting them in a way that is not dualistic. It stresses the value of Aristotle's orienting question without proposing an ethnocentric answer, and it also affirms Dewey's insistence on the idea that no moral judgment can be made independent of the circumstances in which it arises.

The CMM approach also has potential for sorting out the kinds of ethical issues that arise. For example, the elaboration-transformation model highlights the issue of whether elaboration or transformation is called for under particular conditions, and the available resources for participation in those two modes of liberation. Perhaps less obviously, because the model is meant to apply to personal, relational, institutional, and cultural levels of analysis, it identifies another class of issues involving the tensions among those levels. The use of CMM's analytical procedures requires accounting for unique forms of selfhood and consciousness operating in particular conditions.

CMM theory has been described by some critics as a sort of black hole in space into which all kinds of issues were drawn. This excursion into the implications of the theory for post enlightenment ethics will probably renew that cry. CMM's creators keep dragging it into all sorts of issues that do not seem to be the proper place for communication scholars. I want to explain why this must be so with a very short story. After a battle the Czar was decorating some common soldiers for bravery. He said he would grant each a request. One asked for a week of leave, another for a cash bonus. When the Czar came to a ragged soldier from Chelm and asked what he wanted, the soldier said, "I want to be transferred to another company, my corporal doesn't like me." What a foolish request," responded the Czar. "Why don't you ask to be made a corporal yourself?!"

ENDNOTES

[1]In systemic family therapy, anorexia is viewed as an aspect of the family's pattern of activity, not as a problem in the mind of the identified patient.

[2]The author first encountered this usage of *mad* or *bad* in Evan Ember Coppersmith, "From Hyperactive to Normal but Naughty: A Multi-System Partnership In Delabeling," *International Journal of Family Psychiatry*, 3 (1982): 131–144. Her use of it is probably derived from R. D. Laing, *The Divided Self* (New York: Penguin Books, 1965), 178–205. The author's use of the terms here are informed by Coppersmith's applications.

[3]Sara Cobb, "The Concept of Power In Family Therapy: Towards The Hegemonic Analysis of Discourse," diss. U of Massachusetts, 1988.

[4]*Obligatory* is one of the deontic operators used in the theory coordinated managment of meaning. The other operators are: *legitimate, prohibited, undetermined, caused, probable, blocked*, and *random*. These Operators were adapted from Georg von Wright, "Deontic Logic," *Mind*, 60, (1951): 1–15.

[5]John Dewey, *Theory of the Moral Life* (New York: Irvington, 1980), viii.

[6]Linda M. Harris, "The Maintenance of a Social Reality: A Family Case Study," *Family Process*, 19 (1980): 19–33.

[7]Alasdair MacIntyre, *After Virtue* (Notre Dame, IN: University of Notre Dame Press, 1981).

[8]See, for example, Mara Selvini Palazzoli, Luigi Boscolo, Gianfranco Cecchin, and Giuliana Prata, *Paradox and Counterparadox* (New York: Jason Aronson, 1978).

[9]John Dewey, *Experience and Nature* (New York: Dover, 1958), 1–78.

[10]Gregory Bateson, *Mind and Nature: A Necessary Unity* (New York: E. P. Dutton, 1979), 46.

[11]MacIntrye, *After Virtue*, 49–75.

[12]Henri Pirenne, *Economic and Social History of Medieval Europe* (New York: Harcourt, Brace and World, 1937), 25–38.

[13]Stephen Toulmin and June Goodfield, *The Fabric of the Heavens* (New York: Harper and Row, 1961), 182–209.

[14]MacIntyre, *After Virtue*, 54–56.

[15]Robert N. Bellah, Richard Madsen, William M. Sullivan, Ann Swidles, and Steven M. Tipton, *Habits of the Heart: Individualism and Commitment In American Life* (Berkeley, CA: University of California Press, 1986).

[16]Edward E. Sampson, *Justice and the Critique of Pure Psychology* (New York: Plenum Press, 1983), 138–139.

[17]American Psychiatric Association, *Quick Reference to the Diagnostic Criteria from Diagnostic and Statistical Manual of Mental Disorders, 3rd ed.* (Washington, D.C.: APA, 1980).

[18]Karl Marx, *Capital* (Moscow: Foreign Languages Publishing House, 1959), 84–85. See also Steven Lukes, *Marxism and Morality* (Oxford: Clarendon Press, 1985).

[19]John Rawls, "A Kantian Conception of Equality." In J. Rajchman and C. West (Eds.), *Post-Analytic Philosophy* (New York: Columbia University Press, 1985), 201–214. See also responses to Rawls by T. M. Scanlon and Sheldon S. Wolin in the same volume.

[20]Robert Nozick, *Philosophical Explanations* (Cambridge, MA: The Belknap Press of Harvard University Press, 1981).

[21]Dewey, *Theory of the Moral Life*.

[22]MacIntyre, *After Virtue*, 178.

[23]MacIntyre, *After Virtue*, 190–209.

[24]*Ibid*.

[25]Richard J. Bernstein, *Philosophical Profiles* (Philadelphia, PA: University of Pennsylvania Press, 1986), 115–140. For an alternative interpretation of MacIntryre see Jeffrey Stout, *Ethics After Babel* (Boston: Beacon, 1988).

[26]Bernstein, *Philosophical Profiles*, 130.

[27]Bernstein, *Philosophical Profiles*, 131.

[28]Bernstein, *Philosophical Profiles*, 134.

[29]Frederick M. Dolan, "Nietzsche as Aristotelian: On Alasdair MacIntyre's 'After Virtue'," *New Orleans Review*, 13 (1986): 61–74.

[30]Alasdair MacIntrye, *Whose Justice? Which Rationality?* (Notre Dame, IN: University of Notre Dame Press, 1988), ix.

[31]MacIntrye, *Whose Justice? Which Rationality?* 399.

[32]MacIntyre, *Whose Justice? Which Rationality?* 386.

[33]*Ibid*.

[34]Richard J. Bernstein, *Beyond Objectivism and Relativism*, (Philadelphia, PA: University of Pennsylvania Press, 1985), 80–85. See also Donal Carbaugh, "Comments on 'Culture' in Communication Theory," *Communication Reports*, 1 (1988): 38–41.

[35]Clifford Geertz, *The Interpretation of Cultures* (New York: Basic Books, 1973), 3–33.

[36]Vernon E. Cronen, Victoria Chen, and W. Barnett Pearce, "Coordinated Management of Meaning: A Critical Theory." In Y. Kim and Wm. Gudykunst (Eds.), *Theories in Intercultural Communication* (Beverly Hills, CA: Sage, 1988), 66–98.

[37]Ludwig Wittgenstein, *Philosophical Investigations* (New York: Macmillan, 1958) para. 67.

[38]Geertz, *The Interpretation of Cultures*.

[39]W. Barnett Pearce and Vernon E. Cronen, *Communication, Action and Meaning* (New York: Praeger, 1981); Vernon E. Cronen, Kenneth M. Johnson, and John W. Lannamann, "Paradoxes,

Double Binds and Reflexive Loops: An Alternative Theoretical Perspective,'' *Family Process*, 20 (1982): 91–112; Vernon E. Cronen, W. Barnett Pearce, and Karl Tomm, ''A Dialectical View of Personal Change.'' In K. Gergen and K. Davis (Eds.), *The Social Construction of the Person* (New York: Springer-Velag, 1985) 203–244; Vernon E. Cronen and W. Barnett Pearce, ''How the Milan Method Works: An Invitation to a Systemic Epistemology and The Evolution of Family Systems.'' In D. Campbell and R. Draper (Eds.), *Applications of Systemic Family Therapy: The Milan Approach* (London: Gruen and Stratton, 1985); and Cronen, Chen, and Pearce, ''Coordinated Management of Meaning: A Critical Theory.''

[40]Rom Harré, *Personal Being* (Cambridge, MA: Harvard University Press, 1984), 20.

[41]Harré, *Personal Being*, 65.

[42]Hannah Arendt, *The Human Condition* (Chicago: The University of Chicago Press, 1958), 57–58.

[43]Dewey, *Theory of the Moral Life*, 163.

[44]Donal Carbaugh, *Talking American* (Norwood, NJ: Ablex Publishing Corp., 1988). See also Michael Carrithers, ''An Alternative Social History of the Self.'' In M. Carrithers, S. Collins, and S. Lukes (Eds.), *The Category of the Person* (Cambridge: Cambridge University Press, 1985) 234–256; John Kirkpatrick and Geoffrey M. White, ''Exploring Ethnopsychologies.'' In G.M. White and J. Kirkpatrick (Eds.), *Person, Self, and Experience* (Berkeley, CA: University of California Press, 1985), 3–34; and Paul Hirst and Penny Woolley, *Social Relations and Human Attributes* (London: Tavistock, 1982).

[45]John Shotter, *Social Accountability and Selfhood* (Oxford: Basil Blackwell, 1984), 14–15.

[46]Shotter, op. cit.

[47]Hysook Kim, ''The Reflexive Relationship Between Address Forms and Context: A Study of Korean Spouses,'' diss., U of Massachusetts, Amherst, 1989.

[48]See Cronen and Pearce, ''How the Milan Method Works.''

[49]Aristotle, ''Nichomachean Ethics.'' Trans. Ross. In R. McKeon (Ed.), *The Basic Works of Aristotle* (New York: Random House, 1938), 1095a 16.

[50]Jurgen Habermas proposed an ethic for discourse based on what he called ''universal pragmatics'' and the ''ideal speech situation.'' In reality, Habermas's whole conception is based on a particular language game wherein equal partners disclose their presuppositions. This game would surely be to the disadvantage of a jobless housewife, attempting to get both child custody and financial support, who must confront a former spouse with many resources. Her ability to hide her emotional need for the children may give her the only bargaining leverage she can obtain. Habermas may say this whole situation is very far from the ideal, but what is the value of an ideal if it misguides us in the conduct of real social-political circomstances? See Jurgen Habermas, *Communication and the Evolution of Society* (Boston, MA: Beacon, 1979).

[51]See Pearce and Cronen, *Communication, Action and Meaning*; Cronen, Johnson, and Lannaman, ''Paradoxes, Double Binds and Reflexive Loops''; Vernon E. Cronen and W. Barnett Pearce, ''How the Milan Method Works''; and Vernon E. Cronen, ''Het Individu Vanuit Systeemteotetisch Perspektief,'' *Systeemteoretisch Bulletin*, 3 (1987): 167–197. (English translation is available from the author.)

[52]Bernstein, *Beyond Objectivism and Relativism*.

[53]Cronen, Pearce, and Tomm, ''Dialectics of Personal Change.''

[54]Rom Harré, *Personal Being*, 123.

[55]Rom Harré, *Personal Being*, 127–129.

[56]Howard Gadlin, ''Private Lives and Public Places: A Critical View of the History of Intimate Relations in the United States. In G. Levinger and H. Raush (Eds.), *Close Personal Relationships* (Amherst: University of Massachusetts Press, 1977), 33–72.

[57]Dewey, *Experience and Nature*, 55. See also John Dewey, *The Quest for Certainty* (New York: G. P. Putnam's sons, 1929), and Ludwig Wittgenstein, *On Certainty*. Edited by G.E.M. Anscombe and G.H. von Wright, Trans. Paul and Anscombe (New York: Harper, 1969).

[58]Cronen, Chen, and Pearce, ''Cooordinated management of Meaning: A Critical Theory.''

[59]Nelson Goodman, *Fact, Fiction, and Forecast* (Cambridge, MA: Harvard University Press, 1979).

[60] Cronen, Pearce, and Tomm, ''Dialectics of Personal Change.''

[61]Ernst Nagel and J. Newman, *Godel's Proof* (New York: New York University Press, 1958).

[62]W. Barnett Pearce and Robert J. Branham, ''The Ineffable: An Examination of the Limits of Expressibility and the Means of Communication.'' In B. Rubins (Ed.), *Communication Yearbook* 2 (New Brunswick, NJ: Transaction, 1978), 345–350.

[63]Wittgenstein, *Philosophic Investigations*.

[64]Pearce and Cronen, *Communication, Action and Meaning*, 148–184.

[65]Pearce and Cronen, *Communication, Action and Meaning*, 273–284.

[66]John Dewey, *Human Nature and Conduct* (New York: Henry Holt, 1922) 123–127.

[67]Johnathon Shailor, ''The URP that Ate Mediation.'' Unpublished paper, Department of Communication, U of Massachusetts, 1988. Shailors's work was conducted as part of an interdepartmental university study of mediation processes and mediator training.

3

The Status of Communication Ethics Scholarship in Speech Communication Journals from 1915 to 1985

Ronald C. Arnett, Ph.D.
Professor of Communication Studies

Manchester College
North Manchester, IN

INTRODUCTION

This study, endorsed by the Communication Ethics Commission of SCA, reviewed 128 articles related to ethics of communication published in our disciplinary journals from 1915 to 1985. This extensive review was commissioned because no journal length review of "ethics of communication" literature currently exists, and what efforts do exist were confined primarily to the decade of the 1950s.

This review reflects our discipline's concern for ethics, as revealed by the new Communication Ethics Commission, Ken Andersen's 1982 theme for SCA, "Communication, Ethics, and Values," and our participation in interdisciplinary ethics inquiry. As Callahan and Bok concluded in their "Hastings Center Project on the Teaching of Ethics," numerous academics are recognizing ethics inquiry as relevant, contemporary, and significant despite the current pragmatic mood on university campuses.[1]

FRAMEWORK FOR ANALYSIS

This chapter is intended to serve as a stimulus for discussion, a contemporary benchmark for further research. To accomplish this goal, a descriptive focus guides this inquiry. Before examining the actual literature on communication ethics, the elements that compose the analytic framework of this chapter require attention: (a) a communication ethics definition, (b) descriptions of five categories of communication ethics, and (c) discussion of a conceptual center that ties the diverse research on communication ethics together.

Defining Communication Ethics

The few, but thoughtful, Speech Communication textbook contributors to the ethics of communication question agree on the importance of *choice-making* in a communication ethic.[2] Thayer contends that one must accumulate enough information so one's privately and publicly stated belief structures are grounded in knowing choices, not blind allegiance to particular social institutions (p. 354). Johannesen, in what is now the major work on ethics in speech communication, lists the term *choice* or *significant choice* 25 times in the index to his first edition—more than any other term. It is, however, Thomas Nilsen who is best known for the choice-making perspective in communication ethics.

> When we communicate to influence the attitudes, beliefs, and actions of others, *the ethical touchstone is the degree of free, informed, and critical choice on matters of significance in their lives that is fostered by our speaking. We shall call this significant choice*. (p. 46); Emphasis in original

Most recently, Bormann emphasized that an ethical decision necessitates choice; praise or blame is not appropriate for actions not knowingly chosen.[3]

The relationship between communication ethics and choice making can be traced to Aristotle's emphasis on a practical discourse tradition, *phronesis*, that seeks to mediate between universal truths and the concrete situation;[4] such action is referred to as *deliberate choice*. Focus on deliberate choice via practical discourse can be found in Aristotle's *Nichomachean Ethics*, Gadamer's philosophical hermeneutics, Richard Bernstein's practical alternative to the objectivistic/relativistic dichotomy, and MacIntyre's use of Aristotle's practical reasoning in understanding ethical issues.[5] A tracing of our indebtedness to a *phronesis* tradition is beyond the scope of this chapter, but it is apparent that the choice-making tradition naturally embraces multiple approaches communication ethics. This chapter reviewed five choices or categories grounding communication ethics.

Categorizing Approaches to Communication Ethics

In discerning the choices or categories for organizing communication ethics articles in our disciplinary journals, this author turned initially to four introductory communication ethics articles. Jensen[6] provided a beginning categorization of the choices represented in communication ethics research: (a) Judeo-Christian, (b) democratic, and (c) scientific descriptive. Johnson[7] surveyed the disparity between the many Speech instructors proclaiming that ethics "should be" taught (90%) and the few who actually teach communication ethics (28%) (pp. 58-61). Johannesen,[8] as guest editor of *Communication*, devoted an entire volume to various approaches to communication ethics. Finally, Chesebro[9] summarized five major areas of communication ethics research (pp. 104-107). (Interestingly, more than half of the articles written on ethics in communication were published after 1969.) This article adopts four of Chesebro's categories and adds another, narrative ethics. The following five categories guide this review: (a) democratic ethics; (b) procedural, standard, and code ethics; (c) universal-humanitarian ethics; (d) contextual ethics; and (e) narrative ethics.

The rationale for the above communication ethics categories is two-fold. First, this categorization has precedence in the field. Second, the category of narrative ethics was added, due to recent interest in the work of Hauerwas, MacIntyre, and Fisher.[10] The primary guidelines for inclusion of articles in this review was the use of the terms *ethics*, *morals*, or *values* in the title of the article and the article's immediate relevance to the communication ethics issue. While some articles appropriate to this study may have been overlooked and others potentially could have been placed in more than one category, a representative picture of "the status of ethics scholarship in speech communication literature" is provided. A bibliography of ethics articles published in speech communication journals is provided at the end of this review, according to the above ethics categories.

Conceptual Center

Even though five categories are used to examine the diversity of communication ethics scholarship, one theme runs throughout the research—a public/private dialectic. Bensman and Lilienfield[11] suggest that, when major issues are dealt with in a public fashion, a dialectical need for a more private orientation emerges, and vice versa. Of the five categories, three attempt to publicly announce some form of ethical standard—democratic, universal/humanitarian, and codes. These three approaches are counterbalanced by a contextual approach to communication ethics which relies more on individual decisions at the moment—a more privatized ethic. Only a narrative ethic attempts to go beyond this public/private dialectic with a creative synthesis. Each communication ethic category is examined within the framework of this public/private dialectic.

DEMOCRATIC ETHICS

Democratic communication ethics are based on a public *process* ethic, an open airing of diverse opinions and control by majority vote. The Jeffersonian ideal of the best ideas rising to the surface of debate is the key to democratic ethics. Traditional speech courses, such as argumentation and free speech, keep this public effort to weigh and consider ideas a mainstay of our discipline.

In fact, the democratic communication ethics category is the best known in our discipline, has been used in every previous examination of the literature in communication ethics, and is consistent with our disciplinary roots in Greek democracy.[12] Seventeen articles were reviewed in this category, with the earliest being Miller, and with Hart and Redding providing the most recent contributions.[13] The following concepts and metaphors are representative of this approach: democracy, self-determination, linking democracy and conscious rational choice, debate and open discussion, freedom of dissent, cooperative controversy, democracy as a methodology for discussion, and recognition of the value of diversity of opinion.

Some contemporary social analysts claim that democratic metaphors are under attack in today's more competitive and less sharing environment. Daniel Yankelovich has stated that American youth are now more willing to limit the importance of principle and cut corners by using questionable means to get ahead, and some insist that the University campus today has too much "hard-heartedness, self-centeredness, possessiveness, materialism and driving competiveness reflected on campus by students, faculty and administration."[14] Roderick Hart offers a similar message. He challenges the Speech Communication instructor to counteract the prevailing mood of our times by not abandoning "courses in communication [that] teach us to accept boat-rocking, protests, and free speech as necessary and desirable part of the American tradition."[15]

In another 1985 article, Charles Redding states his distress when a business speaker stated, "We don't particularly need boat-rockers" (p. 245).[16] Redding's point, like Hart's, is that our discipline has traditionally encouraged boat rocking and whistle-blowing when necessary.

Perhaps it is still important to inform introductory communication students about Wallace's four *habits* required in democratic communication ethics: (a) *habit of search* (search for information that both confirms and questions one's own premises), (b) *habit of justice* (present all the information openly and fairly), (c) *habit of preferring public to private motivation,* and (d) *habit of respect for dissent.* Such respect for information gathering and presentation aids in the actualization of Cicero's hope of giving the majority the power to limit the elite and "expert" class.[17]

Wallace's *habit of permitting dissent* is consistent with Haiman's[18] belief that an unusual imbalance of power coupled with an unwillingness to listen legitimizes protest and dissent in the streets. Short-circuiting open discussion is in direct violation of democratic ethics.[19] As Day[20] suggests, open discussion is the methodological door to democracy.

The emphasis on open discussion paved the way for Brown and Keller's[21] merging of interpersonal communication and democratic ethics, no longer limiting this orientation to rhetorical scholarship.

> We have said the idea [interpersonal communication ethic] is not a new one. . . . A number of years ago Thomas Nilsen set forth what he regarded as the paramount values of democracy. They were: 'A belief in the intrinsic worth of the human personality; a belief in reason as an instrument of individual and social development; man's fulfillment of his potentialities as a positive good.' The values he mentions, interestingly enough, could be translated almost completely, into Erich Fromm's 'humanistic values.' They seem to us to represent an extraordinarily cogent statement of a value system on which an ethical rhetoric could be established. (p. 79)

Brown and Keller's work emphasized the connection between interpersonal communication and a democratic ethic. In addition, it describes the kinship between a democratic interpersonal communication ethic and humanistic psychology, founded by Carl Rogers and Abraham Maslow. Rogers' inclusion in all four editions of *Bridges No Walls* indicates his close connection to interpersonal communication, and Rogers' biographer called his approach as American as apple pie and democracy.[22]

The democratic ethic in the humanistic approaches of Rogers and Brown and Keller in our field stresses the right to be heard. Instead of "one person, one vote," their view seems to be "one person, one voice to which we must listen."[23] Keller discusses the possibility of being committed to a position and simultaneously being open to new information; listening to dissent and encouraging constructive change is central to a healthy democracy.[24] As John F. Kennedy stated, "Those who make peaceful revolution [dissent] impossible will make violent revolution inevitable."[25] Perhaps the best ideas rise to the surface if we have the courage to listen to the powerless as well as the powerful.

Significance for Communication Studies

The results of the Yankelovich poll and the warning words of Hart and Redding indicate that the "old time" emphasis on democratic ethics is not passe but is still an important issue for speech communication classrooms. However, only the research implications from Redding relating to organizational communication push the democratic ethics category into new terrain; he asks the relevance and significance of the ethic for the corporate world. Such inquiry is timely in an era of the business oriented student in speech communication. Thus, use of the democratic ethics paradigm for analyzing applied communication settings and for rhetorical criticism is still a significant research endeavor.

The democratic ethic in communication studies is a public process for forging mass collaboration on ideas, customs, and rights. The inalienable rights in a democratic ethic are grounded in the next communication ethic, universal/humanitarian perspective.

UNIVERSAL/HUMANITARIAN ETHIC

The universal/humanitarian approach also seeks a public ethical posture. But it is a public announcement of principles, not a public decision-making process. The universal/humanitarian approach to communication ethics requires a select intellegentsia to announce principles that should guide communicative behavior. However, the principles are *not created* by the intelligentsia; rather they are universal, a priori principles announced, supported, and if necessary, fought for by an enlightened and insightful minority. A universal/humanitarian communication ethic is the model of the Old Testament prophets and Plato's philosopher king. This elite orientation is at odds with the democratic love of process and mass participation. However, without such an ethic, high and lofty goals for human conduct would not likely be available for the masses to consider.

Twenty-five articles were categorized within the universal/humanitarian perspective, from Pellegrini to Eubanks and Lake.[26] This approach recognizes fundamental characteristics that constitute civilizing values. Metaphors representing this ethical position include: humanness, culture, wisdom, levels of morality, dignity, social value, human values, reasonable man (person), humane knowledge, principles, critique of ethical relativism, character, commitment, responsibility, and human rights.

The universal/humanitarian category represents a search for a position more permanent than ethical relativism. Johnstone[27] describes the universal/ humanitarian ethic as a rhetorical mission of generating "humane knowledge." Rhetoric is a vehicle through which people gather their wisdom as they test propositions in everyday communication. Johnstone contends that humane knowledge is universal, in that it is potentially available through discourse and invited by civilizing values that encourage a search for higher ideals and principles. Johnstone's pursuit of humane knowledge adds to Flynn's[28] reference to Quintilian's urging that the orator study moral principles, by suggesting that morality is made visible in discourse, not in isolation.

The communicative task from a universal/humanitarian perspective is to uphold values of culture and wisdom that focus, according to Eubanks, on "the *high dignity and essential worth of the individual human person* as homo sapiens, or 'the symbol-using animal' " [emphasis in original][29] Eubanks calls for a rebirth of two terms in communication: *culture* and *wisdom*. He laments that, today, culture is used primarily in an anthropological sense instead of simply implying a quality education. He conceives of wisdom as the vehicle through which culture is creatively put to use. The work of Johnstone and Eubanks suggests that the *potential* for humane knowledge at one historical moment may not be so considered at another. Thus, the potential is universal, but the particular expression is historically grounded.

An even firmer universal position is present in the work of Kohlberg and Weaver. Lower[30] describes Kohlberg's stages of moral development (often viewed as a universal description) as an assessment of the moral character of a speech:

(1) Preconventional level of moral development
  (a) Stage one: There is an overt response to punishment.
  (b) Stage two: Recognizes the importance for instrumental action and the necessity to satisfy one's own needs.
(2) Conventional level of moral development
  (a) Stage three: Importance is attached to being a nice boy or girl and behavior is judged by attributed intention.
  (b) Stage four: Is typified by being a rule follower.
(3) Post-conventional level of moral development
  (a) Stage five: One is willing to follow a social contract with the possibility of changing the rules to fit the unique situation.
  (b) Stage six: One chooses ethical principles that are uniquely applied to human situations, such as justice, reciprocity, and equality. (pp. 178–191)

Kohlberg's levels of moral development are universal in that they are perceived to be concrete stages with the postconventional level of moral development permitting growth of "humane knowledge" and ethical principles.

Johannesen[31] identifies Weaver's communicative ethic as conforming to this universal/humanitarian perspective because of his acceptance of Platonic idealism and the importance he places on universal principles.

> As a Platonic Idealist, Weaver believes in the reality of transcendentals, the primacy of ideas, and the view that form is prior to substance. Reality for him is a hierarchy in which the ultimate Idea of the Good constitutes the value standard by which all other existents could be appraised for degree to which things and ideas in the material world conform to their archetypes and essences. (p. 127)

Reality for Weaver is independent of the person; it consists of principles that are lasting, given, and good. The task of rhetoric is to infuse universal principles into human interaction, providing a picture or vision of an Ideal by which the human can better himself or herself. Arguments are then hierarchially judged by their approximation of an ethical Ideal defined a priori to human interaction: (a) argument from rational definition, (b) argument from similitude, (c) argument from cause/effect, and (d) argument from circumstances. Arguments from genus and similitude are preferable to those initiated from cause-effect reasoning and circumstances because they more closely approximate an a priori Ideal, independent of the current moment.

Lake[32] describes Weaver's rhetoric as a deontological ethic of duty and obligation. It is an ethic which establishes a responsibility to work for the "recovery of the ceremony of 'innocence,' of that clearness of vision and knowledge of form which enable us to sense what is alien of destruction. . ." (p. 425) Weaver urges us to stretch—to reach for a vision of higher ideal, a moral landscape beyond the present situation.

Significance for Communication Studies

Weaver, through the eyes of Johannesen and Lake, affirms the universal even more than does Johnstone. But in both cases, it is communication or rhetoric that is needed to actualize the humane knowledge or the ultimate Idea of Good. The a priori ideal of the universal/humanitarian ethic emphasizes civilizing values grounded in principles, not anthropocentricism. Viktor Frankl's[33] work is a prime example of this approach where ethical principles are *dis-covered*, not created by the person. In short, rhetoric and communication theory using this approach conceptualize the person as necessary but not sufficient for ethical decision making. The universal/humanitarian communication ethic requires *public* proclamation of a priori higher principles that have permanence and universality.

The universal/humanitarian approach can best be viewed as an ethic or standard from which criticism or appeals to higher ideals can commence. For this approach to further mature, the historicality/standard question, which only Johnstone's work in this area has begun to address, must be explored. Bernstein[34] may assist in such inquiry. In general, however, application, not new theory construction, is most likely to emerge from this approach to communication ethics.

CODES, PROCEDURES, AND STANDARDS IN COMMUNICATION ETHICS

The final contribution to the public side of the public/private dialectic of ethical positions is Codes, Procedures, and Standards. Like the universal/humanitarian approach, this orientation relies on a select number of guardians of appropriate ethical conduct. Only in this case, the members *create* the codes and procedures; they are not discovered a priori principles. Thirty-six articles were categorized together from Knower to Bennett.[35] Rating scales, standards, codes of ethics, procedures for argument, testing and/or measurement of values, ethical proof, and guidelines are used to describe this approach to communication ethics.

The establishment of a code or standard is often critiqued as an inflexible approach to ethics by those trained in the aftermath of Thomas Kuhn's[36] description of multiple paradigms. Yet, in persuasive fashion, this group of articles argues that codes and standards commit people to a public stance. The very realization that something ought to be done implicitly recognizes the existence of a standard, as Haiman[37] explains:

> Our question now becomes, not 'Is it done?' or 'Is it necessary?' but 'Ought it to be done?' When we raise the question as to whether something ought to be done we imply that there are certain standards or criteria by which we can judge and evaluate it. (p. 7)

As a discipline, we have grappled with Haiman's "Ought it to be done?" in articles concerning debate, the ethics of ghostwritten speeches, and procedures for arguing value-laden propositions. Murphy's position, rejecting debating both sides of an issue, is in contrast with Dell's position that debating both sides of a proposition is academically justifiable. Even though supportive opinion rests with Dell, 93%, the issue for some still remains, "What procedural code should we permit to govern a debate contest?"[38]

The argument between Bormann and Auer concerning ghostwriting reveals a similar set of questions. In 1961, Bormann stated that, for a speech to be ethical, it must satisfy one of two standards: (a) it must be written by the individual delivering the speech, or (b) the real author must be credited at the beginning of the oration. Auer's standard is a contrary pragmatic position suggesting that we must simply hold a speaker accountable for ideas spoken, whether written by him/her or another.[39]

Rieke and Smith suggest two basic standards for the debate activity itself. First, investigation should be encouraged over gamesmanship. Second, a variety of techniques should be established to permit more quantity and quality time to be devoted to the examination of evidence. Again concerning debate, Warnick attempts to establish a standard for implementing a value debate by formulating a standard from which one can, to a degree, judge the 'truth' value of a value proposition.[40]

Rice[41] calls for a code of ethics for the Speech Communication Association. He provides a lengthy description of guidelines for constructing a code, and he discusses the problems such a code would alleviate for the communication discipline.

The most recent contribution in the standard genre is Bennett's[42] proposal to limit what he terms *negative communication*. He defines negative communication as interactions which discourage challenging content assumptions in discourse, rationalize the status quo, negate innovation, and press facts "into the service of already determined idealized versions of reality" (p. 275). Bennett quotes McGee's warning that a view uncritically accepted without a countermyth decays, leaving behind only a word or *ideograph*, instead of a conceptually powerful rhetorical vision (p. 283). Bennett proposes a series of propositions of standards to minimize "systematic negative communicative strategies that subvert possible new realities while reaffirming existing categories of 'preferred thought' " (p. 287).

Significance for Communication Studies

Standards and codes are important to most organizations in crisis and in beginning identity formation, as long as they are not taken too legalistically. The value of codes lies more in their ability to promote discussion than in the total regulation of behavior. Communication research in this area is particularly fruitful for emerging applied areas of communication such as organizational consulting.

The final category in the public/private dialectic of ethical positions is the contextual communication ethic. This approach provides a private counterweight to the effort to make ethical decisions public.

CONTEXTUAL ETHICS

Although one can differentiate between contextual, relativistic, and emotivist ethics, for the purpose of this review they are gathered together because of their private reliance on individual discernment at the moment of decision. The twentieth century has been the era of contextual and relativistic ethics. The work of Einstein, Heisenberg, Polanyi, Kuhn, and MacIntyre all contributes to this ethic. In this communication ethic decisions emerge more from the private self, not from a democratic process, a priori principles, or agreed-upon standards and codes.

Sixteen articles were organized under the contextual category, with Schrier and Bormann offering initial and contemporary contributions to this approach.

The terms *choice, variability, flexibility, critique of absolutes and universals, rule violation, audience and context adaptation,* and *belief* as a *value* manifested in a specific situation are vocabulary associated with this approach. Condon reminds us that values and ethics are generally not universal, but culturally or contextually rooted. Even when an ethical standard is carried out across cultures, its implementation is generally unique. Condon's message is akin to that of Schrier 50 years earlier. "There is no separate standard of ethics for public speakers; each case of persuasion must be judged in the light of the particular instance" (pp. 476-477).[43]

Erlich suggests that variations in the context or the needs of the moment encouraged Thoreau to speak on behalf of John Brown and for Towne and Stringfeller to support the civil disobedience of the Berrigan brothers. As Burgess suggests, no matter what metamoral perspective one attempts to work from, in the moment of crisis an individual decision must be made that may or may not conform to standards and principles normally affirmed.[44]

As the contextual requirements in a communicative exchange shift, even lying becomes, at time, appropriate. One group of authors (Camden, Motley, and Wilson) posed the question: Is contextual lying a communicative competence or not? The contextual lying question becomes even more significant in light of the fact that some communicative actions are more irreparable than others, according to Cox. Thus, it is possible that some people lie in order to avoid a potentially "irreparable communicative exchange."[45]

Significance to Communication Studies

A contextual perspective on ethics justifies different communication standards for different audiences, cultures, and relationships. Perhaps the majority of today's students are taught a contextual ethic, implicitly and/or explicitly. This approach has been the dominant theme of the latter part of the twentieth century. The research in this area has made its contribution with emphasis on subjectivity, historicality, and critique of absolute ethical standards. However, further research in communication ethics is more likely to focus on the last category, narrative ethics. Narrative ethics extends beyond the public/private dialectic of communication ethics positions.

NARRATIVE ETHICS

Many of the articles in this final category would have been placed in the universal/humanitarian and the contextual genres prior to the contributions of Hauerwas, MacIntyre, and Fisher.[46] This section includes articles directly related to narrative ethics, and others that have paved a conceptual path to this approach.

Articles on or related to narrative ethics number 24 with Free and Fisher[47] offering initial and recent contributions. Words and phrases associated with narrative ethics are as follows: *narrative, Homer, story, community, drama*, and *homo narrans*. This storytelling orientation—like the Biblical narrative—requires, not a set of rigid laws to follow, but a story to guide people, a willingness to bring into dialogue the story and the contemporary moment, and a desire to find a vision without locking the follower into an uncompromising pattern or technique.

Although Fisher's narrative approach is the most recent potential contribution to the study of communicative ethics, it did not emerge spontaneously without assistance from conceptually distant cousins. Over 20 years ago, Chesebro[48] conceptualized Burke's pentad as a synthesis of various approaches to communication ethics. Chesebro correlated each element of Burke's pentad with five different approaches to ethics of communication.

1. Purpose—Democratic ethics
2. Agent—Individual humanitarian ethic
3. Agency—Ethical means consistent with society's prescriptions
4. Act—Communication process, related to freedom of speech ethics
5. Scene—Context or contextual ethics.

The primary connection between narrative and Burke's pentad is the importance of story or narrative for the enactment of any drama.

Crable,[49] in another explication of Burke's dramatistic approach, used Burke's pentad to ground ethics in the realm of moral action (a combination of teleological and deontological), not adherence to an inflexible code of ethics. In such an approach it is not the code, but how the code is used in the narrative or drama, that is crucial to the ethics of human communication. The code is not the ending, but the starting place, of an ethical drama.

A narrative ethic provides a flexible guideline tied to a community that nourishes the vision, as illustrated by Hauerwas' analysis of the "rabbit community" in *Watership Down*. Only when a narrative guideline emerges from the community in public fashion can it guide. Fisher states that individual and privatized ethics are contrary to public disclosure, which requires the community to openly discuss guiding stories.[50]

This community focus has also been addressed in some earlier related articles. To experience community, one must be involved in the story. Andersen[51] broadens community involvement with his 300% formula of responsibility in communication—100% for the speaker, another 100% for the receiver, and a final 100% for nonparticipants in the conversation. Andersen suggests that both those directly and indirectly involved must recognize that argument or the offering of counterstories is central to a story-telling ethic and community formation.

Argument within community in today's complex society needs to be grounded in standards sensitive to a pluralistic community. Brummett[52] calls for community standards sensitive to a pluralistic set of participants.

> The relativist's problem of judging across social boundaries occurs more often in philosophy than in fact. German Nazis *ought* to know better because they *do* share community with Jews, Slavs, Yankees, and the dissenters of their culture. (p. 298; emphasis in original)

Brummett's desire to ground ethics in pluralistic community standards that must be actualized rhetorically is akin to Alasdair MacIntyre's.[53] Both are concerned about rhetoric and community standards, only MacIntyre explicitly discusses the notion of narrative. In a description of MacIntyre's work, Frentz[54] defines narrative as the forging of past and future into the temporal present.

> Narratives are dramatic stories with beginnings, middles, and ends which give individual actions meaning, provide unity and self-definition to individual lives, and facilitate improvement of the impersonal good for humankind by showing the future as potential extensions of the present. (p. 5)

Narrative or story provides a community with a why or context for action and rhetoric of practice. As Frentz suggests, MacIntyre forged Homer (story) and Aristotle (practical action) into a narrative that propels one to action, not just aesthetic enjoyment of the story line. Fisher also uses MacIntyre's approach in his discussion of narration and community. For community to emerge, ethical standards must come forth in the public debate within a community.

For Fisher,[55] the narrative paradigm unites the literary or aesthetic and the argumentative and persuasive traditions with four major features. First, the notion of story transcends many modern dualisms that confront us, such as fact–value, reason-emotion, and public-private. Second, a lasting story has a value and moral dimension to it. Third, reason itself is grounded in the background of story, not the dry waste of unconnected facts. Fourth, and perhaps most importantly for Fisher, narrative offers a way of engaging more participants in public moral argument. *Rationality* of the *experts* with the *appropriate* credentials limits discussion and asks an audience passively to accept expert opinion. However, from a story-telling perspective, the expert is a story-teller and the audience participates in the narrative. Argument is permitted as rival experts become people with contrasting stories with the audience involved in each (pp. 10-15). As in Andersen's 300% statement of communication ethics responsibility, the audience becomes actively involved.

Significance for Communication Studies

Narrative ethics is the most novel of the five approaches discussed in this review. The recent interest implies more research is needed in this area. Fisher himself continues this line of inquiry in his 1985 comparison of the narrative paradigm to social scientific and humanistic theories.[56] Specifically, narrative ethics seems to provide two helpful insights. First, it can be seen as the ethical counterpart to Bernstein's[57] philosophical conclusion that "keeping the conversation going" is a necessary first step in locating an alternative to objectivism and relativism. In ethical terms narrative provides an alternative to dogmatism and relativism—or what this chapter has termed the *public/private dialectic*. Second, a case can be made that all ethical approaches are dramas or stories from which human actions can be understood and evaluated.

The narrative ethic has close kinship with the universal/humanitarian perspective. A key difference, however, is that the universal/humanitarian ethic is a priori grounded in an ideal, while narrative is rooted in community. In short, the former can only be approximated in discourse, while the latter is constituted in the common communication life of a people. When the community theme is forgotten we move from narrative to individual speech. Observation of future research in this area will determine if community remains the formative place of narrative. Also, we will need to examine the lack of community vocabulary and lack of community in contemporary society.[58]

SUMMARY EVALUATION AND FUTURE RESEARCH DIRECTIONS

The charge of the Communication Ethics Commission of SCA was to examine the status of ethics of Speech Communication research in our journals. Each of the ethics categories described—democratic ethics, universal/humanitarian ideals, standards and codes, contextual responses, and narrative—has tradition and a contemporary contribution for our discipline. Only a narrative communication ethic is likely to go beyond use in applied communication research and criticism and contribute new theoretical insights.

In summary, the five categories are not equally insightful for understanding contemporary ethical problems in communication, as evaluation at the end of each section revealed. The democratic communication ethic is part of our history or story as a country and discipline and is still worthy of instruction and application. Codes and standards assist the ethical formation of new organizations and can be a fruitful starting place for ethical discussions related to an organization. The universal/ humanitarian ethics of Plato's a priori principles act as a foundation for religious and ideologically oriented rhetoric. However, none of these efforts at *public* announcement of ethics via democratic *process*, discernment of universal principles, or negotiated codes is likely to provide new theoretical insights. Similarly, the *private* approach of contextual communication ethics is of more value in pedagogy and in application than in new theory construction.

Interestingly, the newest approach to communication ethics research, narrative ethics, seeks to go beyond a public/private dialectic of ethical orientations and most closely is associated with classical studies. Frentz, Fisher, and MacIntyre ground their work in Homer and Aristotle. Narrative scholarship is demanding in that it requires knowledge of the *public* tradition and a willingness to bring into dialogue the *private* questions of the contemporary moment. Gadamer provides an excellent model of this form of scholarship in his work with Plato's dialogues.[59]

The effort to go beyond the public/private dialectic of ethical approaches places us in the heart of the most important philosophical question today—how do we affirm standards with our contemporary understanding of historicality of knowledge and insight? This is the central question in the Haberman-Gadamer debate and the major issue for Bernstein, MacIntyre, and Hauerwas, in philosophy and theology, respectively. These scholars do not have a narrative ethic totally conceptualized; it is in the beginning stages. We, as a discipline, can productively enter this conversation with the work of Fisher and Frentz leading the way. As Fisher[60] states, the narrative paradigm is:

> A response to the exigence of our time identified by Gadamer: 'In the age of science, is there any way of preserving and validating the great heritage of knowledge and wisdom?' That way is to formulate a theory of human communication that recognizes permanence and change, culture and character, reason and value, and the practical wisdom of all people.

Whatever approach to communication ethics one pursues, it seems that we must be guided by the practical wisdom that, if we are to be concerned about ethical issues in communication and do not wish to place ourselves at the mercy of expert opinion, then argument, debate, and public discourse over what is and is not ethical must continue. If we are to be good choicemakers, we must actively pursue opportunities to ask ethical questions about the process and the content of communication. For, as Johannesen quotes Charles Frankel, " 'All that follows from the fact there are no experts in morals is that morals are everybody's business.' "[61].

NOTES

[1]J. Chesebro, "A Construct for Assessing Ethics in Communication," *Central States Speech Journal*, 20 (1969): 104–114; J. V. Jensen, "An Analysis of Recent Literature on Teaching Ethics in Public Address," *The Speech Teacher*, 8 (1959): 219–228. And see K. E. Anderson, "Communication Ethics: The Non-Participant's Role," *Southern Speech Communication Journal*, 49 (1984): 219–228; D. Callahan and S. Bok, *Ethics Teaching in Higher Education* (New York: Plenum, 1980).

[2]R. L. Johannesen, *Ethics in Human Communication* (Prospect Heights, IL: Waveland, 1978); T. Nilsen, *Ethics of Speech Communication, 2nd ed.* (Indianapolis, IN: Bobbs-Merrill, 1974); L. Thayer, Ed., *Communication: Ethical and Moral Issues* (New York: Gordon & Breach, 1980).

[3]E. G. Bormann, "Ethics and Small Group Communication," *Speech Association of Minnesota Journal*, 12 (1985): 20–25.

[4]C. L. Johnstone, "An Aristotelian Trilogy: Ethics, Rhetoric, Politics, and the Search for Moral Truth," *Philosophy and Rhetoric*, 13 (1980): 1–24.

[5]Aristotle, *Nicomachean Ethics* (Indianapolis, IN: Hackett, 1985); H. Gadamer, *Dialogue and the Dialectic: Eight Hermeneutical Studies on Plato* (New Haven: Yale U P, 1980); R. Bernstein, *Beyond Objectivism and Relativism: Science, Hermeneutics, and Praxis* (Philadephia: U of Pennsylvania P, 1983); A. MacIntyre, *After Virtue: A Study in Moral Theory* (Notre Dame, IN: U of Notre Dame P, 1981).

[6]op. cit.

[7]R. C. Johnson, "Teaching Speech Ethics in the Beginning Speech Course," *The Speech Teacher*, 19 (1970): 58–61.

[8]R. L. Johannesen, "Issues Editor's Introduction: Some Ethical Questions in Human Communication," *Communication*, 6 (1981): 145–157.

[9]op. cit.

[10]S. Hauerwas, *A Community of Character* (Notre Dame, IN: U of Notre Dame P, 1984); MacIntyre, op. cit.; W. R. Fisher, "Narrative as a Human Communication Paradigm: The Case of Public Moral Argument," *Communication Monographs*, 51 (1984): 1–22.

[11]J. Bensman and R. Lilienfeld, *Between Public and Private: Lost Boundaries of the Self (New York: Free Press, 1979).*

[12]J. L. Golden, G. F. Berquist, and W. E. Coleman, *The Rhetoric of Western Thought, 2nd ed.* (Dubuque, IO: Kendall Hunt, 1978).

[13]O. C. Miller, "Are We Pharisees or Publicans?" *Southern Speech Bulletin*, 1 (1936): 5–10; R. P. hart, "The Politics of Communication Studies: An Address to Undergraduates," *Communication Education*, 34 (1985): 162–165; C. Redding, "Rocking Boats, Blowing Whistles, and Teaching Speech Communication," *Communication Education*, 34 (1985): 245–258.

[14]V. Schmid, "The Pastor's Duty to Stand Sentry," *The Christian Century*, 100 (1983): 1127–1128.

[15]op. cit., 162.

[16]op. cit., 245.

[17]E. Rogge, "Evaluating the Ethics of a Speaker in a Democracy," *Quarterly Journal of Speech*, 45 (1979): 419–425.

[18]F. S. Haiman, "The Rhetoric of the Streets: Some Legal and Ethical Considerations," *Quarterly Journal of Speech*, 53 (1967): 99–114.

[19]F. S. Haiman, "Democratic Ethics and the Hidden Persuaders," *Quarterly Journal of Speech*, 44 (1958): 385–392.

[20]D. G. Day, "The Ethics of Democratic Debate," *Central States Speech Journal*, 17 (1966): 5–14.

[21]C. T. Brown and P. W. Keller, "An Interpersonal Ethic for Communication," *Journal of Communication*, 6 (1968): 73–81.

[22]H. Kirschenbaum, *On Becoming Carl Rogers* (New York: Dell, 1975).

[23]Brown and Keller, op. cit.

[24]P. W. Keller, "Interpersonal Dissent and the Ethics of Dialogue," *Communication*, 6 (1981): 298.

[25]M. L. King, Jr., "Vietnam and the Struggle for Human Rights," in *War and the Christian Conscience: From Augustine to Martin Luther King, Jr.*, ed. by A. Marrin (Chicago: Henry Regnery, 1971) 304.

[26]A. M. Pellegrini, "Public Speaking and Social Obligations," *Quarterly Journal of Speech*, 20 (1934), 345–351; R. T. Eubanks, "On Living in the House of Humanities," *Southern Speech Communication Journal*, 48 (1982): 1–10; R. Lake, "Order and Disorder in Anti-Abortion Rhetoric: A Logical View," *Quarterly Journal of Speech*, 70 (1984): 425–443.

[27]C. L. Johnstone, "Ethics, Wisdom, and the Mission of Contemporary Rhetoric: The Realization of Human Being," *Central States Speech Journal*, 32 (1981): 177–188.

[28]L. J. Flynn, "The Aristotelian Basis for the Ethics of Speaking," *The Speech Teacher*, 6 (1957): 179–187.

[29]R. T. Eubanks, "Nihilism and the Problem of a Worthy Rhetoric," *Southern Speech Journal*, 33 (1968): 194.

[30]F. J. Lower, "Kohlberg's Moral Stages as a Critical Tool," *Southern Speech Communication Journal*, 47 (1982): 178–191.

[31]R. L. Johannesen, "Richard M. Weaver on Standards for Ethical Rhetoric," *Central States Speech Journal*, 29 (1978): 127.

[32]op. cit., 425.

[33]V. Frankl, *The Unheard Cry for Meaning: Psychotherapy and Humanism* (New York: Simon, 1978).

[34]op. cit.

[35]F. H. Knower, "A Suggestive Study of Public-Speaking Rating Scale Values," *Quarterly Journal of Speech* 15 (1959): 30–41; W. L. Bennett, "Communication and Social Responsibility," *Quarterly Journal of Speech*, 71 (1985): 259–288.

[36]T. Kuhn, *The Structure of Scientific Revolutions, 2nd ed., enl.* (Chicago: U of Chicago P, 1970).

[37]F. S. Haiman, "A Re-Examination of the Ethics of Persuasion," *Central States Speech Journal*, 3 (1952): 4–9.

[38]R. Murphy, "The Ethics of Debating Both Sides," *The Speech Teacher*, 6 (1957): 1–9; G. W. Dell, "In Defense of Debating Both Sides," *The Speech Teacher*, 7 (1958): 31–34; D. Klopf and J. McCroskey, "Ethical Practices in Debate," *Journal of the American Forensic Association*, 1 (1964): 16.

[39]F. Haiman, E. G. Bormann, and J. J. Auer, "Ghostwriting and the Cult of Leadership," *Communication Education*, 33 (1984): 306–307.

[40]R. D. Rieke and D. H. Smith, "The Dilemma of Ethics and Advocacy in the Use of Evidence," *Western Speech*, 32 (1968): 223–233.

[41]G. P. Rice, Jr., "Do We Need a Code of Ethics?" *Association for Communication Administration Bulletin*, 18 (1976): 7–13.

[42]op. cit.

[43]W. Schrier, "The Ethics of Persuasion," *Quarterly Journal of Speech*, 16 (1930): 476–486; Bormann, op. cit.; J. Condon, "Values and Ethics in Communication Across Cultures: Some Notes on the North American Case," *Communication*, 6 (1981): 255–267.

[44]H. J. Erlich, " '. . . And By Opposing, End Them. . . ' The Genre of Moral Justification for Legal Transgressions," *Communication Quarterly*, 23 (1975): 13–16; P. G. Burgess, "The Rhetoric of Moral Conflict: Two Critical Approaches," *Quarterly Journal of Speech*, 56 (1970): 120–130.

[45]C. Camden, M. T. Motley, and A. Wilson, "White Lies in Interpersonal Communication: A Taxonomy and Preliminary Investigation of Social Motivations," *Western Journal of Speech Communication*, 48 (1984): 309–325; J. R. Cox, "The Die is Cast: Topical and Ontological Dimensions of the *Locus* of the Irreparable," *Quarterly Journal of Speech*, 68 (1982): 227–239.

[46]op. cit.

[47]W. M. Free, "Aesthetic and Moral Value in *Bonnie and Clyde*," *Quarterly Journal of Speech*, 54 (1968): 220–225; W. R. Fisher, "The Narrative Paradigm: An Elaboration," *Communication Monographs*, 52 (1985): 347–357.

[48]op. cit.

[49]R. E. Crable, "Ethical Codes, Accountability, and Argumentation," *Quarterly Journal of Speech*, 64 (1978): 23–32.

[50]Hauerwas, op. cit.; Fisher, "Narrative Paradigm."

[51]op. cit.

[52]B. Brummett, "A Defense of Ethical Relativism as Rhetorically Grounded," *Western Journal of Speech Communication*, 45 (1981): 286–298.

[53]op. cit.

[54]T. S. Frentz, "Rhetorical Conversation, Time, and Moral Action," *Quarterly Journal of Speech*, 71 (1985): 1–18.

[55]Fisher, "Narrative," 10–15.

[56]Ibid.

[57]op. cit.

[58]R. N. Bellah et al., *Habits of the Heart: Individualism and Commitment in American Life* (Berkeley, CA: U of California P, 1985).

[59]H. Gadamer, *Dialogue and the Dialectic: Eight Hermeneutical Studies on Plato* (New Haven, CT: Yale U P, 1980).

[60]Fisher, "Narrative Paradigm," 354.

[61]Johannesen, "Issues," 155.

Part II

Individual Systems of Account Making

4

Discursive Community and the Problem of Perspective in Ethical Criticism

Frederick J. Antczak

Rhetoric Department
University of Iowa

FINDING A FOCUS: SUBJECTIVITY OF PERSPECTIVE AS A CRITICAL PROBLEM

> Tell me what you saw,
> and I'll tell you who you are.
> —Robert Rosenberg

The occasions for raising ethical questions about persuasive texts appear in tantalizing variety, in ways both theoretical and practical. Yet, unless its peculiar problem of perspective is addressed, ethical criticism risks failing to be a form of criticism at all. This chapter proposes to outline that problem of perspective, to suggest a new critical focus, and to examine its capacities.

The impulse to make ethical judgments of texts has of course ample theoretical provocations, from Plato's *Gorgias* and *Phaedrus* through the Romans' explorations of what it meant to be "a good man speaking well" on to Kenneth Burke's exhortations to view language as a constitutively human mode of action.

Ethical questions are pressed at least as urgently by the vagaries of contemporary persuasive practices, which seem not merely to invite, but to cry out for, sharper ethical analysis. At a time when our leading political candidates call each other liars, racists, classists, and worse, it seems that even their harshest criticisms fall far short of capturing much of what is most disturbing in the ways they argue. But strangely, while we lack sufficiently rich and diverse ways of talking about the ethical issues that emerge from the study of public discourse, those issues nonetheless promise to sustain a very lively and enlightening debate. It would surely be productive to find new ways of talking about questions like: what are the obligations of cigarette advertisements, especially given government-mandated warning labels, by way of information about health risk? Is it somehow culpable morally to sell a recreational vehicle known for its proclivities to roll over with the slogan "never a dull moment"? How are we to read one televangelist's seeming indictment of the Author of all Goodness for a form of extortion: namely, that God would "take him home" if a certain fundraising goal was not met by deadline, no pun apparently intended? How are we to evaluate the claims to sincere repentance and reform by other televangelists who in the same breath refuse to submit themselves to any Church authority[1] beyond their own conscience? What are we to make of a marine colonel who admits that yes, he's certainly lied before, knowingly, even under oath, shredded evidence, obstructed investigations, held his private purposes above the law and beyond Constitutionally mandated Congressional oversight, but nevertheless and therefore he's not the sort of hero-next-door to be lying *now*, to *us*, when facing public investigation and possible indictment? and who unblushingly ornaments this argument, an argument ostensibly about his personal character, with the flag and the uniform he claims to hold dear—"Checkers," as it were, with a less reticent prop man?

Though these situations suggest both occasions and needs for pursuing ethical knowledge and advancing ethical judgments of texts, it is still not clear how such judgments are to be reached, or how they could qualify as verifiable knowledge. The problem with formulating and pursuing ethical questions in a way that can be tested and refined by critical debate, and with conducting such debate so that it might ultimately issue in something we can regard as ethical knowledge of texts, is that we lack a stable and sharable focus for such criticism. About this problem of perspective in ethical criticism, Edwin Black has remarked,

> The moral judgment of a text is a portentious act in the process of criticism, and . . . the terminal character of such a judgment works to close critical discussion rather than open or encourage it. Moral judgments, however balanced, however

> elaborately qualified, are nonetheless categorical. Once rendered, they shape decisively one's relationship to the object judged. They compel, as forcefully as the mind can be compelled, a manner of apprehending an object. Moral judgments coerce one's perceptions of things.[2]

It seems that, by its nature, ethical judgment involves the critic's subjectivity. His or her subjective commitments and preferences, though they have no necessary relationship to the text being criticized, nonetheless powerfully shape how the critic may see that text—what is viewed as unworthy of comment, what captures attention as deserving analysis, and so on. Moreover, there is nothing to prevent so personal a perspective from being at odds, apparently irreconcilably, with the different ethical perspectives adopted by others. Insofar as it cannot escape involving and reflecting the subjectivity of the critic, ethical criticism by its nature always risks failing to be a mode of criticism at all—failing, that is, to find a stable and sharable focus capable of performing the essential (if not exhaustive) critical tasks of illuminating the text, generating testable claims about it, and thereby invigorating critical exchange as to issue, at least sometimes, in a kind of knowledge of the text.

Perhaps the most startling example of this is provided by Black himself. When Black examined (pp. 113–118) the uses of an ethically suspect rhetoric—the Radical Right's uses of the metaphor "the cancer of communism"—he wrote as if he recognized an obligation to support his description of those uses; he gave careful and insightful explications of how each nuance of the metaphor worked. Some critical functions, namely descriptive functions, clearly seemed to him to require his characteristically acute, extensive, and painstaking support from the text. In contrast, Black offered in support of his subsequent ethical evaluation only this flat statement:

> What moral judgment may we make of this metaphor and of discourse that importantly contains it? The judgment seems superfluous, not because it is elusive, but because it is so clearly implied. The form of consciousness to which the metaphor is attached is not one that commends itself. It is not one that a reasonable man would freely choose, and he would not choose it because it does not compensate him with either prudential efficacy or spiritual solace for the anguished exactation it demands. (p. 118)

However carefully text-based matters of description were for Black, it was admissible and appropriate for evaluation to take place through a perspective that the critic *brought* to the text, *imposed* on it by his personal and unargued choice. The choice of perspective did not have to be treated as if it could be warranted by the text in some publically examinable way, nor, consequently, did it have to be treated as if it were a matter that required a reasoned defense. Black left little room for critical disagreement or diversity here, left open few ways to challenge or test or qualify or refine (or, for that matter, even agree with and validate) his central critical assertions, assertions about what it means to be a reasonable man, what prudential efficacy amounts to for different people, what spiritual solace might consist in. Nor did Black's ethical criticism suggest anything about how critical debate in this mode, with its evaluative perspective asserted without explication or further support, could be sustained and extended when such assertions conflict. When even one of our very best critics encounters such problems, they seem all the more formidable and serious. And if ethical criticism is indeed inescapably subjective, what can ethical critics do if they disagree—or if their agreement has the slightest qualification or nuance—but shout at each other or fall silent?

Black's ethical perspective reveals a good deal about *him*; we can find a great deal, a very great deal, to admire in the courage and eloquence with which he took this stand at a time when it seemed most needed to be heard and most likely to be resisted in the ugliest of ways.[3] That respect notwithstanding, we learn from Black much more about what it would be to see texts (and the world) through *his* critical vision with *his* value commitments than we do about what aspects of the text might warrant, invite, or at least admit of its being read this way. We learn almost nothing about what might make the results of reading in this way susceptible to testing and refinement in critical debate.

Or, for an instance that involves you and your activity as reader more immediately, consider the examples I offered earlier in the attempt to persuade you of the need for ethical criticism of public address. A reader might begin to infer something from, say, my voicing the question about the obligations of cigarette advertisers: I remain curious about the possibility of further obligation, even beyond the government-mandated warnings. Thus it might reasonably be inferred that I am at least willing to entertain the notion that the doctrine of the Invisible Hand (in this instance, that consumers are best left to be trusted to get the message if enough of them die) might conceivably not, in this case and perhaps others, produce optimum public policy. Or something might be gleaned from the fact that, in discussing televangelists, I am willing to apply, with apparent irreverence, legalistic categories to the edicts of God (one rejoices that Abraham blinked no such hesitation when commanded to sacrifice Isaac). Or put more precisely, I am willing to apply such categories to the alleged edicts of God as filtered through a televangelist who happened also to be a Chairman of the Board and CEO of a corporation; a corporation that happened to fall sufficiently deeply in debt that, in order to stay afloat, it had to generate quick cash; a cashflow need that happened to arise at the very moment when God, in His ineffable wisdom and dandy timing, chose to call him to this unusually subjunctive accounting.

You can even discern a little bit about what I want to think of you, for example from my writing style: in my long and complicated sentence structure, I am trusting you to be both able and willing to hold lots of things in your attention all at once, and to sort out with me the interrelations on the basis of grammatical hints that are sometimes tryingly obscure.

Perhaps a great deal could be inferred about me from my sardonic characterization of Oliver North. That I find him unblushingly contradicting himself is clear from my choice to put that "nevertheless and therefore" in his mouth; that I find his list of transgressions a long one, perhaps suggesting some form of systematic premeditation, is hinted in my stylistic choice to omit connectives in order to convey a stacking up of North's "neat ideas." You can tell a good bit about what kind of relationship I am offering when I invoke Richard Nixon's "Checkers" speech as the punchline to this sarcasm. I am calling upon you in the respect of your membership in a certain group, the community of scholars for whom a reference to that speech is differently evocative than for ordinary folk. For the sarcasm to have the real bite I clearly want it to have, you have to be (at least for the time of reading) one of those sorts of people who, though they might admire the technical shrewdness of the imagemaking, have logical problems and ethical reservations about the speech. In those criticisms, you may not be learning much about the original texts, but you can learn a fair amount—enough already, I would expect, to build a tentative pattern of expectation, a working sense of character—about me.

Or rather about "me." It would be an intentional fallacy that would rightly set Wimsatt and Beardsley[4] spinning to infer that you knew anything very certain about me, the existential person. If I were inept, I could very easily have been creating an effect I had not intended. If I were more adroit than that, I might still be lying for effect; or there may simply be, for whatever reason, some distance between my personal attitudes, their shadings and accents and emphases on the one hand, and my public stances on the other. The "real" author stays well beyond the reliable reach of such easy inferences, and to some extent even beyond protracted patterns of such inferences across different texts over many years. And, without wanting to be flip, that's not a staggering critical loss. As it is relatively less important to know what the real Shakespeare or Whitman or Salinger or deMan intended in their deepest being—less important relative to what they created in their texts—so it is relatively less important to know what the historical person who delivered a speech or the critic who wrote a criticism of it "really" meant by it.

It may seem strange to critics of public address to hear that it is relatively less important to know what, say, Richard Nixon intended by "Checkers." But that existential Nixon is irretrievable; we simply can never know the intention he had for the speech. Nor can we reliably ask him, since he may remember infirmly or may—could this be imagined—stretch the truth for some reason. In any case, his answer would simply create a new text, itself in need of another analysis and interpretation.

But isn't this is a peculiar point at which to find ourselves stymied? Almost no one lives in the belief that ethical criticism of texts is altogether impossible. Most of us feel capable, as Wayne Booth[5] points out, of having some reasoned and defensible position about whether a daily 8-hour hit of *MTV*, *Love Boat* reruns, *Wheel of Fortune*, *Rambo* cartoons, and *Lifestyles of the Rich and Famous* would be a bad trip for our children (and whether we would be discharging our obligations if we left them utterly on their own to just say no). Not only is it desirable, it is often frankly necessary to make ethical assessments about texts of many different sorts—we do it all the time, and sometimes with a good bit of confidence. Yet it would seem at best a self-deception to pretend that any reader or listener can avoid bringing something of his or her own personal perspective to such assessments; and when those assessments are shared, they tend apparently by their nature towards becoming a form of coercion themselves—an ethically questionable reduction of critical discourse to the untethered subjective preferences of the critic. How could criticism with such inherently personal bases ever be anything more than a reflection and an imposition of subjective taste? How then can ethical criticism ever hope to be a mode of developing arguments about the ethical quality of texts, and of sharing, testing, and improving those arguments in reasoned debate?

POSSIBILITIES FOR INTERSUBJECTIVITY: COMMUNITY IN THE TEXT

> In a world of flux, where self and culture are in a process of continuous and reciprocal change, the ground of judgment on which we can best rely is the ground we make with each other when we talk. Our sense of character and relation is in the end the firmest foundation of value and basis of criticism.
>
> —James Boyd White[6]

Texts surely evoke, indeed they enlist, the personal in their interpretation. Some of the more dyspeptic ethical critics (Plato, Marx, Weaver, Marcuse; the Reverend Donald Wildmon, Andrea Dworkin, Larry Flynt, Ed Meese) do at their worse moments demonstrate vividly how ethical criticism readily *could* subjectify and thereby privatize the personal in criticism. But it is not clear that, for purposes of critical judgment and discourse, "the personal" need necessarily mean the inaccessibly subjective or the unarguably, untestably private. Instead we may infer one approach to the problem of subjectivity in critical perspective from the nature of what we do when we read or listen. We might explore the ethical implications of treating the text as a commonly held and negotiated, constitutively public thing—a kind of critical *res publica* on which and around which to constitute discussion—and of coming consequently to regard the role of "the personal" in the process of reading and response as in some measure accessible, sharable, even improvable intersubjectively. By finding focus in that process, ethical criticism can perform the functions of illuminating texts and invigorating critical discourse about them.

Such a focus can be found in the relationship the author forms with the reader in the process of reading the text. Every text has such aspects of relation, dimensions of character that are recoverable, indeed are public in nature. A text is always somehow the scene of an active engagement of one character with another, an interaction that is therefore proper to regard as ethical and properly the object of ethical inquiry. We may not be able to recover much of critical import about the historical author or know it with adequate or arguable certainty; what we can know, however, is the character enacted in the discourse, the *implied author* of a text—the "Nixon" or "North" or "Black" or "Antczak" who is an aspect of the text itself, with whom any reader interacts as they read, about whom we may make critical statements testable by other readers of the discourse.[7] The implied author is manifested in a variety of publically accessible ways: in the tone he or she adopts, in the kinds and quantities of signals he or she gives the audience about how to read that tone and, on another level, the reliability of such signals. The author is further manifested in the attitudes he or she invites or discourages the audience to hold toward the world, toward institutions or groups or individuals within it, toward the emotions and ideas, causes and drives, that matter to them, and of course toward the author himself or herself and the authority he or she earns to talk this way.

But that description oversimplifies the act—or rather the complex interactions that make up the process—of reading. In its persuasive activity, every discursive text also functionally defines an *implied audience*[8] which it invites its reader or listener to join, or at least to approximate, for the time of reading. Readers are offered particular roles to play in their interaction with the text; they are allowed certain ways of functioning out of what they already are, know, feel, care about, and are discouraged from others. They are focused on certain angles of perception and dispositions of response, certain possibilities of character to realize or neglect in the interaction of reading and understanding the text. Readers are taught how functionally to join those who note, follow, and appreciate the author's moves. They learn how to be and move among those who are swayed by the sorts of proofs the author privileges—who start from the assumptions, recognize the truths, share the values, feel the sentiments, are driven by the passions, take the stands, reach the judgments, and make the commitments that the discourse requires in order to achieve its clearest intelligibility and effect.

Thus we can—in a publically accessible, intersubjectively testable way—formulate and argue critical claims about a text's implied author and implied audience as they interact in the process of reading. Carrying those concerns further, we can even attempt to describe, with some degree of intersubjectively testable precision, what sort of relation, what sort of *discursive community*[9] is enacted between the implied author and the implied audience as the text unfolds.

In other words, I propose that work in the ethics of rhetoric may be focused on the *ethos* of rhetoric enacted in each text, the way of life in language practiced in the activities of reading and interpretation into which it invites readers, the interaction of implied author and implied audience in which it engages them.

Ethical criticism with such a focus differs from previous varieties of ethical criticism in that it is in less of a rush to be evaluative. The critic must start with description of the text in terms of its intention, as best it can be inferred from the discourse itself. The critic must go on to locate the means used to assume and share authority, to persuade the audience, and to reconstitute the rhetorical relation with that audience. Only then the critic evaluates the possibilities and limits of such a relation—but, even here, not exclusively in terms he or she imports, but rather as they are shaped by the text's own terms. The critic must describe the world of perception and action that seems to confront him or her in the terms the text provides, seeing and evaluating as the text permits and enables him or her to. The purpose of such criticism is to articulate the moral possibilities and limits of this particular way of life in language; to describe in a way that others may test what it is to live and move in the discursive community that is constituted, the shared way of life in language that is continuously reconstituted in this way.

Two basic sorts of questions[10] would enable us to examine such[11] rhetorical concerns as ethical ones. The first sort concerns the *vision* in terms of which the world is to be seen and characterized for purposes of morally charged persuasion and action in the given text. Here we might inquire:

- What are its characterizing terms of description and evaluation? How do they work with one another to create the discourse's constitutive *topoi*, the lines of argument it takes to be authoritative? How do these terms work to rank-order the possibilities for appeal, and for intersections of motive?
- In what language are specific rhetorical situations with ethical import to be recognized, the thinkable alternatives for attitude and action to be characterized and made determinate for conscious and freely willed choice? With what values, assumptions, kinds of attention, and notions of authority is that language freighted and articulated?
- How do these terms clarify some possibilities (and obscure others) for sustaining or denying, extending or transforming the immediate community of discourse and the wider world in which it is given to operate?
- On a larger scale, what forms and modes of reasoning are practiced in the text as if they were valid and authoritative? What is the specific function and relative force accorded to deduction from general probability, to induction from particular example or anecdote, to analogy, story, narrative, or to the explication of aphorism?
- Which shifts and transitions does the text assume will and should pass without question? Which does it acknowledge some need to defend? How much and

what kind of need, and of what might the defense be constituted? What is regarded as unanswerable argumentative trump, and what need not be answered?

By pursuing these questions, critics can begin to determine what one can and cannot say, what one can and cannot do, or even aspire to do, through discourse constituted in the text's characterizing way. They may begin to formulate testable claims about just who it is they have to become in relation to the author, in relation to the text in its habits of language and dispositions of persuasion, in order to belong and to move appropriately and effectively in the sort of world the text establishes and enacts, and what it can mean to be and move that way.

These questions lead to larger issues of *character*, issues made intelligible by being placed in the context of morally relevant community. Critics will want to know:

- How is the discourse inclusive and exclusive? What roles does it offer or preclude for the variety of potential members of the audience, and for other parties affected but not directly addressed by the text? On what principles is this inclusion and exclusion done, how explicitly, how consistently, and how justly, especially as the text gives us to see justice?
- What relation exists between the discursive community constituted and enacted in the text and the overall culture that supplies the materials from which the text is formed? How are the potential materials for discourse treated? What is discarded without explanation or afterthought, what may be pillaged, what may be treated partially, and what comes with strings attached?
- Finally, what are the dimensions of that relation? In what ways and to what degrees is the discursive community recognizably committed to the maintenance and systematic extension, or to the destruction, or to the transformation of these cultural resources? to the recognition or denial or reshaping of their past? to the promise of a future for its author and its audience, its materials, and any others who inhabit such communities?

This sort of ethical criticism, criticism concerned with character in discursive community, will be brought into focus, not by the critic's asserted evaluations, but by sharable, testable, even improvable description of the text—description of the specific relation constituted *in the text* and enacted in the activity of reading into which it invites its readers and engages them. Thus discursive community offers a perspective for criticism both grounded in the text and incorporating in a public way the subjectivity of the reader. As James Boyd White puts it,

> The true center of value in a text, its most important meaning is to be found in the community it establishes with its reader. It is here that the author offers his reader a place to stand, a place from which he can observe and judge the character and events of the world he creates, indeed the world itself.[12]

What is important for critical discourse here is that the community that a given text constitutes and enacts, however deeply it involves the subjective and the personal, has a kind of recoverable public existence that may be the object, not only of personal response and evaluation, but also, and in a prior way, of sharable description and reasoned debate.

All of this of course implies distinctly interactive notions of what competent reading is and of what critical engagement with a text requires, cognitively and affectively, objectively and subjectively: every competent reading of a text is a reading capable in some measure of recreating and participating in the intersubjective functions that the text needs its reader to perform—understanding what the text needs its reader to understand, responding as it needs its reader to respond. Comprehension and feeling are in some part public functions, testable and mutually informative in text-anchored discussion and text-driven debate. Yet these functions of understanding and response, notwithstanding their public character, always proceed in some other part from personal experience and personal commitment. That is to say, every reading of a text's moral charge and force—at least every reading that can claim to be personally engaged—along with every argument for and about that reading, inescapably has roots in the reader's personal experiences. Each *must* gain orientation and direction from his or her own personal commitments.

Ethical criticism emerges from a notion of the process of reading and criticism as an intersubjective interaction with both personal and public elements. This understanding does not purge subjectivity, for it cannot. Rather, it incorporates subjectivity—or even more accurately, it recognizes how subjectivity is *already* incorporated—in any competent reading. The reader here is not seen as altering the text; instead, in a public and reason-able way, he or she ethically contextualizes its reception and interpretation.

Focusing ethical criticism of the text on the discursive community it constitutes and enacts can make even that subjectivity both an object of critical attention and a resource of critical direction. An ethical criticism focused on discursive community offers different and more hopeful prospects for the illumination of texts and the invigoration of critical discourse about them. It affords its practitioners an object of criticism held in common but variously approached. It is an object authority over which is not to be imposed subjectively but earned intersubjectively. It permits a plurality of revealing angles of critical vision as each of us—equipped with our particular perspectives, experiences, and commitments, but not stranded by them—participate in the processes of inference and interpretation that the text requires in order to read it. Thus the problem of subjectivity of perspective can be, if you will, *talked into* the possibilities of intersubjectivity in ongoing and meaningful critical discourse.

ENDNOTES

[1]For a lighthearted but profound look at "the wages of sin" and the failure of profiteering televangelists to take their place in any tradition of interpretation or be answerable to any community authority, see Henry Fairlie, "Evangelists in Babylon," *The New Republic* 27, April 1987, 22-25.

[2]Edwin Black, ''The Second Persona,'' *The Quarterly Journal of Speech* 56, April 1970, 109.

[3]I am indebted to Professor Christine Oravec for helping me to appreciate more fully the virtues of Black's article in relation to its time and circumstances. While I persist in the reservation articulated here, I am even more firmly convinced that the article as a whole is not only enlightening critically, but admirable ethically.

[4]W. K. Wimsatt Jr. and H. C. Beardsley, ''The Intentional Fallacy,'' reprinted in Wimsatt, *The Verbal Icon* (Lexington, Kentucky: University of Kentucky Press, 1954).

[5]Wayne C. Booth, '''How I Loved George Eliot': Friendship with Books as a Neglected Critical Metaphor,'' *The Kenyon Review* 2, 1980, 5.

[6]James Boyd White, *When Words Lose Their Meaning: Constitutions and Reconstitutions of Language, Character and Community* (Chicago: University of Chicago Press, 1984), 282.

[7]Booth, *The Rhetoric of Fiction* (Chicago: University of Chicago Press, 1960), 169–266.

[8]The critical concept of ''implied audience'' I employ here is synthesized from my readings of Booth, ''Friendship with Books,'' Stanley Fish, *Surprised by Sin: The Reader in Paradise Lost* (Berkeley, California: University of California Press, 1967); Wolfgang Iser, *The Implied Reader: Patterns of Communication in Prose Fiction from Bunyan to Beckett* (Baltimore: John Hopkins University Press, 1974); and White, *When Words Lose Their Meaning*. This is, I believe, an area where rhetorical theory might be further invigorated by infusions of ''reader response'' theory.

[9]While my concept of ''discursive community'' arises out of White, op. cit.(especially 14-18), it differs in three ways: I explicitly search out discursive community in new sorts of texts, including the oral texts of public address in the traditional sense; it is focused more explicitly on purposes of ethical criticism; and it is aimed more consciously at extending critical discourse about ethical issues.

[10]See White, op. cit., 10–20. It would be fair to characterize my critical enterprise here as an attempt to make explicit what seems to have been left implicit in the works of White and Booth, and to make those contributions more directly relevant to the study of public address in the traditional sense.

[11]It deserves reiterating that the concerns I examine here are *not* the only ones deserving of ethical examination, and that this approach to ethical criticism is only one of the variety of approaches that would be required by a complete ethics of rhetoric.

[12]Op. cit. 17.

5

Communication Ethics as Tolerance, Understanding, and Unity

Karen Joy Greenberg

Communication and Theatre Department
Trenton State College

If I am not for myself, who will be for me?
And if I am only for myself, what am I?
And if not now, when?[1]

SYSTEMS OF CRITICISM AND PRELIMINARY ASSUMPTIONS

This chapter on the ethical dimension of communication provides analyses of some of our most common individual and social[2] systems of moral criticism and presents insights on how we create and maintain these systems. It also directs us to use these systems to achieve tolerance, understanding, and unity.

Several assumptions undergird it. Among them are: that contemporary Western epistemology is ontologically limited, that methods of account-making based on this epistemology are therefore limited, and that some facets of this epistemology are nonetheless too invaluable to discard.

Contemporary Western epistemology is ontologically limited in that it is ethnocentric in nature. Only self-generated premises are valid in this world-view. The resulting tautology provides contemporary Western epistemology with a vital force, but simultaneously makes suspect this epistemology's suitability as a perspective for analyzing and evaluating incommensurate moral orders.

Even if contemporary Western epistemology attributed cogency to a plurality of systems, it would remain restricted in its ability to provide solutions to human discord. Contemporary Western epistemology lacks parsimony and contains many incompatible elements. It assigns relative worth to patterns of reasoning[3] but urges us to be magnanimous in our choice of methodology. Consequently and absurdly, contemporary Western epistemology touts the eminence of dialectic while promoting the superiority of prescriptive and descriptive account making.

Another problem with this world view is its reinforcement of the status quo. Select institutions, such as psychiatry, business, and monied art,[4] are treated as exclusive, whereas other institutions are repeatedly denied changes in their social status. Proponents of Western medicine, for example, frame acupuncture, chiropractic therapy, homeopathy, medical herbalism, and osteopathy/naturopathy as quackery. Proponents of Western business frame Gaean and other "nontraditional" approaches to industry as antiestablishment.[5] Likewise, proponents of European art forms frame non-Western and primitive forms as invalid.[6] Ironically, contemporary Western epistemology's emotion-based system of values conflicts with its logic-based system of proofs.[7] As a result, this epistemology yields a moral order based on dogma.

Despite contemporary Western epistemology's systemic redundancy, paradoxes, and blind modes of validation, it is difficult for us to use other means of comprehending reality. In part, we support the existing system because of its self-validation. In part, we support it because we have been acculturated by this system and find that "being authentically human is not easy. Indeed, it can sometimes be quite painful."[8] Contemporary Western epistemology thus remains the basis for our conversations on communication ethics.

Accordingly, our account-making is both generated by and limited by contemporary Western epistemology. Our work on epistemic expansion fails at the level of legitimizing, coordinating, and integrating new insights into the status quo. Discourse that departs from warranted systems is regarded as "grand" or "superficial." Discourse that makes this kind of departure in order to illuminate creative ethics is even more harshly judged.[9]

The rhetorics of nouveau clergy, of alternate political leaders, and of resource reformers is regarded as "symbolic bullying," and for that reason devalued. The rhetorics of Rabbi Meir Kahane, of Reverend Jesse Jackson, and of Ralph Nader, for example, have been often disqualified as the rhetorics of the antiestablishment.[10] The rhetorics of unconventional clergy, of rebellious leaders, and of ahierarchical resource managers are more severely appraised. These latter rhetorics are regarded as so extreme as to be untouchable. Given this type of regard, the rhetorics of groups such as the International Society for Krishna Consciousness, the Contras, and the prisoners of the Soviet Union's corrective labor camps have fared poorly.[11] Even though we could argue that these rhetorics are recognized, hence credible, because they are "known," our reception of rhetorics of defiance contrasts greatly with our reception of "symbolic nurturing" rhetorics of institutionally backed clergy, of elected leaders, and of conservative resource managers. Compare the typical responses to rhetorics of defiance with those given to rhetorics of proponents of the indigenous culture. Think of how we respond, for example, to the discourse of Oral Roberts, Ronald Reagan, and Lee Iacocca.[12]

All the same, we adjudicate account-making methods by their means as well as by their ends, in that we reserve legitimacy not only for communication that adheres to conventional ideology, but also for communication that adheres to conventional modes of transcription. Concepts that flow free of legitimized discourse, and discourse that operates independent from legitimized ideologies are disbelieved. "Nonideological rhetorics" such as the Zen meditation state, habits, comas, foresight, and dreams, and "nonrhetorical ideologies," such as autistic imagings, make-believe, spiritual possession, trances, and empathic states are often ascribed little worth.[13] We praise our state of affairs to the detriment of a more expansive vision.

The extent to which we allow the constraining effects of contemporary Western epistemology to influence our attitudes and actions is also the extent to which our conventional account-making methods such as rhetorical and communication theory fall short of meeting our needs. As long as we remain locked into our epistemology, our thoughts and performances about reformation are

> stupid and hypocritical. Either reforms are designed by people who claim to be representative, who make a profession of speaking for others, and they lead to a division of power, to a distribution of this new power which is consequently increased by a double repression; or they arise from complaints and demands of those concerned.[14]

As scholars, as a privilege social group, we talk about ideals and implore other individuals to strive toward them. Yet, at the same time, we frequently chose not to act in ways that could promote greater social unity.[15] The academe's linguistic control of psychological and sociological classifications for ideas and behaviors works to segregate academics from the rest of society and also defeats many of the academy's attempts to empower the rest of society. The academic enigma merely perpetuates the academic hegemony. Unless we and other socially empowered individuals opt to demystify our communication we essentially help our society remain ideologically stuck. We ought to rethink the boundaries of our epistemology and use this reconceptualization process as the springboard for more critical work.

By granting realism a place in our experiences, we can escape status quo restrictions. We can reify theories for their heuristic power, their breadth, their range, their logic, their appropriateness, and their parsimony,[16] and inculcate dialogue as a means to: "engage in a continual process of making judgments about aspects of [our] lives, [identify] the general rules implicit in these judgments, [and modify] the original judgments in light of their appropriateness of these general rules and so on."[17] We can change our thinking from "either/or" to "both/and" and become more able to respond to the consequences of using powerful references such as "communication," "ethics," and "communication ethics."

Communication

We use the concept *communication* to generate and sustain knowledge. Communication makes meaning for us as individuals because it helps us to establish our individual borders. " 'Self' [is] related to the interactive knowledge gaining strategies of interrogation and disclosure."[18] Communication makes meaning for us as communities, too, because language is "the specific medium of understanding at the sociocultural stage of evolution. . . . [It] is the medium through which speakers and hearers realize certain fundamental demarcations."[19] We use communication to represent our life experiences by endowing it with aesthetic, technical, or philosophical form; with laws, rules, or systems bases; or with social contexts.

When we utilize communication's aesthetic/technical/philosophical demarcation, we look at life as, respectively, ceremonial and cultural, active and civic, or introspective.[20] We make sense out of a romantic breakfast, a graduate seminar, and an evening mass, respectively, as: a chance to savor the beauty of a dear one's love words, a chance to perform academic protocol, and a chance to demonstrate reverence for God; as an opportunity to reconsummate adulthood, an opportunity to engage in greater levels of scholarship, and an opportunity to be a better Christian; or as an occasion to find one's self through intimate sharing, an occasion to use intellectual stimulation for introspection, and an occasion to increase self-discovery through spirituality.

When we employ communication's laws, rules, and systems of division, we look at our experiences as governed by nomic necessity, by universal occurrences of acts; by practical necessity, by particular occurrences of acts; or by logical necessity, by theoretical occurrences of acts.[21] We make sense out of the above three experiences as: breakfast follows waking and sleeping, Wednesday is seminar day, and evening mass takes place on weekdays; my lover feels good about our relationship this morning, this afternoon's seminar will focus on the writings of Hans-Georg Gadamer, and I will attend mass at 7 p.m.; or putting flowers on the table might make my lover linger longer, giving a prepared answer in seminar might make the professor notice me, and practicing my religion might make me a better parent.

We use communication contexts, too, to organize our experiences. Unlike the technical/aesthetic/philosophical and laws/rules/systems distinctions, these rubrics are mutually exclusive. Communication is singularly intrapersonal, interpersonal, group, rhetorical, *or* mass mediated.[22] The romantic breakfast uses interpersonal communication since it involves exchange between members of a dyad, the seminar uses group communication since it involves a small number of people working together on a common goal, and the evening mass is rhetorical since one person is speaking to many.

Communication is one of our "god-terms," one of our "expression[s] about which all other expressions [can be] ranked as subordinate and serving dominations and powers. Its force imparts to the others their lesser degree of force, and fixes the scale by which degrees of comparison are understood."[23] Communication compels us as individuals and as members of society to regard and to react to life. "All cultural and social phenomena and all human experiencing are made possible by, and are shaped by [communication]."[24]

Ethics

In addition to "communication," we use the concept *ethics* to generate and sustain knowledge. Ethics is epistemic, because ethics is a branch of philosophy and because philosophy is supersedant to other modes of thinking about the universe. "The traditional distinction . . . still considers as branches of philosophy the three standard "normative" sciences of logic, ethics, and aesthetics, concerned with standards, methods and tests of thinking, conduct, and art, respectively."[25] Philosophy is architectonic to logic and aesthetics, is "the mother of virtually all intellectual disciplines, including the physical Sciences [sic] and the nascent psychological sciences."[26]

When "ethics" is synechdochical for "philosophy," it garners a variety of connotations, including: "morals" ("normative ethics"), "propriety," "obligations," "virtue," "moral choice," "the study of moral choices," "acceptable behavior," "prescribed moral action," "an aspect of public ethic," "a form of critical thinking," "the logic of ethics," "metaethics," "theoretical ethics," and "philosophical ethics."[27]

> The student of ethics will nevertheless have to get used to a variety of terminologies; he [or she] will find plain "ethics" used for what we have just called "morals" ("normative ethics" is another term used for this); and he [or she] will find, for what we have just called "ethics," the more guarded terms "the logic of ethics," "metaethics," "theoretical ethics," "philosophical ethics," and so on.[28]

Ethics can be comprehended equally well as a system whose foci are stases (norms), values, and virtues, and whose functions are prescription, description, and metatheorizing.[29]

Norms inform about typicality, and emphasize affordances, prohibitions, and obligations. In the expressions "pussycats ordinarily chase sparrows rather than rainbows,'' and ''large whiskers are needed to chase rainbows,'' norms mark the act of chasing rainbows. Values create preference, approve, commend, and grade.[30] Values emphasize goodness and badness. In the expressions ''I pick the purple cat,'' ''I prefer purple cats to indigo ones,'' ''that purple-spotted feline is acceptable for my reality-spotted home,'' ''praise be rainbow-finding felines,'' and ''it is better to own a rainbow-chasing than a sparrow-chasing cat,'' values mark the act of chasing rainbows. Virtues emphasize moral excellence and nonexcellence, the fulfillment of function.[31] In the expressions ''pussycat Nirvana is rainbowness,'' and ''serendipity is an aspect of Nirvana,'' virtues mark the act of chasing rainbows. Prescriptions command, exhort, advise, guide, and commend.[32] In the expressions ''cats ought to chase rainbows,'' ''I think it would be wise if my oldest cat stopped chasing rainbows,'' ''this is where to put your paws to chase a rainbow,'' and ''Cleo, chase that rainbow,'' prescriptions mark the act of chasing rainbows. Descriptions inform about the qualities of an individual or an object.[33] In the expressions ''Timon is a good rainbow chaser,'' and ''lightening rods can be used to divine rainbows' locations,'' descriptions mark the act of chasing rainbows. Last, metatheorizing involves introspection, the analysis of coordinated talk.[34] In the expressions ''since the time that CDR started chasing rainbows, he moved closer to Nirvana,'' and ''when my pussycat meows in C sharp, he is boasting about his rainbow chasing exploits,'' metatheories mark the act of chasing rainbows.

''Ethics,'' like ''communication,'' has a richness of significations as well as great heuristic power. It is another of contemporary Western epistemology's pivotal concepts.

Communication Ethics

Communication ethics, too, is a pivotal concept. Created by the meshing of ''communication'' and ''moral orders,'' ''communication ethics'' has the power and variety of each of these concepts as well as the power and variety that results from their nexus. ''Every human society is a moral order [which] emerge[s] through communication.''[35]

Sometimes ''communication ethics'' is epitomized as the essence of knowledge because it is ''the ethics of communication'' the moral practice of communicative acts. Other times ''communication ethics,'' is seen as epistemic because it is conceptualized as ''communication's ethics.'' as accounts of communication practices.

In the former case, ''communication ethics'' is doctrine, absolute. It determines whether or not an attitude or action is ''prescribed by a correct rule for the situation in which it occurs.''[36] In this interpretation, ''communication ethics'' is

> productive of arguments and architectonic of attitudes. It provides the principle, in both the sense of beginning point and of guideline, for the construction of an

> architectonic productive art of rhetoric and philosophy which can be used to create a method productive of the arts and a subject matter substantive to the problems of an age of technology.[37]

For example, instructors' "legitimized reality creating power is more weighty and is less often questioned than [is] the legitimized reality creating power of our [sic] students,"[38] Given the "ethics of communication," instructors have the "right" to ask students personal questions, but not vice versa.

In contrast, when "communication ethics" is held to be the "major measure of communicative achievement,"[39] a more relativistic view of communication is utilized. In this interpretation, "communication ethics" is a system of

> probability and not scientific certainty, the communicator by definition possesses a certain measure of freedom to determine the structure of his [or her] message. During the exercise of this freedom, the concept of "choice" becomes apparent. Precisely because of the probable nature of rhetoric, the rhetor knowingly or unknowingly selects from his [or her] experiences and observations those elements of the persuasive process which best enable him [or her] to affect change in a given audience.[40]

The instructor who asks a student a personal question in order to help in crisis is evaluated differently from an instructor who asks the same student the same question in order to satisfy a curiosity.

Whether regarded as separable from, or as intrinsic to, our thoughts and deeds, "communication ethics," like its parents, "communication" and "moral orders," is a world-making construct. Unlike its parents, "communication ethics" has a special power that results from its twinning of ideology and rhetoric.[41]

TOLERANCE AND INDIVIDUAL SYSTEMS OF CRITICISM

We can use "communication ethic's" ideological/rhetorical twinning to illuminate our acceptance or denial of, our identification with, and our integration of our ideas into reality constructs. We can use the power of this reference to raise questions about our imperfect ideologies and our imperfect rhetorics. Both our individual and social systems of account making can be explained from this *topos*.

Looking first at individual systems of account making, we see that they are important because of the human need to construct and maintain a sense of self.

> One of the most severe of all problems . . . is that of trying to interpret all the confusing signals from the outside as to who one is. In this case, the potential for intralevel and interlevel conflict is tremendous. The psychic mechanisms have to deal simultaneously with the individual's need for self-esteem and the constant

> flow of evidence from the outside affecting self-image. The result is that information flows in a complex swirl between levels of personality; as it goes round and round, parts of it get magnified, reduced, negated, or otherwise distorted, and then those parts in turn get further subjected to the same sort of swirl, over and over again-all of this in an attempt to reconcile what is, with what we wish were. . . .
>
> The upshot is that the total picture of "who I am" is integrated in some enormously complex way inside the entire mental structure, and contains in each one of us a large number of unresolved, possibly irresolvable inconsistencies. These undoubtedly provide much of the dynamic tension which is so much a part of being human.[42]

There are several types of account-making systems that individuals generally use. These systems include: ones that delegitimize references for community means of shaping reality, that delegitimize public constructs; ones that delegitimize references for individual means of shaping reality, that delegitimize private constructs; and ones that delegitimize both public and private constructs.[43]

Asocial Individuals

Asocial individuals define their boundaries by delegitimizing public constructs. They act as if "nothing is to be assumed as necessary, in accounting for any fact, unless it is established by evident experience or evident reasoning, or is required by the articles of faith."[44] Punk rockers, Gray Panthers, and neonazis, for example, define their individual boundaries this way.

Punk rockers would remain yet another generation's semianonymous adolescents, defined only by their appreciation for a specific class of music, if they did not further separate themselves from society by their unusual haircuts, clothing, and mannerisms.[45] Conversely, if society did not respond to punk artifacts and actions, the rockers might look and act less extreme.

The Gray Panthers, too, achieve their identity through distinction. These elders' socially discordant, often militant, behaviors sets them apart from other elders, specifically, and from the establishment, in general. Like their younger counterparts, the Gray Panthers would be less successful in attracting attention if their attitudes and actions were more mainstream or if the mainstream did not react so extensively to them.[46]

Notwithstanding, both the punk rockers and the Gray Panthers, as well as other individuals who define their boundaries asocially, often suffer from their reliance on this type of distinction.[47] To successfully create a self-identity, asocial individuals have to be atypical. However, when asocial individuals become too unusual, these cease to be socially recognizable and lose the rhetorical power gained by their uniqueness. Consequently, many successful asocial individuals depend on other attributes, such as illicit drugs and membership in asocial groups, to distinguish their moral orders.

Sometimes asocial individuals use their special status to justify special acts rather than use their special acts to attain a special status. Individuals such as America's neonazis fall into this category.

> People with preferences find sympathy and friendship among others who share these preferences. They spend more time with their friends than with others, and the preferences become elaborated and sharpened. This puts them more out of step with the others, and when they perceive this, they retreat still more exclusively into the company of their friends, and so on. The result is isolation. Couple this with intense specialized interests, and we see the formation of a cult.[48]

Neonazis employ the status given asocial people as a mandate for carrying out their devices. A member of a neonazi lynch mob was recently quoted as saying "[w]e are racial and she was black. We don't like the black minority or other immigrant races. We're into white supremacy."[49]

Regardless of why asocial individuals define themselves by rejecting public reality constructs, they are often repulsed by more ideologically neutral communities. Communities define themselves by what they are not, by their essential or ontological opposites,[50] and need special classes of people for their supply of negative models and for their supply of "horrible, reproachable, or sadistically fascinating" discourse.

Some communities treat the rhetoric of atypical minors and of adults with extraordinary illnesses in this fashion. Children and adolescents who are survivors of physical, emotional, or sexual abuse are often shamed, threatened, or otherwise manipulated into silence. Worse, when the conflicting social messages of "always tell authorities about your experiences" and of "never tell authorities about experiences that might embarrass them" cause some of these survivors to engage in self-destructive behaviors such as alcoholism, drugs, eating disorders, or suicide, as means of escaping their social double binds, society often creates more paradoxes for them by punishing them for their coping mechanisms and by reinforcing their victim status by forbidding them to name their tormenters.[51] Likewise, individuals suffering from AIDS often find that disclosing their diagnosis is a political rather than an private statement.[52] Society frequently uses AIDS survivors as illustrative of moral poison instead of treating them as disease-stricken individuals who ought to receive community assistance with their healing. Unfortunately, both of the above types of persons are often stigmatized, incarcerated, ostracized, or isolated instead of being loved or supported, because they fill some communities' needs for "unethical" models.

Although public and private restrictions on the acceptability of asocial systems of account making do not stymie truly transcendent individuals, these restrictions do create barriers. Many individuals are frustrated when they attempt to make their lives more meaningful by establishing boundaries via nontraditional systems.

Controvertible Individuals

Antithetical to social individuals are controvertible ones. The latter define their boundaries by delegitimizing private constructs, by treating "the [rhetorical] relationships we use in weaving the intricate web of meaning [as] the real fabric of human life."[53] Some members of austere religions, and some residents of intentional communities (collective settlements) define themselves in this way. These individuals reject the creative options utilized by many men and women in favor of more rigid standards defined by their own conscious. Contemporary Hasidic Jews, for instance, scrupulously avoid the morality of contemporary Western society. They see themselves as the "bulwarks" of Jewish Orthodoxy,

> besieged from every direction by what they perceive as a decadent, morally bankrupt world, they shun its preoccupants, rebel against many of its social conventions, spend as much time as possible in their neighborhood fortresses, and devote themselves to perpetuating the ideals of Jewish religious life.[54]

Participants in collectives, too, disavow popular mores in favor of their own. For example,

> The evangelical Protestant ashrams are all characteristically dedicated to the way of selfless action and social service. . . . They are based on the Gandhian principles and message that ashrams are not only places for spiritual striving; they must also be oriented to social reconstruction.[55]

Controvertible individuals' systems of account making are epistemically viable; as long as controvertible individuals can distinguish themselves from society, society can distinguish itself from them. Propaganda and humor are among the devices used to create this schism. Direct mail, films, and posters are used, for instance, to segregate.[56] It is also true that humor is used to segregate.

> [H]umor emasculates those against whom it is directed; it renders than less potent, and worse, it attempts—and sometimes succeeds—to make them a constant object of derisive laughter. . . . From the earliest colonization in the seventeenth century to the present, many groups have been the object of humor stereotyping. While usually directed against the powerless—the politically ineffective and economically deprived—the humor stereotype has also been employed against upwardly mobile minority groups.[57]

Like asocial individuals, controvertible individuals are sometimes separated from the rest of society even when they would rather be integrated into it. In this century, Jews sometimes find it difficult to obtain jobs and housing, and ashram members sometimes find themselves the center of public spectacle rather than of public harmony. Communities use controvertible individuals as exemplars of the negative and use their rhetoric as representative of communication aberrations.

Despite the hardships inherent in the controvertible style of self-definition, some individuals, especially ones who have previously succeeded in establishing their identities by delegitimizing private constructs, use this class of rhetoric. These people fail to establish their individual ethics only when society incorporates their perspectives into the mainstream—thus eliminating their controvertible distinctions—or when the tensions of maintaining controvertible views become so great that they become functionally impaired or obsessive.[58] Granted that public restrictions on the acceptability of controvertible systems of account making do not deter special people, these restrictions do make it challenging to live according to a controvertible moral order.

Ecumenical Individuals

Unlike asocial and controvertible individuals, ecumenical individuals define their boundaries by integrating public and private constructs. They strive for an epistemic "mean" and act as if "[i]t is in the nature of moral qualities that they can be destroyed by deficiency on the one hand and excess on the other."[59] Some creators of scientific and religious paradigms have defined their individual boundaries in this manner. For example, Albert Einstein, the father of relativity theory, claimed that "the only justification for our concepts and system of concepts is that they serve to represent the complexity of our experience; beyond that they have no legitimacy."[60] Lao Tzu, founder of Taoism, came to the same conclusion;

> The sage relies on actionless activity . . .
> Puts himself in the background; but is always to the fore.
> Remains outside; but is always there.
> Is it not just because he does not strive for any personal end
> That all his personal ends are fulfilled?[61]

Ecumenical individuals' systems of account making are not only epistemically viable but are preferred by individuals who have had prior success with integrating public and private constructs. Students of akido tend to be less bigoted than students of pointe. Critical thinkers tend to be more creative than positivists or relativists.[62] Ecumenical individuals see options in places where others see merely constraints.

Nonetheless, individuals who define their boundaries ecumenically often suffer because of their need to validate both public and private norms.

> One who walks the narrow ridge knows the joy of the community of dialogue but also knows the tragic limitations resulting from the drawing of the demarcation line

> each day anew, the continual rediscovery of the boundary between self and other in community through which we pass forward and honor reality while we do so. The dialogical journey of the "narrow ridge" requires us to be together sometimes and at the other times to walk alone."[63]

The more successful that ecumenical individuals are in creating boundaries, the more that they need both types of realities against which to demarcate themselves. Often ecumenical individuals collapse from conflicting stresses. Many of them become plagued by heart attacks, paralysis, or nervous breakdowns.[64] In addition, ecumenical individuals are sometimes forced to stay within their ideological systems. Some communities are so invested in using this type of individuals' ethics as bogeyman that communities goad ecumenical individuals into martyrdom. Women have been urged to testify in rape cases despite threats to their physical safety,[65] and educators have been pushed to critique ideas despite denied tenure, research support, or professional recognition.[66] Ecumenical individuals are too often used as scapegoats.

Ecumenical individuals are safer than are either asocial or controvertible individuals from public discount, but they are susceptible to the absurdities of both asocial and controvertible moral orders. The ecumenical stance can appear to be an epistemic wasteland. Ecumenical systems of account making involve systemic realignment, a process immaleable by human will that is often painful and difficult. "To live this way is to risk losing everything that we have held onto for reasons of external (false) security."[67] Most individuals are not suited to the rigors of an ecumenical way of life.

As articulated above, the ways in which we define ourselves as individuals are socially constrained and epistemically imperfect. We can overcome these limitations, though, if we enable all types of systems of ethics to harmoniously coexist. If we accept the fact of being of moral orders that are unlike our own, then we can allow for a variety of ways to making meaning. Further, if we can comprehend these other systems, then we can enhance the ways in which we are already making meaning. The "light" in our lives will come from the opening of our minds, from our allowing for the existence of divergent, even disturbing views.[68]

UNDERSTANDING AND SOCIAL SYSTEMS OF CRITICISM

One way in which to both acknowledge and to compute incommensurate moral orders is to explore their manifestation at the social level. It is important to analyze and evaluate moral systems at this level, because we tend to live in communities rather then in isolation. Social systems of account-making direct "attention both to the characteristics of persons as processors of information and to the interpersonal rule systems as the locus of action. Both of these are necessary for an explanation of the forms in which human communication occurs."[69] Like individual systems of account making, community systems can be classified as asocial, controvertible, or ecumenical.

Asocial Communities

Asocial communities define their boundaries by delegitimizing the constructs of the greater public. These communities gain rhetorical power, the ability to respond to negative symbols, and the ability to create positive symbols from their deviant behavior. Some animal rights groups and some street people define themselves in this manner. Some animal rights groups raid research facilities, steal (animals), and deface private property because they believe that they can more aptly assess appropriate treatment of animals than can society. "[T]hey have adopted the rhetoric of national liberation movements and a conviction that their cause puts them above the law."[70] Street people, too, sometimes treat the common moral order as subordinate to their own moral order. Some homeless people appropriate subway station benches, sidewalk heat vents, bus station bathrooms, and municipal garbage cans for food and shelter at the expense of breaking social rules.[71] To these people, survival ethics are more important than civil law.[72]

Asocial modes of account making are preferred by communities with a history of successful, but socially independent systems. "Success" does not mean lack of cost, but means relative cost. As long as freedom or peaceful death for laboratory animals remains a priority to their crusaders, then the punishments they might incur will not deter them from challenging public standards. Similarly, as long as the illicit use of private and public facilities spells existence for the homeless, this community will not be dissuaded from their acts by legal reprobations.

Communities that define their boundaries asocially often suffer from dissonance, though, because they are reliant on a alien public for their status. In wartime, for example, there would probably be less discreet treatment of street people and no animals left to liberate. In wartime, street people might become leaders rather than "degenerates," and members of animal rights groups might find themselves battling research institutions, not for creatures' freedom, but for food. In a wartime scenario, these asocial groups might lose their identifying status, because special status is not ordinarily assigned to typical groups.

The greater community does try to maintain the integrity of atypical ones, though. Some segments of society classify other segments as exemplifying "crude, impious, or untranscribable" behavior when the former need to define themselves as engaging in "proper, obedient, and readily comprehensible" ways of life.

When few or no groups step forward to fill the role of the notorious, the populace itself, often creates this distinction among its constituents. For instance, when explicit racial, religious, ethnic, and gender-based discrimination lose acceptability, alternative ideological whipping posts gain much greater legitimacy. Members of the New Age Movement have been condemned to the ranks of Satan worshippers in some communities,[73] and readers of Salman Rushdie's *The Satanic Verses* have been protested against, injured, or killed, worldwide.[74] New Agers have been spurned for their food choices, their sexual habits, their political prerogatives, and their family groupings. Readers of *The Satanic Verses* have been threatened, nations have banned the book, and the work's author has incurred an international price on his head. Both the New Age Community and the community of readers of *The Satanic Verses* have received the thumbs-down distinction from the status quo at times during which other means of rallying social forces were less desirable.

Despite the fact that public restrictions on the acceptability of asocial systems of account making do not alter the activities of truly self-sufficient communities, these restrictions do create obstacles. Some asocial communities find themselves pulled closer to the ideological center because of these barriers.

Controvertible Communities

Farthest from asocial communities on the ideological spectrum are controvertible communities. Controvertible communities regard inherent moral systems as the foundation for human dialogue and as the basis for community association.[75] To controvertible communities, "truth is the outcome of consensus: if everyone says it is so, it is so."[76]

Some media, for instance, define their boundaries in this way. They depend on outside constructs to guide their responses to reality. The radio communications available to troops fighting in Southeast Asia in the 1970s, for instance, were censored by an American government preoccupied with, among other things, American military morale. Despite the fact that certain of the enlisted persons' constitutional rights were violated, and despite the fact that an underground, alternative radio system developed, the legitimized form of this medium conformed to the standards of the American military.[77] The censorship of television programs is another example of how the media have altered their message to suit the mores of a larger community. In reaction to irate messages from sufficient numbers of audience segments, many television networks air audio or visual warnings before showing graphically sexual or violent programs. This practice is maintained, although these warnings do not often affect viewers' selections.[78] Film, too, has responded to society. When *The Last Temptation of Christ* was released, for instance, it was protested in so many communities for having a "blasphemous" nature that its run was shortened, and in some cases, altogether curtailed.[79] In each of these cases, "morally questionable" discourse was changed to satisfy status quo norms.

Interestingly, groups such as the media that define themselves by pleasing larger communities become increasingly reliant on those communities for their validity. The more invested that the media become in satisfying their public, the more difficult it is for the media to criticize the public. "The more messages are tied to real behavior and events, the less they can be manipulated and controlled."[80]

The opposite is true as well; the more that behaviors are tied to messages, the less power of choice a public has. When we opt to sacrifice our conceptually outermost groups, we lose some of our freedoms. When society designates as irreverent the work of the Guardian Angels or of abortion centers, for instance, society closes some doors.[81] Sometimes the public that controvertible communities try so hard to satisfy is happy only by the nullification of those communities and by the rubrification of their discourse as threatening, as persecuting, or as otherwise problematic.[82] Although status quo restrictions on the viability of controvertible systems of ethics do not keep truly transcendental communities from following a controvertible way of life, these restrictions do make it difficult for them to prosper.

Ecumenical Communities

Unlike either asocial or controvertible communities, ecumenical ones define their boundaries by integrating public and private reality constructs. They hold that human conflict can be overcome by the joint energies of participants and audiences.[83] To ecumenical groups, social understanding is based upon ideological compounds.

Some youth shelters define their boundaries in this manner. These organizations entwine their own agendas with those of society's in order to construct a unified system of ethics. The Covenant House in New York City, for example, is a haven for homeless and runaway children that provides "food, clothing, shelter, medical attention, educational and vocational training, and counseling to kids with no place to go,"[84] but does so without patronizing or judging them. Some of the kids who participate in this program have addictions, and some are prostitutes. Even though these youths are required to abide by the house's rules while residing there, they are never ridiculed for their life choices, but merely encouraged to change what they can. The Covenant House has a simple vision;

> Kids should not be bought and sold. They should not be exploited. It should not be indefinitely dangerous to be alone and homeless on the streets of our cities. There must be a place where they can all get help. And when they need it: before it's too late. And from people who love and respect them. With no strings. No questions asked. And in a place where nobody gets excluded.[85]

Were the Covenant House less consistent about Covenant property ground rules or more persistent about judging street mores, fewer adolescents would use it as a sanctuary.

Ecumenical communities' ethics are preferred by communities that have had prior success with integrating public and private constructs. The Covenant House, for instance, began with one man opening his door to a handful of street children and has grown into a network of centers. Yet communities that define their boundaries ecumenically often suffer because of their dual identity. They struggle to challenge the rules, rituals, mysteries, and hierarchies that coordinate large numbers of people while concurrently acting to support those people. A youth center that harbors young offenders is "catholic" because of its indiscriminatory treatment of its residents and the hope that this type of community offers the "hopeless." Yet, it needs to be sufficiently "catholic" to receive outside support, too.

Needless to say, ecumenical communities, akin to the more polar asocial and controvertible ones, sometimes find themselves the target of social wrath.

> Developing critical capacities in ourselves and others invites criticism from those who are ruffled by being asked awkward questions. It will frequently be in the interests of some . . . systems of account-making *not* to have people become critical thinkers. Critical questioning is the last thing those in positions of power who are autocratically seeking to retain the status quo wish to see.[86]

One priest's loving custody of a handful of juvenile offenders is more likely to be overlooked than a network of juvenile shelters. Whereas the former is merely one member of the clergy's private business, the latter can be read as a public threat to sanctioned youth programs. When empowered segments of social wish to retain their status, and when they perceive that this status is based on relative virtue, the empowered often publically deride alternative systems. In the case of youth shelters, neighborhoods have publically questioned their zoning, safety, nutritional and educational standards, sleeping arrangements, and so on. The more successful that ecumenical communities are in defining themselves, the more that publics criticize them.

Another example of the problems that ecumenical communities face is internal rupturing. Ecumenical businesses, as a case in point, often collapse from the conflicting stresses of public and private obligations. For example, companies that invest in overseas production may be providing economic support to neighboring nations by spreading their resources, but may also be granting their support at the expense of local needs. Impending employment problems in Japan typify this problem. After extensively investing in overseas factories, Japan is discovering that it may have an unemployment problem.[87] Companies that increase their employee benefits but decrease the numbers of their employees would be another example of a community that might explode while integrating internal and external values. Some of these businesses die altogether, whereas others transform.[88]

Sometimes ecumenical communities try to leave the ideological middle but are forced to return to that place by a greater public that lacks negative exemplars. Public legal services, and war, have sometimes been preserved for this purpose. Public legal services have been criticized by both their leaders and by outsiders. In 1987, for instance, W. Clark Durant and the Reagan Administration were against the continued funding of the Legal Service Corporation, an agency that funds local legal aid groups.[89] Likewise, war has been used to establish order when "the politics of dissent threatens in fact to de-legitimize existing political/military authority."[90] In both cases, ecumenical communities are influenced so extensively that they remain politically neutral.

Although ecumenical communities are safer than asocial or controvertible ones from the harms of public discount, they are still susceptible to certain woes. Many ecumenical communities are ultimately frustrated in their attempt to create identity by integrating public and private constructs. Their nightmare is the epistemic wasteland or conceptual nether world where support is scant and the resolution of crises is painful and difficult.

> Peoples' thinking cannot remain static in this fast-moving world. People must acquire new information. . . . [but they] cannot react to every bit of information to which they are exposed, . . . they organize the information into categories. When a given category becomes important to a culture's survival, it is broken up or differentiated into smaller units. The practical result is that if people from other cultures do not differentiate a knowledge area in the same way, they may be seen as ignorant or at best backward.[91]

Despite their plusses, ecumenical communities are often seen as ignorant of social ethics and as backwards in their attitudes and actions.

All of the ways in which communities attribute meaning to morality; by delegitimizing public reality constructs, by delegitimizing private reality constructs, or by delegitimizing both, are epistemically incomplete strategies. Because all of these strategies are lacking, we need to adopt inclusive, rather than exclusive way of communicating, and we need to understand each others' moral orders. "To have a public we must overcome fragmentations of interests. Fragmentation of interests is overcome if we can recognize [our] common[ality]."[92]

UNITY AND FUTURE SYSTEMS OF CRITICISM

In addition to acknowledging the existence of a variety of systems of ethics and in addition to grasping the essence of these systems, we could benefit from making meaning through them. To gain even more epistemic power, we must experience multiple modes of truth building.

To experience these modes, we need to seek them and to integrate them into our private and public selves. We need to look at life through others' moral orders as well as to look at it through our own. All of our voices must be legitimized, comprehended and used if we are to transcend the bounds of our status quo.

(Rhetorical) enlightment will come to us if we go to it.

The new world is being built as we open to the higher power of the universe within us and consciously allow that creative energy to move through us. As each of us connects with our inner spiritual awareness, we learn that the creative power of the universe is within us. We also learn that we can create our own reality and take responsibility for doing so. The change begins with each individual, but as more and more individuals are transformed, the mass consciousness is increasingly affected.[93]

ENDNOTES

[1]Joseph H. Hertz, trans., 1.14 *Pirke Aboth: Sayings of the Fathers* (West Orange, NJ: Behrman House, 1945) 25.

[2]Concepts such as *social* and *community* are context dependent throughout this chapter; these concepts refer to collections of people as small as two and as large as the global population. They refer to demographically specified groups, to temporally specified groups, and to groups specified by a variety of other means.

[3]Some patterns (i.e., empirical and hermeneutical ones) are treated as more credible than others (i.e., critical ones).

[4]Alasdair MacIntyre, *After Virtue, 2nd ed.* (Notre Dame, IN: Notre Dame UP, 1984) 30.

[5]Linda Marks, "The Gaean Business," *Many Hands: Resources for Personal and Social Transformation* (Fall 1987) 27.

[6]Amei Wallach, "Beautiful Dreamings: Aboriginal Art as a Kind of Cosmic Road Map to the Primeval," *Ms. Magazine* (March 1989) 63.

[7]T. Edward Damer, *Attacking Faulty Reasoning* (Belmont, CA: Wadsworth, 1980) 92.

[8]Romona Shephard Adams, Herbert A. Otto, and Deana Shephard Cowley, *Letting Go: Uncomplicating Your Life* (New York: Macmillan, 1980) 86.

[9]For more detail on the severity by which certain rhetorics are judged, see the discussion of political argument typology in Charles Stewart, Craig Smith, and Robert E. Denton, Jr., *Persuasion and Social Movements* (Prospect Heights, IL: Waveland, 1984) esp. 17–36.

[10]"Kahane Arrested in Kansas After Scuffle with Hecklers," *The New York Times* 20 Nov. 1986: B19; "The Political Paradox of Jesse Jackson: Public Calls Him a Front-Runner But Says He's Unelectable," *The Christian Science Monitor* 21 Dec. 1987: 3; and Edmund Levin "Lighten Up Those Anti-Bork Appeals," *The New York Times* 26 Sept. 1987: 27.

[11]Tommy H. Poling and J. Frank Kenney, *The Hare Krishna Character Type: A Study of the Sensate Personality,* Studies in Religion and Society: 15 (Lewiston, NY: Edwin Mellen, 1986) 1–5; Allan Nairn, "The Contras' Little List: An Aide to 'President Calero' Talks About 'Bad Guys' Slated for Assassination," *The Progressive* 51.3 (Mar. 1987): 24–26; Aleksandr I. Solzhenitsyn, *The Gulag Archipelago, 1918–1959: An Experiment in Literary Investigation,* Vols. I–II, Trans. Thomas P. Whitney (New York: Harper & Row, 1973); Aleksandr I. Solzhenitsyn, *The Gulag Archipelago Two, 1918–1959: An Experiment in Literary Investigation,* Vols. III–IV, Trans. Thomas P. Whitney (New York: Harper & Row, 1975); and Aleksandr I. Solzhenitsyn, *The Gulag Archipelago Three, 1918–1959: An Experiment in Literary Investigation,* Vols, V–VIII, Trans. Harry Willetts (New York: Harper & Row, 1978).

[12]Terry Muck, "God and Oral," *Christianity Today* (Mar. 20, 1987): 17; Aaron Wildavsky, "Presi-

dent Reagan as Political Strategist,'' *Society* 24(May/June 1987): 56–62; and Alex Taylor III, ''Living as a Legend,'' *Fortune* 116 (Aug. 3, 1987): 43.

[13]See: Michel Foucault, *Madness & Civilization: A History of Insanity in the Age of Reason,* Richard Howard, trans. (New York: Vintage, 1973) 286–289; Brian Fay, *Social Theory and Political Practice,* Controversies in Sociology: 1, T. B. Bottomore and M. J. Mulkay, eds. (Boston: George Allen, 1975); Karen Joy Greenberg, ''A Zen Approach to Epistemology: A Different Light on a Tired Topic of Communication Theory,'' ms., Amherst, MA: U of Massachusetts, May, 1984; and Karen Joy Greenberg, ''Hebraic Rhetoric: A Neglected Fundamental Rhetoric,'' SCA Convention, Chicago, Nov., 1984.

[14]Michel Foucault, *Language, Countermemory, and Practice: Selected Essays and Interviews,* Donald F. Bouchard, ed., Donald F. Bouchard and Sherry Simon, trans. (Ithaca, NY: Cornell UP, 1977) 208–209; cf. Clifford Geertz's discussion of account-making of other people's subjectivity in *Local Knowledge: Fact and Law in Comparative Perspective* (New York: Basic Books, 1983) 70; and cf. Richard Hofstadter's discussion of common descriptions of religious and secular institutions in *Academic Freedom in the Age of the College* (New York: Columbia UP, 1955) 211.

[15]Karen Joy Greenberg, ''The Deficit of Research on Instructional Communication's Accountability,'' ms. Rindge, NH: Franklin Pierce College, Mar. 1988, 7–8.

[16]Stephen Littlejohn, *Theories of Human Communication, 3rd ed.* (Belmont, CA: Wadsworth, 1989) 29–30.

[17]Stephen D. Brookfield, *Developing Critical Thinkers: Challenging Adults to Explore Alternative Ways of Thinking and Acting,* Alan B. Knox, Consulting Editor, Adult and Continuing Education, Higher Education Series (San Francisco: Jossey-Bass, 1987) 13.

[18]Charles R. Berger and James J. Bradac, *Language and Social Knowledge: Uncertainty in Interpersonal Relations,* The Social Psychology of Language: 2, Howard Giles, gen. ed. (London: Edward Arnold, 1982) 94.

[19]Jürgen Habermas, *Communication and the Evolution of Society,* Thomas McCarthy, trans. (Boston: Beacon, 1976) 1, 66.

[20]George A. Kennedy, *Classical Rhetoric and its Christian and Secular Tradition from Ancient to Modern Times* (Chapel Hill, NC: North Carolina UP, 1980) 15–17.

[21]See: Vernon Cronen and Leslie K. Davis, ''Alternative Approaches for the Communication Theorist: Problems in the Laws-Rules-Systems Trichotomy,'' *Human Communication Research* 4.2 (1978): 120–128; Donald Cushman and Gordon C. Whiting, ''An Approach to Communication Theory: Toward Consensus on Rules,'' *The Journal of Communication* 22 (1972): 217–238; W. Barnett Pearce, ''Consensual Rules in Interpersonal Communication: A Reply to Cushman and Whiting,'' *Journal of Communication* 23.2 (1973): 160–168; and W. Barnett Pearce and Don Cushman, ''Generality and Necessity in Three Types of Theory About Human Communication, with Special Attention to Rules Theory,'' *Human Communication Research* 3.4 (1977): 344–353.

[22]Littlejohn, *Theories*, 13–14.

[23]Richard Weaver, *The Ethics of Rhetoric* (South Bend, IN: Gateway, 1953) 212.

[24]Richard B. Gregg, *Symbolic Inducement and Knowing: A Study in the Foundations of Rhetoric* (Columbia, SC: South Carolina UP, 1984) 51.

[25]John Herman Randall, Jr., and Justus Buchler, *Philosophy: An Introduction* (New York: Barnes & Noble, 1942) 8.

[26]Walter B. Weimer, *Notes on the Methodology of Scientific Research* (Hillsdale, NJ: Erlbaum, 1979), 72, ctd. in Paul H. Boase, ''Philosophy/Psychology and Rhetoric/Communication,'' ms., Athens, OH: Ohio University, n.d., 9.

[27]J. O. Urmson, ed., "Ethics," *The Concise Encyclopedia of Western Philosophy and Philosophers* (New York: Hawthorn, 1960) 136; William Lillie, *An Introduction to Ethics* (New York: Barnes & Noble, 1948) 313; and Larry R. Churchill, "The Teaching of Ethics and Moral Values in Teaching: Some Contemporary Confusions," *The Journal of Higher Education* 53.3 (1982): 297.

[28]Urmson, "Ethics," 136.

[29]Karen Joy Greenberg, "Ethical Dimensions in Instructors' Manuals for the Basic Course in Communications," diss., U of Massachusetts, 1987, 26.

[30]Lillie, *An Introduction*, 315.

[31]G. B. Kerfred, *"Arete', Agathon, Kakon,"* Paul Edwards, Editor-in-Chief. *The Encyclopedia of Philosophy*, Vol. 1 (New York: Macmillan, 1967) 147–148.

[32]Lillie, *An Introduction*, 321.

[33]Lillie, *An Introduction*, 324–325.

[34]James Mark Baldwin, ed., "Ethical Theories," *Dictionary of Philosophy and Psychology*, Vol. 1 (Gloucester, MA: Peter Smith, 1960) 346.

[35]Vernon E. Cronen and W. Barnett Pearce, "Microprocesses in the Social Construction of Persons," International Interdisciplinary Conference on Self and Identity, Cardiff, UK: University College, 1983, 4.

[36]Fred Feldman, *Introductory Ethics* (Englewood Cliffs: Prentice Hall, 1978) 64.

[37]Richard McKeon, "The New Rhetoric as an Architectonic and Productive Art," *The Center Magazine* (March 1980) 53.

[38]Karen Joy Greenberg, "The Issue of Teaching Ethics in the Introductory Speech Course," ECA Convention, Atlantic City, May, 1986, 1.

[39]Carroll C. Arnold and Kenneth D. Frandsen, "Conceptions of Rhetoric and Communication," in *Handbook of Rhetorical and Communication Theory,* Carroll C. Arnold and John Waite Bowers, eds. (Boston: Allyn and Bacon, 1984) 16.

[40]James L. Golden, Goodwin F. Berquist, and William E. Coleman, *The Rhetoric of Western Thought, 3rd ed.* (Dubuque, IO: Kendall/Hunt, 1976) 270.

[41]Klaus Krippendorff, "An Epistemology for Communication," *Journal of Communication* 34.3 (1984): 21–36.

[42]Douglas R. Hofstadter, *Gödel, Escher, Bach: An Eternal Golden Braid* (New York: Basic Books, 1979) 693–694.

[43]This delineation is based on Rom Harre's delineation of knowledge into private/public, individual/collective, and active/passive dimensions. Rom Harre, *Personal Being: A Theory for Individual Psychology* (Cambridge, MA: Harvard UP, 1984) 48–49.

[44]Ernest A. Moody, "William of Ockham," Paul Edwards, Editor-in-Chief, *The Encyclopedia of Philosophy,* Vol. 8 (New York: Macmillan, 1967) 307.

[45]Matthew Rolston, "Looks That Shook the World: From the Beginning, Rock and Roll was Defined by Sight as Well as Sound," *Rolling Stone* (Apr. 23, 1987); 86–88.

[46]Francessa Lyman, "Maggie Kuhn: A Wrinkled Radical's Crusade," *The Progressive* 52 (Jan. 1988): 29–31; and Slava Lubomudrov, "Congressional Perceptions of the Elderly: The Use of Stereotypes in the Legislative Process," *The Gerontologist* 27.1 (1987): 77–81.

[47]Raoul Naroll, *The Moral Order: An Introduction to the Human Situation* (Beverly Hills, CA: Sage, 1983) 392–395.

[48]William Bruce Cameron, *Modern Social Movements: A Sociological Outline* (New York: Random House, 1966) 20.

[49]Katherine Bishop, ''Neo-Nazi Activity is Rising Among U.S. Youth: Groups of 'Skinheads' Rally to Racism and to Rock and Roll,'' *The New York Times* (13 Jun. 1988): 12.

[50]Ogden, C. K. and I. A. Richards, *The Meaning of Meaning*. (New York: Harcourt Brace, 1923) 33.

[51]See: Anonymous, *Go Ask Alice* (New York: Avon, 1986); Ellen Bass and Laura Davis, *The Courage to Heal: A Guide for Women Survivors of Child Sexual Abuse* (New York: Harper & Row, 1988); and Kathryn B. Hagans and Joyce Case, *When Your Child Has Been Molested: A Parent's Guide to Healing and Recovery, Putting the Pieces Back Together* (Lexington, MA: D.C. Heath, 1988).

[52]See: Leonard J. Martelli, Fran D. Peltzt, and William Messina, *When Someone You Know Has AIDS, 1st ed.* (New York: Crown, 1987); Neil M. Passariello, ''Living with A.I.D.S,'' *Update: Newsletter of the Brattleboro AIDS Project* 2 (Winter 1989) 3–5; and Richard Restak, ''The AIDS Virus has no 'Civil Rights,' '' *Miami Herald* (15 Sept. 1985): 1E.

[53]Susanne K. Langer, *Philosophy in a New Key: A Study in the Symbolism of Reason, Rite, and Art* (New York: Mentor: 1951) 75.

[54]Lis Harris. *Holy Days: The World of a Hasidic Family* (New York: Summit, 1985) 54.

[55]Helen Ralston, *Christian Ashrams: A New Religious Movement in Contemporary India,* Studies in Religion and Society: 20 (Lewiston, NY: Edwin Mellon, 1988) 69.

[56]One starting point for basic information on propaganda is Bruce Lannes Smith, Harold D. Lasswell, and Ralph D. Casey, *Propaganda, Communication, and Public Opinion: A Comprehensive Reference Guide* (Princeton: Princeton UP, 1946) esp. ''Bibliography,'' 121–392.

[57]Joseph Baskin, *Humor and Social Change in Twentieth Century America* (Boston: Trustees of the Public Library, 1979) 30.

[58]Naroll, *The Moral Order,* esp. 191.

[59]Aristotle, *The Nicomachean Ethics,* J. A. K. Thomson, trans. (Baltimore, MD: Penguin, 1953), 58.

[60]Albert Einstein, *The Meaning of Relativity, 5th ed.* (Princeton, NJ: Princeton UP, 1922) 2.

[61]Witter Bynner, trans. *Tao Te Ching: The Way of Life According to Lao Tzu* (New York: John Day, 1944) Chps.[sic] 2 and 7. Ctd. in Huston Smith, *The Religions of Man* (New York: Harper & Row, 1958) 203.

[62]Donald P. Warwick, *The Teaching of Ethics in the Social Sciences,* The Teaching of Ethics: VI (Hastings-on-Hudson, NY: Institute of Society, Ethics, and Life Sciences, 1980) 29.

[63]Maurice Freidman, ''Forward,'' *Communication and Community,* Ronald C. Arnett (Carbondale, IL: Southern Illinois UP, 1986) xviii.

[64]Kenneth S. Bowers, ''Toward a Multidimensional View of Personality and Health,'' *Journal of Personality* 55 (Jun. 1987): 343; and N. Stedman, ''The New Balance; Learning to Let Go of 'Having it All' May Just Mean Ending up with a Whole Lot More,'' *Health* 18 (Oct. 1986): 22.

[65]''Rape Victim Jailed in Refusal to Testify Against Defendant,'' *The New York Times* (26 June 1986): A19.

[66]Greenberg, ''The Deficit of Research on Instructional Communication's Accountability,'' 5, 7.

[67]Shakti Gawain, *Living in the Light: A Guide to Personal and Planetary Transformation* (San Rafael: Whatever, 1986) 70.

[68]Jagadish Chandra Chatterji. *The Wisdom of the Vedas.* (Wheaton, IL: The Philosophical Publishing House, 1973) 90.

[69]W. Barnett Pearce and Vernon E. Cronen, *Communication, Action and Meaning: The Creation of Social Realities* (New York: Praeger, 1980) 169.

[70]Ben A. Franklin, ''Going to Extremes for 'Animal Rights,' '' *The New York Times* (30 Aug. 1987): E7.

[71]Dennis Hevesi, ''Running Away,'' *The New York Times Magazine* (2 Oct. 1988): 30–42 and 59–64.

[72]A. M. Maslow explains that, in the hierarchy of human needs, physiological needs, such as food, and safety needs, such as shelter, are more important than are esteem needs, such as social legitimization. A. M. Maslow, *Motivation and Personality* (New York: Harper & Row, 1954) 80–93.

[73]Constance E. Cumbey, *The Hidden Dangers of the Rainbow: The New Age Movement and Our Coming Age of Barbarism* (Lafayette, LA: Huntington House, 1983).

[74]Herbert Mitgang, ''Rushdie Novel Brings Bomb Threats,'' *The New York Times* (14 Jan. 1989): 13.

[75]Richard McKeon, ''Dialectic and Political Thought and Action,'' *Ethics* 65.1(1954): 28.

[76]F. G. Bailey, *The Tactical Uses of Passion: An Essay on Power, Reason, and Reality* (Ithaca, NY: Cornell UP, 1983) 20–21.

[77]''Vietnam Radio,'' *All Things Considered* National Public Radio. #871111, 1987.

[78]Joshua Meyrowitz, *No Sense of Place: The Impact of Electronic Media on Social Behavior* (New York: Oxford UP, 1985) 245–246.

[79]Alexander Stevens, ''Film Review: *The Last Temptation of Christ,*'' *Leisure Weekly* (20 Oct. 1988): 18–19.

[80]Meyrowitz, *No Sense*, 109.

[81]Todd S. Purdem, ''Police Dilemma on Restaurant Row,'' *The New York Times* (14 Jun. 1988): B2; and Clifford May, ''U.S. Seeking Pyrotechnics Expert in Bombing of Abortion Clinics,'' *The New York Times* (20 Feb. 1987): B3.

[82]Samuel M. Edelman, ''The Rhetoric of Tragic Choice: The Epidictic Uses of Literature as Resistance During the Holocaust'' SCA Convention, Nov., 1987; cf. Foucault, *Language,* 219.

[83]W. Barnett Pearce, ''notes,'' ms. Communication 894B: Communication Among Incommensurate Social Realities. Amherst, MA: U of Massachusetts, Feb. 18, 1986. 6; Paul W. Keller and Charles T. Brown, ''An Interpersonal Ethic for Communication,'' *The Journal of Communication* 8(1968): 80; and Kenneth E. Andersen, ''The Ethical Contributions of ''Non-Participants in a Communication Activity,'' SCA Convention, Denver, Nov., 1985.

[84]Bruce Ritter, *Sometimes God Has a Kid's Face: The Story of America's Exploited Street Kids* (New York: Covenant House, 1988) 123.

[85]Ritter, *Sometimes,* 115.

[86]Brookfield, *Developing,* 65.

[87]Leslie Heim, ''Japan is Paying for its Strong Yen—in Jobs,'' *Business Week* (June 9, 1986): 47.

[88]Alan Bayless, ''Technology Reshapes North America's Lumber Plants: Yet Industry Faces Shake-Out as Some Mills Can't Afford to Upgrade,'' *The Wall Street Journal* 16 Oct. 1986: 6; and Ralph E. Winter, ''Upgrading of Factories Replaces the Concept of Total Animation: Suppliers and Workers Face Tighter Quality Conditions—'Just in Time' Inventories-How Unisys and Huffy Do It,'' *The Wall Street Journal* (30 Nov. 1987): 1 and 8.

[89]Michael S. Gallagher, "The Future (?) of Legal Services for the Poor," *America* (May 16, 1987): 395–396.

[90]Robert L. Ivie, "Metaphor and the Rhetorical Invention of Cold War 'Idealists'," SCA Convention, Denver, 1985, 1.

[91]Richard W. Brislin, Kenneth Cushner, Craig Cherrie, and Mahaelani Yong, *Intercultural Interactions: A Practical Guide,* Cross-Cultural Research and Methodology Series: 9 (Beverly Hills: Sage, 1986) 304.

[92]Gerard A. Hauser and Carole Blair, "Rhetorical Antecedents to the Public," *PRETEXT: An Interdisciplinary Journal of Rhetoric* (Summer 1982): 142.

[93]Shakti Gawain, *Living in the Light: A Guide to Personal and Planetary Transformation,* 3–4.

6

The Principles of Fidelity and Veracity: Guidelines for Ethical Communication

Josina M. Makau

Ohio State University

Gandhi once said that the "means are the ends in the making." This prophetic voice seems to hold little sway over the large sector of the American community which holds up Oliver North as its ideal public servant. By January 1989, North, awaiting trial on charges of criminal conspiracy and obstruction of justice, "will have pocketed more money from his lecture efforts than he earned in his entire military career."[1] To his admirers, North represents the pinnacle of positive values: love of country, respect for authority, purity of heart, champion of freedom. To ethicists,[2] however, North's prominence is a natural outcome of our relativist age, an era dominated by contextual ethics in which the focus has been placed upon " 'private' reliance on individual discernment at the moment of decision."[3]

This chapter will not address the mysteries or lessons associated with North's rise to the status of an American folk hero. It will, however, suggest that an ethical perspective grounded by two related principles of communication ethics—the Principles of Fidelity and Veracity—provides a framework for making viable ethical judgments within a variety of practical contexts. As such, widespread acknowledgment of, and adherence to, the Fidelity and Veracity Principles would serve as a powerful antidote against the tendency to reduce situational ethics to relativism. Such a move would also redirect ethicists', practitioners', and consumers' attention to the communication *process*. This would both mitigate against the academic tendency to reduce ethical principles to arbitrary formist hierarchies and challenge the popular tendency to focus on the ends of communication.

RELEVANT PROBLEMS

The study of normative ethics is concerned with finding *true, valid, acceptable*, or *viable* principles, rules, or norms of ethical practice. Communication ethicists seek principles, rules, or norms for ethical communication which both account for and transcend the many differences between communication contexts. Most communication ethicists seek to avoid the well-documented pitfalls of ethical relativism, a perspective which essentially leaves ethical judgment to the wholly subjective and often arbitrary whims of any given actor.

A number of ethicists continue to search for general principles which transcend differences between contexts. Many of these theorists remain convinced that, in the final analysis, ethical guidelines "are the same for all communicators, no matter whether they speak as politicians, statesmen, businessmen, or department managers."[4]

Richard Weaver's well-known effort to find such general guidelines is representative of many platonic approaches to communication ethics. Weaver attempted to provide a fixed-weight hierarchy of arguments, from the most ethical to the least, to serve as a guideline for ethical rhetorical practice. Weaver concluded that one of the least "admirable subvarieties" of argument is the "appeal to circumstance" often employed in "arguments based on effect."[5]

Yet this type of formist ethic creates arbitrary and potentially counterproductive constraints on the argumentation process. Martin Luther King's effects-based arguments in support of nonviolent civil rights advocacy often appealed to the specific circumstances of the civil rights movement. Applying Weaver's hierarchy to an analysis of King's arguments, the critic would be led to conclude that argumentation by definition would somehow necessarily have been superior to the types of appeal King used. The critic's primary justification for this position would likely be concern that King's rhetoric preyed on the audience's "sentiments." Yet it would be difficult to show that King's appeals to "sentimentality" were somehow less ethical than George Wallace's definitional arguments for segregationist policies.

In a similar vein, generalized admonitions against widely used strategies of persuasion fail to guide responsible practice. Speech Communication scholar Arthur Kruger's objections to emotional appeals illustrate this problem. He argues that reliance on pathetic appeals is inherently unethical. But nearly all the works of poets, novelists, composers, and artists rely heavily upon emotional appeals. Acceptance of Kruger's views preclude even the possibility of writing an ethical poem.[6]

A brief look at differences across a few specialized contexts helps to demonstrate further problems with the platonist's fixed-weight hierarchical perspective of communication ethics. The field of advertising provides a good starting point for such a review. Harvard University Professor of Business Administration Theodore Levitt argues that consumers "expect and demand that advertising create" symbols which show us "what life *might* be, to bring the possibilities that we cannot see before our eyes and screen out the stark reality in which we must live" (emphasis in original).[7] Whether or not Levitt's assessment of audience demands is warranted, he is surely correct in distinguishing the audience's *expectations* of the advertiser from its expectations of a number of other communication practitioners. It seems safe to assume that many audiences understand that the advertiser's primary function is to sell the consumer a product. Given this basic recognition of purpose, audiences generally remain calm when they learn that advertisers employ a variety of persuasive strategies to sell their clients' products.

Citizens in a representative democracy also understand that their president uses the State of the Union Address in part to gain support for his or her policies. Yet they generally view the primary purpose of this speech as providing the public with information needed to make reasonable judgments regarding the nation's leadership and policies. If the president employs Madison Avenue advertising strategies to manipulate the public during a State of the Union Address, the public would have strong justification for serious concern about the president's strategy of communication.

Canon 7 of the American Bar Association's Code of Professional Responsibility helps further illustrate the role context plays in providing grounds for ethical judgments. Under Canon 7 ("A lawyer should represent a client zealously within the bounds of the law"), the Code asserts that, "where the bounds of the law are uncertain, the action of a lawyer may depend on whether he or she is serving as advocate or adviser." Later, under the same Canon, the Code declares that "the responsibility of a public prosecutor differs from that of the usual advocate; his or her duty is to seek justice, not merely to convict." To the extent that we recognize and account for such distinctions, we help advertisers, legal advocates, and other public communicators make informed ethical judgments.

Perspectives which fail to adequately account for the richness of variation found within and across communication contexts provide little assistance to artists, politicians, advertisers, journalists, documentarians, university professors, or other communication practitioners who seek viable boundaries for ethical practice. Yet viable boundaries for ethical practice are precisely what practitioners and consumers need in today's relativist climate.

Sensing the inadequacies of the fixed-weight hierarchies of ethical standards offered by platonists, communication practitioners and consumers seek practical guidelines for ethical communication. Unfortunately, this search has too often taken place in an atmosphere tainted by positivist reductionism. Throughout this culture, students, teachers, and parents have succumbed to the popular cartesian dichotomy between certainty on the one hand and arbitrariness on the other. Accepting this false dilemma, communication practitioners and consumers in this culture have tended to draw the false and often harmful inference that it is not possible to make reasoned ethical judgments.

As early as 1974, University of Chicago Professor Wayne Booth highlighted some of the dangers associated with this widespread adherence to relativism:

> As our political life is more and more conducted with the deceptive techniques borrowed from commercial advertising, politicians become less and less interested in an exchange of good reasons; voters become more and more cynical; exposes of corruption become more frequent and less effective; and finally, a point will be reached, if it has not already been passed, when there is insufficient public trust for democratic processes to work.[8]

According to Booth, "an open society living by a rhetoric of deception cannot long endure."[9]

As Booth suggests, the stakes for the body politic are high. Our culture's prolonged acceptance of the positivist view that an absence of certainty relegates decision makers and actors to arbitrariness, continues to leave us vulnerable to the dangers associated with relativist ethics.

The remainder of this chapter suggests that widespread understanding of and adherence to the Principles of Fidelity and Veracity would provide a powerful safeguard against these dangers. The discussion will show that, unlike formist principles associated with platonism, the Principles of Fidelity and Veracity provide viable, flexible, yet nonrelativist principles of communication ethics.

THE PRINCIPLES OF VERACITY AND FIDELITY

Communication is a social process, the success of which depends upon participants' adherence to mutually accepted norms. Communication theorists Sara Newell and Randall Stutman write accordingly that "a working consensus on norms in various social settings allows social life to progress smoothly." They note further that "these expectations for behavior vary from general social norms (the expectations strangers may share) to relational rules (unique expectations developed within a particular relationship)."[10]

At the heart of effective interpersonal communication is mutual trust, in part resulting from fulfillment of the mutually accepted expectations referred to by Newell and Stutman. Similarly, communication theorists from Aristotle to Burke have shown that effective public communication depends at least in part upon an audience's trust in the speaker or author's sincerity and goodwill. Fulfillment of the mutually accepted expectations discussed by Newell and Stutman plays an important role in establishing and maintaining this requisite trust.

Psychologists have also long recognized the central role trust plays in the quality of relationships between people. Not only is mutual trust widely seen as a key ingredient to the well-being of relationships, a sense of trust is considered essential to an individual's overall psychological well-being.

The Principles of Fidelity and Veracity derive from this recognition of the central role trust plays in healthy communication interaction. These basic principles—related to one another through their mutual attention to trust—differ from platonist principles in two significant ways. First, the Veracity and Fidelity principles focus on the communication *process* and stress the *relational* nature of this process. Second, these principles provide variable, rather than fixed-weight, ethical guidelines.

The Principle of Fidelity[11] holds that bona fide promises are to be kept. Related is the Principle of Veracity, which gives strong presumptive weight to truth telling. This principle holds that lies "are not neutral from the point of view of our choices"; they "require explanation, whereas truth ordinarily does not."[12] As the discussion below will suggest, successful communication depends, at least in part, upon the receiver's presumption that the communicator is acting in accordance with these two principles.

Philosopher Richard Brandt notes that nearly everyone agrees that the making of a promise creates "a *prima facie* obligation."[13] Similarly, ethicist Sissela Bok notes that "trust in some degree of veracity functions as a *foundation* of relations among human beings; when this trust shatters or wears away, institutions collapse" (emphasis in original).[14]

Both the Principles of Fidelity and Veracity appear formally universal. Yet closer examination reveals that each is context sensitive. The Principle of Fidelity, for example, generates practice-relative obligations. Fully formed, the principle holds that making a promise entails obligations only if the promise is bona fide. To be bona fide, a promise must meet the following two conditions:

1. The promise must be made in appropriate circumstances, and
2. There must be no excusing or releasing conditions.

Included as appropriate circumstances are the promise maker's sanity, consciousness, competence, intent to be taken to be making a promise, intent that the promisee believe the promisor intended to fulfill the promise, and the absence of duress when making the promise. The most prominent excusing condition is any extreme, unanticipated cost. Releasing conditions include the unanticipated inability to fulfill the promise, unanticipated radically changed circumstances, mutual knowledge that neither the promisee nor the promisor have an interest in fulfillment of the promise, and the promisee's explicit release of the promisor from making the promise.

Releasing conditions release communicators from their promises, while excusing conditions only change the intensity of the promise maker's obligation. When excusing conditions are mutually understood to overshadow the obligations of the promise, then the promise maker is fully released.

Suppose, for instance, that Ingrid has promised her brother Vic that she will call him on Tuesday. According to the Principle of Fidelity, Ingrid has a prima facie obligation to call Vic only if her promise is bona fide. That is, she must have made the promise in appropriate circumstances and without any excusing or releasing conditions.

Appropriate circumstances would be defined by Ingrid's sanity, consciousness, and competence; Ingrid's interest in fulfilling the promise; her intent to be taken to be making a promise; her intent that Vic believe she intended to fulfill the promise; and the absence of duress when making the promise. The most prominent excusing condition would be any extreme, unanticipated cost. This would be particularly relevant if Ingrid's promise is made impulsively. Releasing conditions would include the unanticipated inability to fulfill the promise; unanticipated radically changed circumstances; mutual knowledge that neither Ingrid nor Vic has an interest in fulfillment of the promise; and Vic's explicit release of Ingrid from the promise. While excusing conditions would not entirely release Ingrid from her obligation to fulfill the promise, releasing conditions would.

As the example above illustrates, application of the Principle of Fidelity requires attentiveness to contextual variables. The circumstances in which a promise is made help determine whether it is bona fide and hence subject to the obligation entailment of the Fidelity Principle. In some settings, for example, communicators share an awareness that a promise is made without the accompanying intent that the promisor be taken to making the promise. Obvious hyperbole in campaign speeches serves as an example. Or, sometimes, neither the promisor nor the promisee has an interest in fulfillment of the promise. Promises made for the sake of civility or decorum during a United Nations reception might fit this category.

Similarly, the Principle of Veracity generates a *presumption* to tell the truth, but allows for circumstances in which varying degrees of deception are expected and accepted. Sissela Bok's thoughtful analyses of truth telling and deception are instructive here.

Bok distinguishes between deception and lying. Deception is the broader category, including any message meant to mislead, whether it is stated, disguised, photographed, or presented in any other communication form. Lying is a form of deception which involves any statement which communicates an intentionally deceptive message, a message meant to make others believe what we ourselves do not believe.[15]

Bok describes different kinds of lies, each with their own rationale. *White lies* are falsehoods "not meant to injure anyone, and of little moral import." Common uses of white lies are to avoid hurting feelings, to be polite, to flatter, "to throw cheerful interpretation on depressing circumstances, or to show gratitude for unwanted gifts."

Bok persuasively argues that even seemingly benign white lies have the potential to do significant harm. She notes, for example, that "disagreeable facts come to be sugar-coated, and sad news softened or denied altogether." For decision makers, such misinformation can have disastrous consequences far more harmful than the negative consequences of truth telling. Perhaps more importantly, regardless of the ultimate outcome resulting from a specific white lie, this form of deception deprives the person being lied to the freedom to make an informed choice. As such, white lies are often more insidious than they are benign.

Similarly, *paternalistic lies* and lies told to protect the sick and dying are often perceived as justifiable. These types of lies are often told with "the intention of guarding from harm," yet they often lead "both through mistake and through abuse, to great suffering. The 'protection' can suffocate; it can also exploit."[16] Just as white lies prevent decision makers from accurately assessing their options, lies told in an effort to protect someone often result in hurting the very people they are intended to help. Paternalistic lies deprive the person lied to the opportunity to make an informed choice about his or her circumstances. From the perspective of the deceived, this outcome might be much more harmful than it is helpful.

Sometimes otherwise ethical communicators succumb to the temptation to deceive on behalf of a good cause. Legal advocates are particularly vulnerable to this temptation. These practitioners are taught to provide passionate arguments in support of their clients. Yet our adversarial system of justice can serve its purposes only if legal advocates take seriously the Principle of Veracity. Manipulating juries through deceptive means endangers the tender thread upon which our system of justice depends.

Other types of seemingly justifiable lies include lies in a crisis, lies protecting peers and clients, and lies for the public good. Like white lies and paternalistic lies, these forms of deception all seem justifiable on the surface. Yet critical analyses reveal that the people whose interests were designed to be protected by these types of deception are often ultimately more harmed than protected by the deception. Careful consideration of the long-term consequences of these types of lies, particularly from the perspective of the deceived, reveals the importance of beginning with a strong presumption in favor of truth-telling.

To help communicators assess whether their intentional deception is justified, Bok suggests that communicators evaluate the circumstances from the standpoint of the deceived. She proposes that communicators ask themselves, "If I were the person being deceived, would I consent to the deception if given a choice?" Or "If I were being deceived, would I believe the deceiver had the right to deceive me? On what grounds?"

Feminist writer Adrienne Rich provides a useful summary of the Veracity

Principle's strong presumption against lying, "lies are usually attempts to make everything simpler—for the liar—than it really is, or ought to be."[17]

Despite the Principle of Veracity's strong admonition against lying, the principle does allow for circumstances in which varying degrees of deception are expected and therefore accepted. Bok describes several such communication contexts. According to Bok, people sometimes play "mutually deceptive roles" in "certain bargaining situations." She cites the following as illustrative: "as buyer and seller, defense and prosecution, sometimes husband and wife." She adds:

> In a bazaar, for instance, false claims are a convention; to proclaim from the outset one's honest intention would be madness. If buyers and sellers bargain knowingly and voluntarily, one would be hard put to regard as misleading their exaggerations, false claims, to have given their last bid, or words of feigned loss of interest. Both parties have then consented to the rules of the game.[18]

The field of advertising provides interesting examples of situations in which communicators might consider themselves exempt from the Veracity Principle's strong presumption against deception. Advertisers will readily suggest that the public fully expects advertisements to zealously serve the interests of clients. Asking advertisers to present balanced or accurate presentations of their clients' products would be asking the advertiser to defeat his or her purpose.

But Bok notes that there are three conditions which must be met before deception is justified even in these circumstances:

1. Mutual knowledge of the 'rules' of the game;
2. Mutual consent;
3. Mutual freedom.

If one of the parties is either not fully aware of the rules, not in a position to fully consent, or not fully free to negotiate the rules, then communicators remain obligated to avoid deception.

Advertising to children, or to other people who do not have knowledge of the rules of the marketplace, places a burden on these communicators to seriously consider the audience's perspective. Even in the hard realities of a marketplace in which *caveat emptor* is a widely accepted credo, public communicators have a responsibility to their own well-being, as well as to the public's, to consider the consequences of violating the public's trust.[19]

As the paragraphs above suggest, application of the Principles of Fidelity and Veracity requires careful consideration of contextual variables. These principles formalize moral intutitions and afford grounds for reasoned applications in specific communication contexts. As such, they provide valuable guidelines for communicators in a wide variety of contexts.

CONCLUSION

Although the Fidelity and Veracity Principles offer valuable assistance to communication practitioners and consumers, a number of challenges remain. The most obvious remaining challenge is the effective and responsible *application* of the principles. Bok joins other philosophers, such as Jürgen Habermas and Chaïm Perelman, in advocating a reliance on a public of "reasonable persons" to help guide ethical practice in specific professions. As discussed earlier, Bok proposes further that these "reasonable persons" attempt to base their assessments on the perspective of the person communicated to. This strategy would serve as a powerful starting point for the reasonable and responsible application of the Fidelity and Veracity Principles in specific professional contexts.

History supports the need for major modification in the development of codes of professional ethics and other guidelines for ethical professional conduct. In the past, most professional codes have been written by practitioners in the given field. Neither ethicists, nor the public at large, for example, played a significant role in developing the Sigma Delta Chi Code for professional journalists. The resulting code is laced with internal inconsistencies, entrenched ambiguity, and principles easily susceptible to counterexamples. Adoption of Bok's suggestion that Review Boards and Ethics Committees include people representing a broad spectrum of interests, needs, and values, as well as those highly expert at practical reasoning, would help Sigma Delta Chi and other professional associations develop more viable guidelines for their practitioners.

At the same time, however, history provides numerous examples of this ideal gone astray. The contextual variability permitted by the Principles of Fidelity and Veracity entails that even these guideposts will fail to *ensure* the appropriateness of their application by a public.

Related is the obvious problem that some people will simply choose not to apply the principles. Motivating people to behave ethically is always challenging, but particularly difficult in a culture which encourages practitioners to view ethical practice as potentially costly.

Yet a first major step toward widespread adherence to the Fidelity and Veracity Principles must be acknowledgment of their soundness and viability. This chapter has provided grounds for such acknowledgment.

The chapter has shown that, unlike their platonic fixed-weight counterparts, the Principles of Fidelity and Veracity recognize communication as a relational process. These flexible principles offer a middle ground between absolutist and radically relativist, as well as between elitist and radically populist, approaches to communication ethics. Since these principles are both situational and transcendant, they can account for context without abandoning the possibility of universalizability. Further, because they focus on communication process, these principles have the potential to help mitigate against the trend toward acceptance of an ends-oriented ethic. Finally, these principles address a fundamental challenge to theories of communication ethics; they provide an ethical framework that is within ordinary communication practitioners' intellectual reach and responsive to the ordinary person's moral intuitions.

ENDNOTES

[1]"Ollie North's Road Show," *Newsweek* (August 1, 1988): 24.

[2]This chapter uses the term *ethicist* in the usual sense, referring to philosophers concerned with the study of morality, moral problems and moral judgments. See, for example, William K. Frankena, *Ethics* (Englewood Cliffs, NJ: Prentice-Hall, 1963), 3.

[3]Ronald Arnett, "The Status of Communication Ethics Scholarship in Speech Communication Journals from 1915–1985," *Central States Speech Journal* (Spring, 1987): 51–52.

[4]Karl R. Wallace, "An Ethical Basis of Communication," *The Speech Teacher* (January, 1955): 13.

[5]For standard explications of Weaver's views, see "Language is Sermonic," in James L. Golden, Goodwin F. Berquist, and William E. Coleman, *The Rhetoric of Western Thought, 2nd ed.* (Dubuque, IA): Kendall/Hunt Publishing Company, 1978) 270–294; and Richard L. Johannesen, "Richard M. Weaver on Standards for Ethical Practice," in *Ethics in Human Communication, 2nd ed.* (Prospect Heights, IL: Waveland Press, 1983), 161–175.

[6]For an explication and critique of Kruger's views, see Richard L. Johannesen's summary in *Ethics in Human Communication, 2nd. ed.* (Prospect Heights, IL: Waveland Press, 1983) 14–15.

[7]Theodore Levitt, "The Morality(?) of Advertising," *Harvard Business Review* (July–August, 1972): 91.

[8]Wayne C. Booth, *Modern Dogma and the Rhetoric of Assent* (Chicago: U of Chicago, 1974) 201–202.

[9]Ibid., 202

[10]Sara E. Newell and Randall K. Stutman, "The Social Confrontation Episode," *Communication Monographs*, 55 (September, 1988): 266.

[11]This expression is borrowed from John Rawls' *A Theory of Justice* (Cambridge: Harvard UP, 1971). See, for example, pages 346–350.

[12]Sissela Bok, *Lying: Moral Choice in Public and Private Life* (New York: Vintage books, 1979) 32.

[13]Richard R. Brandt, *Ethical Theory: The Problems of Normative and Critical Ethics* (Englewood Cliffs, NJ: Prentice-Hall, 1959) 388.

[14]Bok, 33.

[15]Ibid., p. 14. See also Gillian Michell's summary of Bok's definition in "Women and Lying: A Pragmatic and Semantic Analysis of 'Telling it Slant,' " *Women's Studies International Forum*, 7 (1984): 375.

[16]Bok, 216.

[17]Adrienne Rich, "Women and Honor: Some Notes on Lying," in *Lies, Secrets, and Silences: Selected Prose 1966–78* (New York: Norton, 1979), 187–188.

[18]Bok, 138–139.

[19]The foregoing discussion of the Fidelity and Veracity Principles borrows heavily from Josina M. Makau, *Reasoning and Communication: Thinking Critically About Arguments* (Belmont, CA: Wadsworth, 1990), 122–129.

Part III

Social Systems of Account Making

7

Conversations About the Ethics of Institutional Persuasion

J. Michael Sproule

Department of Communication Studies,
San Jose State University

By 1900, the seeds of a new era of institutional social influence were sprouting. One hundred years earlier, the chief rhetorical tools of society's persuaders were oratory and pamphleteering. However, by the beginning of the twentieth century, the pattern of mass persuasion by large commercial and political organizations was already in place. Institutional persuaders were now taking advantage of the skills of public relations counsels and advertisers. In turn, new modes of persuasion raised pressing issues for those committed to an ethic of democratic public communication. This essay surveys the effort of 20th-century critics and commentators to build an ethics of communication adapted to modern rhetorical practices.

America's progressives have set the agenda for conversations about 20th-century communication with charges that institutional propaganda threatens democracy. However, the impact of this indictment is tempered by alternate visions of social influence offered by media practitioners, communication scientists, and conservative commentators. As a result of these competing schools of thought, American society has neither fully accepted nor completely adopted the progressive program for ethical mass persuasion.

This essay focuses on three concerns raised by the progressives and the concomitant responses of their intellectual competitors. First, is democracy threatened by ideological barriers that limit access to the public forum? Second, do the vast symbolic resources marshalled in orchestrated persuasive campaigns imply a manipulative destruction of democratic publics? Third, what are the implications for a democratic public opinion when institutional persuaders covertly infiltrate their ideologies into such ostensibly neutral channels of public communication as news, government agency messages, education, religion, and entertainment? None of these important issues have yet been conclusively resolved. Vital light may be shed on these questions, however, when we view them as problems inherent to modern communication ethics, and when we compare the differing answers supplied by competing schools of thought.

THE ETHICS OF IDEOLOGICAL GATEKEEPING

By tradition, the ethics of communication are focused on the personal moral qualities of the speaker. A speaker-centered ethics of discourse was appropriate for the days when social influence meant great speakers presenting significant addresses to relatively small audiences of opinion leaders. By the late 1800s, however, channels of mass communication allowed persuaders to bypass the old elites, diffusing messages directly to the wider public. Party officials and interest group leaders still influenced the opinions of their constituencies; but reporters, editors, advertisers, and public relations counsels now enjoyed a comparable power.[1] In the simpler days of 1800, access to the channels of public communication was relatively straightforward. Democratic expression required only negative prohibitions against official interference with persons who spoke from a local soap box or operated a printing press. However, as newspaper publishing became more expensive, and as mass circulation dailies emerged, new issues of democratic communication ethics came to the fore. What assured Americans that those who controlled the large journals would grant access to diverse expression? The ideology of the nation's media gatekeepers was now a matter to be reckoned with.

"Freedom of the press is guaranteed only to those who own one," observed the noted journalism critic, A. J. Liebling.[2] Liebling's remark underscores the importance of media access as one of today's issues in democratic communication ethics. Constitutional defenses of free speech and a free press were designed for an era when oratory and political broadsides constituted the chief means for diffusing arguments and proposals. During the Revolutionary era, the "communication industry" consisted of approximately 40 newspapers with average circulation of no more than 500 copies. Newspapers generally were published as a sideline by individuals whose primary interest was commercial printing, or the papers functioned as an outlet for a political party.[3] By the 1830s, a new kind of independent, advertising-supported *penny paper* was altering customary modes of social and political communication. Congressional leaders increasingly saw that newspaper coverage allowed a wider forum for their views than did individual speeches.[4]

In 1876, the leading Republican candidate for president, James G. Blaine, discovered that even successful speeches in the House of Representatives were useless if key elements of the press chose to interpret them unfavorably. Blaine gave two impressive addresses to vindicate his honesty against charges that he accepted bribes from the railroads. But because he failed to convince leading independent newspapers and magazines of his innocence, Blaine lost his bid for the Republican nomination. In a subsequent try for the White House, in 1884, opposition from the independent press again kept Blaine from the presidency.[5] With the diffusion of political fact and opinion increasingly under the control of large-circulation independent newspapers, the ethics of political expression became less a matter what individual speakers said and more a function of the habitual practices of the journalism profession. Decisions by reporters, editors, and publishers increasingly influenced the diffusion of political information and expression.

As a whole, the press of the early 20th century was not conscious of its own ideological predilections. Journalistic norms held that good, fair reporting amounted to simple fidelity to facts. Reporters and editors assumed that information was understandable apart from its social context.[6] Yet, the ''factual'' approach to journalism had the effect of masking dominant ideologies. Will Irwin, the journalist progressive, provided the first important social history of news biases. Helping to undermine a view of facts as the essential ingredient of good reporting, Irwin focused on the importance of interpretation. Irwin noted the general tendency of editors and publishers to assimilate the social views of the wealthy and powerful with whom they associated.[7]

The gradual shift to an institution-centered view of communication ethics is nowhere clearer than in early critical probes of alliances between newspaper corporations, business organizations, and advertising agencies. Newspapers of all kinds, and especially the low-cost penny papers, derived an increasing proportion of their income from advertising. During the post-Civil War period, advertising agencies emerged to coordinate the placement of ads in the nation's newspapers and to ascertain that the papers possessed the circulation they claimed. The hold of advertisers and advertising agencies on newspapers increased during the last two decades of the 19th century as department store and national brand name advertising became key sources of newspaper revenue.[8]

Irwin's series provided an early social history of the connections between newspapers and advertising. Irwin cited instances in which business organizations, such as Standard Oil, used outright bribery to influence the editorial policy of newspapers. Further, according to Irwin, the desire to avoid offending major advertisers induced newspapers to omit unflattering stories that might embarrass these sponsors.[9] Reformers of this period were fully aware that their views were often ignored or disparaged by the media. Upton Sinclair published a muckraking description of the biased, unfavorable news treatment given to reformers and reform movements.[10] George Seldes, the renowned press critic, recalls that both Irwin's writings and Sinclair's book were influential in alerting journalists to widespread ideological corruptions in reporting.[11] Attention to systematic biases in the news marked an important transition from an individualistic to an institutional treatment of communication ethics.

The ethics of ideological constraints in news has been a specialty of such contemporary media critics as George Seldes, I.F. Stone, A. J. Liebling, and Ben Bagdikian. Seldes's most famous critique of American journalism came in *Lords of the Press*, and he reprises these views in his 1987 best-selling autobiography. Reviewing the career of William Randolph Hearst and other owners of newspaper chains, Seldes has explained how owners infused the news with their social and political biases.[12] For a time, both Seldes and Stone published independent journals of press criticism. As material for his *In Fact*, published between 1940 and 1950, Seldes relied on items of suppressed news supplied by reporters across the nation. *I.F. Stone's Weekly* (1953–1971) was given over to Stone's careful exegeses of official documents. Stone specialized in giving a leftist critical perspective to propaganda by the U.S. government, especially the military.

Liebling, press critic of the *New Yorker*, combined the approaches of Seldes and Stone. Like Seldes, Liebling was interested in influences on news reporting. Liebling's columns presented the press as generally favoring the case of business as opposed to that of labor. For instance, he focused on the overwhelming editorial support given by American newspapers to the Republican party. Liebling also shared Stone's interest in probing the communications of large corporate and military organizations. Ben Bagdikian, today's most active spokesperson for progressive media criticism, also focuses on the problem of concentration in the ownership and control of modern media. Bagdikian has analyzed the rise of large media chains that, in turn, often have been owned by larger corporate conglomerates. The resulting situation has been one in which interlocking directorates constrict diversity of expression. Bagdikian demonstrates the reluctance of editors to run stories critical of their parent firms, and he has shown instances of where books have been withdrawn from publication at the demand of controlling conglomerates.[13]

Media practitioners have been troubled by progressive critics who claim that modern communication is marred by ideological constraints on who has access to the public. According to key spokespersons of the communication industry, modern communication actually works against ideological constraint by elevating popular opinion over elite views. One of the first spokespersons for the communication professionals was Edward L. Bernays, a founder of the field of public relations. Bernays argued that propaganda is inevitable in a society based on political competition. Further, according to Bernays, competition rendered propaganda harmless, since everyone in a democratic society is free to use it. Nor were critics correct in condemning special interests for using propaganda,

Bernays explained. The public relations efforts of particular organizations actually benefitted society-at-large, because these messages brought into public view crucial information. Bernays took the position that public relations widened democracy since it enabled minority groups to get their views heard by the majority.[14]

Another prominent spokesman for the communication industry has been George Gallup, pioneer market researcher and political pollster. Gallup argued that public opinion polls enhanced democracy because they allow the opinion of ordinary citizens to be freely expressed without distortion by ruling elites. By their fidelity to mass opinion, polls bridge the gap between the people and their leaders during interims between elections. Moreover, Gallup maintained, polls actually are better than elections in revealing public opinion on specific matters of policy. Gallup concluded that polling would lead to the highest possible state of democracy by ascertaining at all times the majority will. In contrast, before polling, political leaders were reduced to divining mass opinion through public meetings and from letters of constituents. Such barometers of opinion actually worked against democracy, said Gallup, because meetings and letters reflected only the views of elite opinion leaders. Because polls bypassed elites, they revealed the true (usually limited) strength of demagogues and dissident movements. The value of polls, Gallup contended, is that they supplied hard data to counteract the biased pretentions of wide popular support asserted by interest group leaders.[15]

Defenses of professional practice by leaders of the communication industry generally have succeeded in maintaining for the practitioners a great freedom of action. But contemporary progressive critics remain unimpressed. They insist that public relations techniques favor those corporations, factions, and interest groups that have the greatest resources to pay professional fees. Critics of today, such as Herbert Schiller and Benjamin Ginsberg, dismiss the idea that political polls are a straightforward extension of democracy. Not only are polls chiefly available to wealthy groups, Schiller argues, the polls favor corporate interests by means of the questions asked. For instance, Schiller shows that the wording of questions about television commercials overstates public acceptance of them. For his part, Ginsberg argues that public opinion polling weakens democratic diversity by undermining the leaders of interest groups. For instance, he cites how the Nixon Administration used poll data to make labor leaders appear out of touch with the "true" opinions of the "silent majority" of workers. Under the strictures of polling, labor "opinion" became less the marshalling of workers by their leaders and more an aggregate of spur-of-the-moment responses by miscellaneous workers to questions asked in a "neutral" frame of reference.[16]

What do contemporary progressives have to say about ideological gatekeeping? Critics of today generally accept the claims of newspaper professionals that overt ideological censorship is largely a phenomenon of the past.[17] They focus instead on the wider issue of how news is made. For instance, Edward Epstein explains how the limited number of network camera crews restricts most national

TV news to events in major urban centers that can be predicted in advance. At the same time, the journalistic desire for *balance* means that diversity of opinion is sacrificed for the sake of covering two mainstream positions.[18] Ron Powers argues that market research has locked local television news into a superficial, issueless "happy talk" format calculated to attract a greater number of viewers.[19] In addition to faulting certain practices of deciding what is news, progressives point to continued selective biases in journalism. Today's critics echo the complaint of Will Irwin that the ethics of news reporting are undermined by subtle class biases in the news. White collar reporters, for instance, have a natural affinity for corporate managers, making for a neglect of the labor point of view.[20]

While progressives have persisted in challenging the democratic ethics of the communication industry, American society has adopted few of their recommendations on how to improve media access. Today, as in the 1920s and 1930s, progressives favor a large-scale program for educating the public about how institutions use the communication industry. However, prospects for progressive educators are worse today than before. During the 1930s, progressivism enjoyed a relatively great influence in public education due to widespread Depression-era disillusionment. However, after 1940, social skepticism was replaced by a concern for national security that came with World War II and the subsequent Cold War. As a result, no contemporary program of propaganda education approaches the scope of that developed by the Institute for Propaganda Analysis during the 1930s. The Public Doublespeak program of the National Council of Teachers of English is today a relatively modest undertaking when compared to the influence of the Institute for Propaganda Analysis, whose materials were used by approximately one million American school children per year.[21]

The limited impact of progressive propaganda criticism in contemporary public education parallels the relatively scant attention given to proposals for restructuring ownership of the commercial communication industry. For instance, Robert Picard now calls for recognition of a "positive press freedom" that would require government subsidies to enable diverse social groups to own American newspapers. Picard's recent suggestion has come no further toward fruition than did Upton Sinclair's 1919 proposal for municipal ownership of newspapers or George Seldes's effort to establish a labor-owned national newspaper in the 1930s.[22] Ideological constraints on access to the public will remain an impetus for many future conversations about communication ethics.

THE ETHICS OF ORCHESTRATED CAMPAIGNS

If institutionally organized persuasion brings constraints on public access, this modern format also fosters large-scale, orchestrated persuasive campaigns. By 1900, news and advertising designed for the masses harkened to a new era of public address. Progressive critics pointed out the potential for society's large persuaders to set in motion a bandwagon effect in public opinion. Critics initially focused on the implications for democratic public communication of innovations in news management. When newspapers forsook their elite subscribers and party subsidies, journalism organized itself around professional standards of newsworthiness. Good reporting became the presentation of important facts in a way that compelled interest from ordinary readers. Would-be persuaders found it necessary to tailor their appeals to journalistic codes of what constituted news.

The counterpart to newspaper gatekeeping was a new breed of communication professional whose trade was grabbing space in the news columns for their clients. While business organizations often had employed bribery to win press coverage for their views, early press agents, such as Ivy Lee, convinced important leaders of commerce that good news coverage could not be bought, but rather needed to be cultivated. During the 1914 Colorado mine strike, for instance, Lee defended the Rockefeller interests by soliciting proindustry statements from Colorado opinion leaders and then circulating this packaged material to the nation's newspapers.[23]

Turn-of-the-century American muckrakers were concerned about the implications for democracy of press management techniques. Did not press agentry allow powerful institutions a disproportionate presence in channels of mass communication? Ray Stannard Baker was convinced that the alliance of institutional persuaders and press agents might undermine popular rule. In 1906, Baker wrote a detailed article for *McClure's* magazine on "How Railroads Make Public Opinion," an expose of how three railroads retained a Boston press agency to combat a Senate bill imposing controls on railroads. The railroad's press agents visited editors and sent out prepared articles, keeping careful track of editorials and news stories printed by the various papers. The press agents also encouraged local business firms (who depended on the railroads for shipping) to influence their local newspapers in directions favorable to the railroads. Railroad press agents also paid travel expenses to allow representatives of small businesses to testify before the Senate in favor of the railroads. Baker acknowledged that the railroads had, in this case, eschewed bribery. Nevertheless, he wondered if modern press agentry did not create a "sanitized," corrupted public opinion.[24]

World War I saw an important advance in press management take hold in government. Staffed by leading journalist progressives, the U.S. Committee on Public Information established press offices and sent out volumes of prepared news, much of which was reprinted verbatim, especially by small rural papers. However, in addition to elaborating on these standard techniques of press agentry, the CPI pioneered techniques for making news. The CPI spent much time creating newsworthy groups, such as Americanization Committees, and events, such as War Expositions, to compel attention from the nation's editors and reporters. By making news, instead of merely sending out press releases, the CPI capitalized on the growing professionalization of news reporting. The stage-managed groups and events guided the news, but by eschewing the tell-tale hand of the official press release, CPI news management also allowed for the appearance of complete journalistic independence.[25]

The work of the CPI stimulated a sense of urgency about the institutional orchestration of opinion. Walter Lippmann and others recognized that society's powerful institutions would remember the lessons of the war years and, increasingly, would apply methods of opinion management to domestic controversies. As a result, Lippmann characterized the basic problem of democracy as one of ethical communication practices. Lippmann argued that twentieth century democracy could function only if the channels of public communication were protected from ideological coloration.[26] Edward L. Bernays, a prewar press agent and wartime CPI official, proved Lippmann's prognostication correct by establishing one of the nation's most innovative public relations firms. Bernays was impressed by the successes of the CPI and decided he could make a good living applying techniques of news guidance to the needs of the nation's large businesses and organizations.

Worries about the debasement of democratic life led progressives to criticize the Bernays method of making news. In a debate with Bernays, Ferdinand Lundberg argued that the notion of a modern free marketplace of propaganda was illusory. Propaganda could never be ethically neutral, since "it costs money, which, usually, is in the hands of antisocial groups dedicated to narrow self-interest rather than to the common wealth." Lundberg maintained that modern propaganda was particularly pernicious because of the stealth with which it was spread by professionals. Lundberg argued that Bernays's entire philosophy of communication was based on a view of the public as a "blind, unintelligent beast" needing to be tamed by handlers who were in the employ of dominant institutions.[27]

In addition to promoting news bandwagons through press agentry and public relations, 20th-century institutional persuaders have refined the resources of advertising. Image-oriented, national brand name advertising grew up as part of the shift in the United States from local production to large-scale national manufacturing. For most of the nineteenth century, commerce was organized around the manufacture of generic products by local entrepreneurs. To the extent that advertising was employed, the messages tended to be descriptions of the product itself that were suitable for wholesale buyers. With the rise of large-scale industry, the problem was now one of capturing a place in the national consumer market for one's merchandise. Producers began to apply brand names to their wares, and advertising shifted from an information-oriented style to a new focus on conveying an appealing brand image. A reduced emphasis on reasons in advertising was appropriate since the ads were now designed, not for wholesalers, but for average consumers who had less interest in technical details. The mass consumer was often satisfied to retain merely a holistic impression of competing brands, based on slogans and pictures.[28]

Muckrakers and progressives were largely unconcerned by developments in commercial advertising. However, when the U.S. government adopted image advertising as a technique to promote wartime fervor, the progressive critics perceived an ethical problem for democratic communication. In addition to issuing press releases and acting to make news, the Committee on Public Information showed that the directness of commercial advertising could be orchestrated for political persuasion. The CPI directly addressed the public by marshalling such media as pamphlets, leaflets, donated advertising space, films, posters, and the 75,000 orators of the Four Minute Men speaking program.

An inevitable corollary of postwar disillusionment in the United States was a new, skeptical view of the CPI. As progressives reassessed the war years, they blamed the CPI's opinion-making machinery for the nation's plunge into a war whose most conspicuous result was to enlarge the British and French empires. The post World War I years saw progressive writers and educators enlist in a propaganda analysis movement to expose the work of modern institutional persuaders. Representative of popular propaganda analysis was Ernest Gruening, who exposed the work of the electric power industry's vast publicity bureaus. Gruening showed that utility campaign leaders often opposed publicly owned power plants, not by argument, but by courting newspaper editors and engineering teachers. He exposed the arrogance of these opinion makers who called backers of municipal utilities "Reds" and passed the costs of their propaganda operation to the public through power plant operating expenses.[29]

Like the popular writers, academicians and educators of the post World War I period saw propaganda as a useful concept for explaining modern social organization and social change. Peter Odegard, the political scientist, used propaganda concepts as a basis for his analysis of the temperance movement.[30] The major journals of academic social science carried articles that probed the propagandas of major public and private institutions. Propaganda became an important feature of social science education through the textbooks of Odegard (political science), Frederick Lumley (sociology), and Leonard Doob (psychology).[31] The place of propaganda analysis in American education was solidified in 1937 with the chartering of the Institute for Propaganda Analysis. Reflecting the progressive mission to help the public cope with media-based social influence, the Institute's bulletin, *Propaganda Analysis*, was widely used by American college and secondary school teachers.

Progressive propaganda critique not only fit Depression-era radicalism, but this humanistic view also matches post-Vietnam disillusionment. Renewed popular attention in our era to the artificial and manipulative dimensions of orchestrated campaigns began with such classics as *The Selling of the President 1968* and *The Politics of Lying*.[32] Book stores today provide a wealth of literature critiquing news management as well as packaged commercial and political advertising.[33] In fact, the last ten years have seen the concept of propaganda return as a significant theoretical framework in American academe.[34]

Today's propaganda critics share the interest of their 1930s predecessors in laying bare the works of institutional persuaders. However, modern criticism goes beyond propaganda analysis in that today's writers directly question the social morality of an advertising-based, image-oriented culture. During the 1950s, when Vance Packard wrote his exposé of motivational advertising and image-based political communication, his critique marked a relatively isolated indictment. Today, however, Packard's contentions are echoed by Stuart Ewen, Neil Postman, and many others who fault advertising approaches as lessening the ability of Americans to perceive issues and rationally assess arguments.[35] Educators of today are working to help students cope with manipulative aspects of contemporary social influence.[36] The result has been to further move communication ethics from the individual to the institutional plane.

Communication practitioners, whose daily labor convinces them that persuasion is more easily assumed than attained, defend professionally orchestrated campaigns as essentially unthreatening to democratic life. One of the earliest defenses of the 20th-century's promotional culture was given by Ivy Lee, who insisted that modern social influence was dangerous only when the sources of messages were hidden.[37] Lee's belief that disclosure of the source of a message precluded a propagandistic effect was echoed in the Foreign Agents Registration Act of 1938, a federal law requiring persuaders to give notice that they were working to promote a foreign government. Bernays extended Lee's defense of public relations by proposing that ethical codes of professional practice could eliminate whatever residual danger that orchestrated persuasion posed for democratic life. Further, Bernays argued, critics overstated the power of public relations to mask the faults of business and other institutions. In fact, Bernays contended, public relations only worked when it was based on an ethic of mutual understanding between persuader and public. Public relations acted to represent the public to the corporation, thereby encouraging business to offer policies desired by the public.[38]

In recent times, leading advertising executives, such as Rosser Reeves and David Ogilvy, make a point similar to that of Bernays, pointing up their limited ability to alter either the attitudes or behavior of consumers.[39] Michael Schudson's comprehensive academic study of advertising similarly casts doubt on the real power of the "captains of consciousness" who labor in an atmosphere of uncertainty and competition. Schudson points to examples of failed advertising and shows that advertisers can neither prove nor explain the effect of their ads on sales.[40]

Since the 1930s, social scientists generally have accepted the claim of practitioners that mass communication is socially neutral in view of the competition of propagandas in the American marketplace of ideas.[41] Such a view allows social scientists to eschew the social ethics of communication practices in favor of studying the process by which communication exerts an impact.[42] Since the 1940s, the paradigm of statistical-experimental communication research has seen its mission as that of making communication more effective for society's large institutional persuaders. This tradition grew up during World War II and the Cold War, when the U.S. government and private foundations financed social science research into wartime problems of building civilian and military morale, assessing enemy propaganda, and developing potent antifascist (and later, anticommunist) propaganda.

World War II seemed to teach that mass persuasion in a democracy was socially unthreatening because the democratic electorate held ultimate control over institutions. As a result of this assumption, virtually no formal limits are now imposed on techniques for orchestrating public opinion. The efforts of contemporary progressives to equalize political campaigning through public funding of elections has produced little actual results. Similarly, there exists considerable resistance today in the Federal Communications Commission, and in Congress, to eliminating commercials on television shows aimed at children. The idea of a democratic marketplace, advanced by communication practitioners, continues to dampen public demand for major changes in the freedom of institutional persuaders, notwithstanding occasional inroads by progressive critics.

THE ETHICS OF COVERT IDEOLOGICAL DIFFUSION

An important theme in the progressive critique of modern public communication is the idea that institutions are able to debase public opinion by covertly infiltrating their ideologies into the public mind. This century's debate over hidden ideological diffusion chiefly centers on five instrumentalities of social influence that are ostensibly politically neutral: news, government agency communication, education, entertainment, and religion. Since each of these five social offices has taken on an idealized image of ideological virginity, progressives watch carefully to make sure that none of these apparatuses functions to endanger liberal democracy. In recent decades, however, conservative business and political spokesmen have complicated the issue of ideological diffusion by raising alarms about the efforts of leftists to co-opt instruments of public deliberation and education. Rightist commentators have frequently stolen the thunder of progressive critics, complicating today's conversation about the ethics of ideological diffusion.

Critiques by progressives of newspaper gatekeeping, described earlier, marked the first effort to present ideological diffusion as something corrosive to the ethic of democratic public communication. Competing with today's progressive exposes of media manipulation is a post-Vietnam rightist critique of news bias. The contemporary decline in overt ideological censorship of news, and the greater freedom of journalists to write analysis stories (in addition to factually oriented ones) both lend fuel to rightist claims about "liberal bias" in reporting. The idea of proliberal distortions of news first entered public consciousness as part of the Nixon Administration's campaign to discredit its opponents.[43] Today, a private group called Accuracy in Media has become the standard bearer of the idea that contemporary news is covertly slanted to the left. Typical of the AIM approach is an attack on the television networks for "negative" reporting of the harms of Agent Orange on veterans.[44]

What are we to make of the simultaneous criticisms of the press for alleged leftist and rightist ideological coloration? Can we say that the criticisms cancel themselves out, and hence that news has attained a true political neutrality? George Seldes, the media critic, answers that the right-wing critique applies only to a small number of visible media outlets, such as the *New York Times* or the major TV networks. These powerful media channels have developed a relative independence from conservative economic and political institutions that traditionally set the tone for commercial journalism. Seldes argues that the vast majority of the press is still under the control of gatekeepers holding a rightist political perspective. However, since media owners and editors now rarely impose overt censorship, Seldes characterizes today's news reporting as vastly better than in past times.[45]

In addition to concerns about ideological manipulations in the news, the modern era has seen a parallel preoccupation with the possible ideological capture of government agency communication. One progressive critique of the CPI was rooted in a belief that this bureau unfairly used its aura of legitimacy to spread a self-serving, but ultimately misleading, propaganda. The dangers of having an executive department orchestrate public opinion were not lost on members of Congress who closely monitored appropriations for the Committee. Republicans were especially sensitive to the possibility that the CPI would give the White House a competitive advantage over Congress, and Republicans harbored suspicions that the CPI sought to promote President Wilson as much as to inspire the nation's war effort.

The establishment of press offices in the many New Deal administrative agencies made clear that the issue of ideological control of government communication would be a lasting one. Will Irwin, the progressive media critic, saw the "quiet and subtle persuasion" of the New Deal as setting precedents dangerous to democratic communication.[46] One like-minded critic compiled the names of public employees whose job was to send out New Deal propaganda disguised as news.[47] Unlike the CPI, whose patriotic aura and brief existence protected it from sustained partisan attack, the promotional efforts of the New Deal prompted systematic counterattacks from political opponents. The House Un-American Activities Committee, controlled by an anti-New Deal faction, devoted as much of its early effort to expose New Deal promotions as to identify avowed communists in government. For instance, HUAC was incensed about the leftist bias in plays produced by the Federal Writers and Federal Theater programs, and several representatives smeared the entire government arts program as being pro-Red.[48] The "issue" of "Communists in government" was a staple of the McCarthy period, an era preoccupied with loyalty oaths and other overt demands for ideological conformity.

American intervention in Vietnam caused progressives to returned to the topic of government propaganda. The effort by the White House, the Pentagon, and the State Department to "sell" the Vietnam War produced the so-called credibility gap. Until 1968, the Johnson Administration was generally successful in monopolizing channels of public communication with prowar views.[49] Decisions on what to broadcast about the war were strongly influenced by the assumption that the Executive Branch properly set the agenda for discussion of the war. Frank Stanton, president of CBS, opposed his news division's plan for a series of debates between leading Congressional hawks and doves, partly on the grounds that dovish speeches might dilute LBJ's power to conduct the war.[50] However, with the Tet Offensive of 1968, and with the rising anti-war movement, dissenting views began to receive wider media attention. The publication of Senator J. William Fulbright's *The Pentagon Propaganda Machine* again brought public attention to the old issue of whether or not one-sided governmental persuasion injured democracy.[51] Issues of government propaganda are prominently featured in such recent books as *The Press and the Presidency* and *Bureaucratic Propaganda*.[52] In addition, Noam Chomsky and Edward S. Herman have produced a considerable body of literature arguing that the American government habitually misleads citizens about foreign policy. For instance, they contend that the White House and the Pentagon suppress unfavorable information about pro-American regimes abroad and that the U.S. government promotes "demonstration elections" to make right-wing dictatorships acceptable to American sensibilities.[53]

Ideological debasement of public education has been a source of concern for critics since the 1920s, when humanists raised alarms about special interest propaganda disguised as educational materials. A 1929 report of the National Education Association examined a host of free handouts, films, and educational contests supplied by private organizations and concluded that "the propagandist is knocking at the school door."[54] College educators, too, pointed to the efforts of such groups as the National Electric Light Association to infiltrate partisan views into the schools, for instance, by subsidizing textbooks authors who expressed congenial views.[55]

The progressive conversation about propaganda in the schools continues to the present day, for instance, in exposes of textbook censorship and in Ira Shor's argument that educational careerism and campaigns for "excellence" both have been used as a cover for the restoration of conservative values in education.[56] However, diluting the impact of today's progressive critique are complaints by rightist critics that the very educators who cry "propaganda" tend themselves to act as propagandists for left-wing ideology. The thesis that progressive educators function as left-wing propagandists dates back to charges by the National Association of Manufacturers that American school texts were derogatory to American business and political institutions.[57] Today, the rightist ideological critique of education continues in the work of textbook censorship groups and the classroom monitoring group, Accuracy in Academia.

The idea that entertainment media may purvey propaganda has become a fourth focus for ethical debates about ideological manipulation in public communication. By the late 1930s, isolationists were insisting that Hollywood movies served to prepare America for intervention in Europe's new war.[58] The House Un-American Activities Committee took up the theme of movie ideology in 1947 with its investigation of possible communist infiltration in Hollywood.

Ideological propagation through entertainment was initially a complaint chiefly of rightists. However, liberal critics today actively pursue the matter of entertainment as ideological tool. J. Fred MacDonald argues persuasively that news and entertainment programs on television served as effective tools for promoting public acceptance of the Cold War. Todd Gitlin frames a thesis that the entertainment industry senses political shifts and steers its programs to catch the drift of ideological currents. Neil Postman takes the wider position that today's public deliberations are saturated with entertainment values and are therefore debased. Postman argues that Americans are largely content to view the world on the basis of pictures on a television screen. News and public affairs programs lose their impact when prepared according to the show business format of short, superficial, and disjointed presentations.[59]

Religious institutions have become a fifth front in today's debate about covert ideological dissemination. At the outset of American entry into World War I, Eugene Debs claimed that, "when Wall Street says 'war,' every pulpit in the land yells 'war.' "[60] After the war, progressives faulted American clergy for acting as apologists for government war policies. Particularly influential was *Preachers Present Arms*, in which sociologist Ray Abrams detailed the effort of clergy to highlight the militancy of Jesus and their eagerness to spread unproven atrocity tales. Further, disillusionment with the war was rampant among clergy during the 1920s, with such prominent ecclesiastical advocates of the Great War as Harry Emerson Fosdick suffering pangs of conscience over the unquestioning support they rendered to Caesar.[61]

The rise of contemporary televangelism has brought the ideological role of religion again to prominence. Progressive critics generally argue that the electronic evangelism of fundamentalists represents a danger to democracy because it purveys a right-wing political and social ideology under the guise of religion. At the same time, the Reagan Administration and its supporters are quick to label religious opponents of nuclear armament policies as improperly intruding into political affairs. The FBI has opened files on various clergypersons and religious groups that vocally oppose aid to the Contras. Clearly, American society has not yet worked out the ethical parameters of church action in the realm of social and political policy.

Today, Americans may turn to a large body of literature presenting the case that covert ideological diffusion is a pressing social problem. Critiques of propaganda in news, government communication, education, entertainment, and religion usually come from the pens of progressives. However, rightist critics have entered the fray, particularly with regards to ideological winds in institutions of news and education. The literature of liberal critique is the more extensive. However, conservatives have probably enjoyed the greatest single success in drawing general public attention to the ethics of ideological diffusion by constantly reiterating their "liberal bias" thesis of news reporting.

First expressed by muckrakers and progressives, concerns about powerful institutions overthrowing popular democracy laid the seeds for a school of propaganda criticism. Since 1900, progressives have worked to build support for reforms of American public communication by exposing ideological barriers to access, by revealing institutional orchestration of public opinion, and by exposing subtle ideological infiltration in news, government agency communication, education, entertainment, and religion. At the same time, however, competing schools of thought have blunted the ability of liberal humanists to create a sense of alarm about ethical problems in America's institution-based public communication. Practitioners and social scientists tend to minimize the humanist critique by casting doubt on whether modern opinion management methods really produce significant effects. Moreover, since the 1960s, conservatives have diluted the potency of the progressive critique by claiming that left-wing reporters and progressive educators are the real ideological culprits. Our national conversation about the ethics of institutional discourse shows no sign of abating.

ENDNOTES

[1]For a thorough treatment of these ideas, see Benjamin Ginsberg, *The Captive Public: How Mass Opinion Promotes State Power* (New York: Basic Books, 1986); cf. Elihu Katz and Paul F. Lazarsfeld, *Personal Influence: The Part Played by People in the Flow of Mass Communications* (New York: Free Press, 1955).

[2]A. J. Liebling, *The Press* (New York: Pantheon, 1964) 32.

[3]Alfred McClung Lee, *The Daily Newspaper in America: The Evolution of a Social Instrument* (New York: Octagon Books, 1973) 18, 29, 711, 728.

[4]Barnet Baskerville, *The People's Voice: The Orator in American Society* (Lexington, KY: U of Kentucky P, 1979) 121–122.

[5]J. Michael Sproule, "Newspapers as Political Persuaders: The Campaign Against James G. Blaine," *Central States Speech Journal*, 24 (1973): 310–318.

[6]Michael Schudson, *Discovering the News* (New York: Basic Books, 1978) 63, 71, 81, 87, 120.

[7]Will Irwin, *The American Newspaper* (Ames, IA: Iowa State UP, 1969). (Original work published 1911)

[8]Schudson, *News*, 93ff.

[9]Irwin, *American Newspapers*, 51–55, 65–66.

[10]Upton Sinclair, *The Brass Check: A Study of American Journalism* (New York: Arno, 1970). (Original work published 1911)

[11]George Seldes, personal interview, Heartland-4-Corners, VT, May 12–13, 1984.

[12]George Seldes, *Lords of the Press* (New York: Julian Messner, 1938), and *Witness to a Century* (New York: Ballantine, 1987).

[13]Ben H. Bagdikian, *The Media Monopoly* (Boston: Beacon, 1983) 29–37.

[14]Edward L. Bernays, *Propaganda* (New York: Liveright, 1928) 11, 109; Bernays, "Melting Pot of Ideas," *The Forum* 99 (1938): 341–342; Bernays, *Crystallizing Public Opinion* (New York: Boni and Liveright, 1923) 216.

[15]George Gallup and Saul F. Rae, *The Pulse of Democracy: The Public Opinion Poll and How It Works* (New York: Simon and Schuster, 1940) 6, 12–13, 17–21, 26, 125, 144–166, 213–214, 267.

[16]Herbert I. Schiller, *The Mind Managers* (Boston: Beacon, 1973) 104-123; Ginsberg, 75–80.

[17]George Seldes, interview; Stephen Hess, *The Washington Reporters* (Washington, DC: Brookings, 1981) 5.

[18]Edward J. Epstein, *News From Nowhere* (New York: Vintage, 1973).

[19]Ron Powers, *The Newscasters* (New York: St. Martin's, 1978).

[20]Michael Hoyt, "Downtime for Labor," *Columbia Journalism Review* (March–April 1984): 36–40.

[21]Benjamin Fine, "Propaganda Study Instills Skepticism in 1,000,000 Pupils," *New York Times* (21 February 1941): 1.

[22]Robert G. Picard, *The Press and the Decline of Democracy* (Westport, CT: Greenwood, 1985).

[23]Ray E. Hiebert, *Courtier to the Crowd* (Ames, IA: Iowa State UP, 1966) 97–102.

[24]Ray S. Baker, "How Railroads Make Public Opinion," *McClure's* 26 (1906): 535–549.

[25]Stephen L. Vaughn, *Holding Fast the Inner Lines* (Chapel Hill, NC: U of North Carolina P. 1980).

[26]Walter Lippmann, "The Basic Problem of Democracy," *Atlantic Monthly* 124 (1919): 616–627.

[27]Ferdinand Lundberg, "Freedom to Distort the Truth," *The Forum* 99 (1938): 343–345.

[28]A nice sense of the emergence of modern advertising is conveyed by Roland Marchand, *Advertising the American Dream: Making the Way for Modernity, 1920–1940* (Berkeley, CA: U of California P, 1985).

[29]Ernest Gruening, *The Public Pays: A Study of Power Propaganda* (New York: Vanguard, 1931) 147, 235–240.

[30]Peter H. Odegard, *Pressure Politics* (New York: Columbia UP, 1928).

[31]Peter Odegard, *The American Public Mind* (New York: Columbia UP, 1930); Frederick E. Lumley, *The Propaganda Menace* (New York: Century, 1933); Leonard W. Doob, *Propaganda: Its Psychology and Technique* (New York: Henry Holt, 1935).

[32]Joe McGinniss, *The Selling of the President 1968* (New York: Trident, 1969); David Wise, *The Politics of Lying* (New York: Vintage, 1973).

[33]Herbert J. Gans, *Deciding What's News* (New York: Vintage Books, 1979); Michael Parenti, *Inventing Reality* (New York: St. Martin's, 1986); Kathleen Jamieson, *Packaging the Presidency* (New York: Oxford UP, 1984); Edwin Diamond and Stephen Bates, *The Spot* (Cambridge, MA: MIT Press, 1984).

[34]See David L. Altheide and John M. Johnson, *Bureaucratic Propaganda* (Boston: Allyn and Bacon, 1980); Terence H. Qualter, *Opinion Control in the Democracies* (New York: St. Martin's, 1985); Garth S. Jowett and Victoria O'Donnell, *Propaganda and Persuasion* (Beverly Hills, CA: Sage, 1986).

[35]Vance Packard, *The Hidden Persuaders* (New York: Mckay, 1957); Stuart Ewen, *Captains of Consciousness* (New York: McGraw-Hill, 1976); Neil Postman, *Amusing Ourselves to Death: Public*

Discourse in the Age of Show Business (New York: Viking, 1985); Donna W. Cross, *Mediaspeak* (New York: New American Library, 1983); Joshua Meyrowitz, *No Sense of Place: The Impact of Electronic Media on Social Behavior* (New York: Oxford UP, 1985).

[36]Hugh Rank, *The Pitch* (Park Forest, IL: Counter-Propaganda Press, 1982), and *The Pep Talk* (Park Forest, IL: Counter-Propaganda Press, 1984)

[37]Ivy L. Lee, *Publicity* (New York: Industries, 1925) 23.

[38]*Crystallizing*, 57; Bernays, *Propaganda*, 62ff.

[39]Rosser Reeves, *Reality in Advertising* (New York: Knopf, 1961); David Ogilvy, *Confessions of an Advertising Man* (London: Pan, 1987).

[40]Michael Schudson, *Advertising, the Uneasy Persuasion* (New York: Basic Books, 1984) 36–43, 85–89, 192–208.

[41]Harold D. Lasswell, "Propaganda," *Encyclopaedia of the Social Sciences, 1933 ed.*, 12: 521-528; and *Democracy Through Public Opinion* (n.p.: George Banta, 1941).

[42]On the social scientist as student of effective persuasive campaigns, see Katz and Lazarsfeld, *Personal Influence*, 17–20.

[43]William E. Porter, *Assault on the Media: The Nixon Years* (Ann Arbor, MI: U of Michigan P, 1976).

[44]"Sour Reaction to Good News," *Aim Report*, March-B 1984.

[45]George Seldes, interview.

[46]William H. Irwin, *Propaganda and the News* (New York: Whittlesey, 1936) 306.

[47]George Michael, *Handout* (New York: Putnam's, 1935) 219–232.

[48]See August R. Ogden, *The Dies Committee* (Washington, DC: Catholic University of America Press, 1945) 90–100.

[49]Daniel C. Hallin, *The "Uncensored War"* (New York: Oxford UP, 1986) 133–158.

[50]Fred W. Friendly, *Due to Circumstances Beyond Our Control* (New York: Random House, 1967) 216–218.

[51]J. William Fulbright, *The Pentagon Propaganda Machine* (New York: Vintage, 1970).

[52]John Tebbel and Sarah M. Watts, *The Press and the Presidency* (New York: Oxford University Press, 1985); Altheide and Johnson.

[53]Noam Chomsky and Edward S. Herman, *After the Cataclysm* (Boston: South End Press, 1979); and *The Washington Connection and Third World Fascism* (Boston: South End Press, 1979); Edward S. Herman, *The Real Terror Network* (Boston: South End Press, 1982); Edward S. Herman and Frank Brodhead, *Demonstration Elections* (Boston: South End Press, 1984).

[54]National Education Association, *Report of the Committee on Propaganda in the Schools* (n.p.: N. E. A., 1929) 5.

[55]Edwin R. A. Seligman, "Propaganda by Public Utility Corporations," *Bulletin of the American Association of University Professors* 16 (1930): 349–368.

[56]Ira Shor, *Culture Wars* (London: Routledge & Kegan Paul, 1986).

[57]"NAM Textbook Survey Arouses Storm," *Publishers' Weekly* 139 (March 1, 1941): 1023.

[58]U.S. Congress, Senate, *Propaganda in Motion Pictures, Hearings*, subcommittee of Interstate Commerce Committee., 77th Cong., 1st sess., 9–26 September 1941: 22–56.

[59]J. Fred MacDonald, *Television and the Red Menace* (New York: Praeger, 1985); Todd Gitlin, *Inside Prime Time* (New York: Pantheon, 1985); Postman.

[60]Clyde R. Miller, "Debs Urges Aid for Bolsheviki from America," *Cleveland Plain Dealer* (17 June 1918): 1.

[61]Ray H. Abrams, *Preachers Present Arms* (New York: Round Table, 1933).

8

Democratization of Communication: Normative Theory and Sociopolitical Process

Robert A. White

Professor
Centre for Interdisciplinary Studies in Communication
The Gregorian University
Rome, Italy

Nearly all of the major policy models for public communications, over the past hundred years or more, have been advanced in the name of the democratization of communication. As one runs through the list of these proposals, one must stop to think about the flaws and contradictions that theorists of a future generation will find in this progressive thinking.

For instance, the libertarian model, epitomized in the thought of John Stuart Mill, attempted to free the press from the shackles of monarchical or oligarchical political censorship and to permit all people to express ideas openly. The beginnings of the popular press in the early nineteenth century, as exemplified by the penny newspaper, saw in advertising one of the means to employ this model, by freeing the media from dependence on wealthy patrons and by placing political interests in the hands of the masses—making it a newspaper that all people could afford and could find attractive.[1] The penny newspaper's emphasis on objectivity, on professionalism in journalism, and on the separation of factual reporting from editorial opinion were seen as means for putting the facts before the public so that the public could make up its mind on public affairs via critical judgment rather than via powerful interests' manipulation.[2]

Another example of *democratization of communication* is the model of the national public broadcasting system developed in the 1920s and 1930s which later extended to many developing countries in Africa and Asia. This system was considered by some of its proponents as one that centralized control in order to insure culturally uplifting education, diversified balance in programming, and the promotion of national unity. The modernization–diffusion concept of development communication was further seen as a plan to make the technology of the developed centers of the world available to the information poor, especially to those people in backward rural hinterlands. The global reach of new information technologies embodied in satellites and computers that was concomitant to this model was hailed by theorists. However, today, each of the above, as well as other, related models of public communication are widely questioned as obstacles to democratization of communication or are considered to be incomplete solutions to the democratization problem.

Thus, critical researchers, persons with some responsibility for national communication policies, must look critically at the way these models of democratization of communication are actually being implemented, especially if their policies profess to be concerned with democratic, participatory communication but in practice are actually leading in other directions. Most important, critical researchers must also question whether proposals for democratic communication will find support in the broader process of democratization of national societies. The institutions of a democratic communication grow out of the particular historical conditions of countries, and this process may follow different paths to reach roughly similar goals, depending on the sociocultural and political traditions of a given society. Yet it is unrealistic to expect democratization of communication if this process is not inherent in the broader process of sociocultural, economic, and political equalization at national and international levels.[3]

This chapter first summarizes the major policy proposals that are frequently mentioned in the literature on democratization of communication. This provides a normative definition of what is commonly included under the rubric of *democratic communication.* A central contribution of the chapter goes beyond this normative definition to outline an analytical model of democratization of communication as part of a social process of concentration and redistribution of social power. The focus point here is on *structural* change.[4] The chapter then examines some of the major trends in contemporary communication policies in the light of this model. This helps us to determine the extent to which the social logic of these policies actually does lead away from an authoritarian pattern of communication and toward the objectives of more democratic communication.

DEFINING DEMOCRATIZATION OF COMMUNICATION

Policy Objectives in Proposals for Democratic Communication

There are at least six major dimensions of the problem of democratization of communication that are currently discussed. The first of these is that of *access to information*. Given the state of development of knowledge in a particular nation or in an international system, many people do not have equitable access to the information necessary for their basic human needs of health, educational, and personal development, occupations, and for significant participation in local or national public decisions.[5] In most cases it is not just a matter of information not being available, but also of it not being available in a form which is usable; the information either is unrelated to information needs or is presented to individuals lacking the socioeconomic conditions to utilize it.[6] The problem of the information rich and the information poor is characteristic not only of different social status groups within a national society, but also of national societies at the international level.

What is needed is not just better extension of communication channels, alternative media, and structural reorganization, but also a radical change in social conceptions of information and communication, namely, from source-oriented to user-oriented definitions of communication.[7]

A second dimension of the democratization of communication problem is that information input is often reserved to a small, professional elite and is largely unidirectional. Under these circumstances, the only direct influence on the input is that of the passive consumer, who may choose not to use the media. Democratization suggests, that communication systems should be reorganized to permit all sectors of a population to *contribute to the pool of information* that provides the basis for local or national decision making and the basis for the allocation of resources in society.[8] All sectors of a population should have the opportunity to contribute to the formation of the national cultures that define their social values. All of the public should have access to the tools of media production and to technical help for making their own programming.[9] Audiences should have the opportunity to *collectively* criticize, analyze, and participate in the communication process.[10]

A third aspect of the problem is that, at present, decision making in all aspects of policy and administration of public communication tends to be the preserve of a small professional elite or, in commercial systems, of financial–advertising interests. A better alternative could be *broad, consensual decision making and permanent coordinating councils* representing all sectors of the population, including minorities, in questions of general policy, questions of the organization and management of media decisions on programming orientation, and questions of the evaluation of programming as well as other aspects of performance.[11] A basic principle for decision making is that communication is an individual and social right and that society only delegates the execution of this right to professionals.[12]

Fourth, if access to, and control of, channels of information is a social good and the equal right of every individual, then these qualities cannot be taken as merchandise or the privilege of an "enlightened elite." The public has a right to demand accountability in the use of power of information. To insure this accountability, the following kinds of measures are considered important:[13] Introduce the representative decision-making structures described above and representative property structures, preferably beyond the simple dichotomy of private commercial or state ownership; develop new concepts of public law governing information and communication systems, and a new legal definition of rights such as the right to participate in the public communication process; finally, there should be forms of financing public communication which protect these rights from any minority monopoly interests.

Fifth, the public philosophy of communication, based on 19th-century liberal social ideals and libertarian principles, is seen as increasingly inadequate. A new public philosophy of communication is proposed which provides a better understanding of information and communication in human and social development and which defines access to information channels and public participation, not just as an expediency to insure an informed labor force or a stable democracy, but also as basic social rights.[14]

Finally, if the public is to exercise its basic rights and provide accountability for social goods, then education for more responsible use of the medial and for more participation in public communications should become an integral part of basic education.

Locating Policy Making Within a Process of Structural Change

The above broad objectives constitute what might be called a public philosophy of communication; they define basic personal and social rights, outline essential communication functions in a society, and propose the ideal institutional organization of communications. To speak of policy, however, means to establish criteria for realizing these objectives within a concrete historical process with its specific political, economic, and sociocultural conditions.[15]

Strictly speaking, democracy implies a participatory decision-making process. Yet, in actuality, the possibility of participation demands a broad equalization of influence within a decision-making process, which, in turn, rests upon an equalization of the bases of social power in a particular society.

In virtually all societies one can observe tendencies toward the concentration of social power, and in some societies there exist immense concentrations of power with a small elite that controls all central political, economic, and sociocultural functions. In such societies there is massive rigidity and resistance to change in structures of power and privilege. But in the same societies, one can observe simultaneous, contrary, reactive sociopolitical movements and proposals for the redistribution of social power.[16] The question is: How does communication policy making and planning for a democratization of communication enter into these contrary tendencies?

At a certain level of concreteness, a policy of democratization can be concerned with both alternative media emphasizing popular access and control and with introducing participatory coordinating bodies. But at some point policy must address problems related to the process of structural change and the redistribution of social power and influence. Communication policy must outline how the democratization of communication and information both contributes to and is derived from the broader process of democratization in a society.

Some societies have more developed and controllable mechanisms for planned intervention and direction of the sociopolitical process than others, but the democratization of communication is almost never simply a process of social engineering. A central argument of this chapter is that forms of democratization of communication such as horizontal channels of communication and more participatory communication cannot be implemented by concocting an elegant, idealistic model at planning desks and by imposing this in arbitrary fashion.[17] History shows that new communication institutions usually are generated by the juncture of political conditions and conflicting demands in a society. The new conceptions of communication are defined with the process of public reactions to authoritarian tendencies, and new patterns of communication emerge as part of the social structure of grassroot sociopolitical movements. Communication researchers and policy makers can contribute, however, by recognizing that movements are creating successful forms of participatory media, new communication languages and new definitions of information. Dissident scholars and technical experts may even be part of these popular movements, and their expertise may help to perfect or implement new communication approaches within movements. Once the value of new experience is recognized, these can be legitimated by careful analysis and brought into more coherent planning and policy formulation.[18]

One aspect of research and policy making for the democratization of communication is the critical analysis of the factors which are contributing to the concentration of power and, more specifically, to point out how the existing communication institutions are contributing that society's concentration of social power.[19] Unfortunately, much critical research has stopped with the negative function of pointing out what is wrong with the present system and has failed to indicate what alternatives are becoming technically, socially, and politically feasible in a given society.

Thus, an even more important part of research and policy making is the analysis of the dynamic factors of social change and the new institutions that are beginning to be demanded as a result of dialectical tensions. This sort of careful analysis is especially important in societies with a massive, rigid concentration of social power where little possibility of change is immediately evident.

A first step is the critical analysis of inequities, of the public alienation and the cases of repression of communication suggesting an urgent need for change. But the major focus must be the public movements that are forming in reaction to the authoritarian structures because here we begin to see the concrete forms of a new direction. The initial concepts for a new policy often appear in the practice of these movements. The further development of a policy is a matter of giving innovative groups the legitimacy and opportunity to expand their role and prove the validity of their ideas on a broader scale. This may also entail the perfecting of organizational and technical aspects invented in the heat of the moment or discovering new uses for innovations. Policy also requires a refining of idealistic concepts so that these are consonant with existing legal, economic and professional traditions. All this is possible, obviously, only if there are sufficient political and social concessions to at least accommodate alternatives. Indeed, change may be more feasible politically if it does not attempt a direct challenge and removal of powerful communication interests, but rather opens the way for new social actors and new media institutions that may eventually have a preponderant role in the society. Communication policy thus becomes the practice of building on and facilitating a concrete historical process.[20]

In short, policy formation *is* the social process, and unless policy making and the social process are themselves participatory, it is unlikely that the result will be a democratic pattern of communication.

ANALYZING INFORMATION–COMMUNICATION MONOPOLY AND DEMOCRATIZATION AS A SOCIAL PROCESS

The Relation of Social Power and Authoritarian Communication Patterns

There are many ways one might approach the relation of social power and communication, but it is helpful to conceive of social power as the ability to impose one's wishes on another in an unbalanced, asymmetrical exchange.[21] When one party in an exchange holds strategic resources needed by the other and there are no alternative sources available, then the dependent party fills the gap by compliance. To sustain this dependency relationship, the party holding strategic resources must maintain the sense of need through its definitions of values and by preventing the dependent party from seeking alternative sources. Usually, the party holding the strategic resources will use a means such as a monopoly of the coercive power available.[22]

From the perspective of communication, a first consequence of this type of asymmetrical power relation is that holders of strategic resources can extract information, but do not have to give significant information in exchange.

Second, holders of strategic resources tend to be sought for exchange and tend to become the center of exchange networks, including the center of exchanges of information. They thus become centers of channels of communication. This centrality is, in itself, a source of social power, because information centers receive many different kinds of information and develop the capacity to codify and use it.[23] The higher the concentration of strategic resources, the more likely it is that the pattern of communication within the system will be rigidly hierarchical, with one major center of communication in, for example, a national or international system. Thus, powerful information centers are able to extract information, through intermediaries, to be relayed back to the center while supplying very little significant information in return to weak, peripheral parties. This mode of operation explains why, for example, peasant communities in the shadow of modern city continue, for centuries, without real communication. For these cases, there has been no communication of precisely the kind of significant information that might affect the power relationship.

Third, individuals who control strategic resources and who are central in communication networks are in a position to define what is and what is not *information* or at least to define what is and is not *valid information*. These individuals define the common *language* into which must fit the structure of that language, or they at least define the dominant symbols which organize information.[24] For example, if technical–economic sectors control the defined strategic resources in a society, then all aspects of life—political, educational, religious, etc.—will tend to be organized in terms of the symbols of technical–economic development.

Fourth, the prestige and status system, following the power structure, becomes in itself, a kind of language. In a society dominated by traditional modernizing elites, peasants are, by definition, incapable of contributing to national decision making. Everything associated with peasant identity is defined as noninformation.

The above analysis could be greatly extended, but it suffices to suggest some of the consequences of the lack of the democratization of communication for media systems. Dominant elites develop ideologies which define these elites as the most efficient patrons to whom the gathering and distribution of information may safely be entrusted. Technology for gathering, storing, transmitting, and displaying information is developed in ways which will activate the channels of communication that elites control. Media formats are defined in terms of the dominant symbol systems, and content is limited to that which can fit into these formats. The *professional norms* and *communication ethics* define *accuracy, truthfulness,* and the *rights* of all involved in response to this power structure. Finally, the public is educated in what is regarded as valid information and provided "proper" tastes for entertainment and information.

In all of this process, there does not have to be any overt, malevolent conspiracy to control a system. Once all of the elements are in place, the decisions of the patrons can be explained as the "logical, efficient, and effective" ways to communicate. The parameters of public discourse become defined, too, so that there may seem to be perfect freedom to voice opinions as long as that right stays within the established rules of the public decision-making process. According to the logic of this type of system, it seems to be democratic in that everybody's "needs" are taken care of and in that everybody not only has access to channels, but is able to "influence" what is communicated.[25]

The Democratization of Communication as a Process of Structural Change

Analyzing the relation of authoritarian communication to the concentration of social power is relatively easy, because there is a large body of critical research dealing with this topic. However, developing a model of the democratization of communication as part of the redistribution of social power is more difficult. The extant critical research, in the mass of studies carried out largely in industrialized liberal democracies, has been concerned with issues proposed by media reform movements, such as the influence of advertising on children or the effects of sex and violence content in the media. Some research touches on more fundamental problems of equity such as the status of women, the status of ethnic minorities in media organizations, or the portrayal of labor organizations and other lower-status minorities in televisions.[26] Moreover, much of the research on democratization has dealt with small, isolated experiments of participation in local media, and has contained little evidence of a redistribution of social power.[27] Generally, reform movements have been limited because they did not enter into fundamental, widespread problems of social equity, and have often been led by groups that did not experience directly the inequities, alienation, and repression of concentrated social power.[28] Also, insofar as this research has been funded for media administrative purpose, it has not been expected to poke too deeply beyond the symptoms of the problem.

The best methodology for determining the factors in a process of structural change which lead toward the democratization of communication may be to begin by analyzing the reorganization of communication patterns within broad, popularly based movements which have sought a profound redistribution of social power.[29] Some of the best examples of this approach are found in the peasant agrarian movements and in the national liberation movements of this century; out of these movements many new models of political, economic, and sociocultural organization have emerged. Although in this chapter it is not possible to do more than suggest broad outlines of this type of analysis, one can at least indicate the kind of factors in a social process that are influential in the development of this type of more democratic communication.

The beginnings of these movements have often been found in situations in which a fairly wide segment of the population has had very unequal access to resources, low prestige, and little chance of individual amelioration due to very asymmetrical power relations. The central issue of these movements has frequently been the sharp deterioration in the allocation of resources for the aggrieved group and the sharp increase in its experience of exploitative conditions during a period of general socioeconomic improvement. For example, in a context of general agrarian modernization, large landholders may have begun to expel semisubsistence farmers from land in order to take advantage of new markets and improved technology,[30] or, in a period of general prosperity, certain urban racial–ethnic groups may have found it increasingly difficult to get employment. Often the key element in activating these types of movements has been individuals or groups that could not get redress for their grievances or that could not solve economic problems through existing, vertical hierarchical structures of communication with the center of their society's administrative power. At a certain point, too, there has been collective awareness that there was no solution through the existing structure of power and communication, that this pattern of communication extracted information for purposes of control but gave no significant information in return, and that the whole symbol system denigrated their identity and their social opportunities. At that point of realization, individuals and groups rejected the hierarchical channels of communication and extended horizontal channels among other aggrieved groups in order to pool information, usually to form a much more symmetrical exchange.[31] These channels may have activated existing information channels among lower status or ethnic groups and may have utilized simple "folk media."

When lower status movements face a massive concentration of social power, it is difficult for these movements to survive unless there are divisions among elites and unless some dissident urban–technical groups are willing to break away from elite solidarity to form supportive alliances with lower status movements. When these dissident elites are trying to challenge established elites, the dissidents often need and depend upon the mass power base that lower status movements offer. These alliances can represent a more symmetrical power relationship and constitute a communication structure between elites and lower status groups that is very different from the hierarchical extractive relationship. On the one hand, dissident elites are willing to communicate their expertise to help scattered lower status protest groups to organize and develop a large-scale intercommunication network. Professionals in media and in education join popular movements to help semi-literates learn to use media technology and participate directly in media production. On the other hand, in these alliances, dissident elites accept popular culture as a valid world view and language and introduce this culture as an authentic communication code defining media formats. Thus, through the communication structure of these alliances, lower status groups gain direct access to national communication channels, and new communication policies begin to take shape.[32]

Many of the characteristics of a democratic communication described above may appear in lower status movements in general. Access and participation are important for sustaining the cohesion of movements, because mass support is often the most important strategic resource to counterbalance the entrenched power of national elites; participation may be the chief legitimizing factor in this mass support, since often these movements place a high value on the inherent right of every participant to be fully informed of decisions and to have the fullest opportunity to be heard. New patterns of access and participation—indeed a new public philosophy of access—are embodied in the structure and ideology of these movements.

Since the network of communication in these movements develops on the periphery of the hierarchical structure of communication, the center of gravity of this alternative pattern of communication is decentralized. It is radically different from a system of communication controlled from above that only allows token local access. In this type of movements' network of communication, points of input are truly at the local, lower status level, because their locus of power and legitimacy lie there. Lower status leadership and constituency also jealously maintain the control of their communication channels in order to guarantee the authenticity of information. These leaders require that the kind of media they use permit local control. This attitude is quite different from the alienation of passive consumers of distant, foreign information sources, and is the basis for a continuing, active, symmetric involvement in the governance of a communication system.

Most important, these movements produce a new set of central symbols that redefine the perception of reality from a lower status perspective to a more democratic perspective and that form the basis of a new language.[33] These new languages reevaluate the identity of the lower status people (e.g., peasants are the bearers of the true values and virtues of the nation, black is beautiful, etc.) and accentuate the positive role of these groups in the development of nations. These reevaluations also legitimate the participation of lower status sectors in national decision making and in the major reallocation of all resources toward them (e.g., educational opportunities, land, technical assistance, etc.). While traditional elites tend to be internationally oriented in their culture and outward looking, lower status groups are much more rooted in the ecology of their residence. Their new languages establish the basis for national cultures congruent with a nations's resources, geography, and history. This type of cultural legitimation undercuts the tendency of elites to legitimize linkages with international organizations and international communication and provides people with an authentic foundation for a policy of self-reliance and delinking.[34]

In this type of practice of social action, there may emerge very innovative uses of media. Perhaps more important than the evolved technology are the evolved symbol systems which define new media languages and the new social contexts that, in turn, determine the languages' use.[35] Out of this combination develop entirely new programming formats which can be increasingly participatory, which can embody kinds of news information, and which get at deep issues that can foster reflective, liberating interactions with audiences. These efforts may start with very simple media such as mimeo newspapers, popular theater, local radio, or audio cassettes, but, once reformatted, can evolve into a very different national information system. Sympathetic media specialists may be involved with this transformation, but with the delegation of the movement itself. Professionalism and technical expertise, which so often serve to separate the media from the people, become redefined and develop in a new mold.

The relation of a social process of power redistribution and the democratization of communication briefly outlined here is perhaps an ideal type built on many cases. Yet some of these processes do exist to a degree in nearly all national contexts. It may be more difficult to detect these distinctions in complex societies, especially in those with a national ideology that insists that the society "has had its popular revolution and does have democratic communication institutions," but the role of critical research is precisely to unmask these types of mistaken assumptions.

DO CONTEMPORARY POLICY MODELS LEAD TOWARD DEMOCRATIC COMMUNICATION?

Dealing with the social processes of concentrated social power and increasingly authoritarian communication is difficult due to the deeply entrenched vested interests of some participants. But a more dangerous problem—and one that especially concerns communication researchers and policy makers—is that some of the major policy models which profess to be the bases for developing democratic communication, and which are the guidelines for present policy, embody many contradictions and inconsistencies. Underlying these policy models, are conceptions of communication development which need to be questioned and reexamined. The third part of this essay will attempt to summarize some of the major problem areas in contemporary communication policies—as these are actually practiced—and examine these in the light of a broader social process of democratization of communication.

The Influence of the Cultural Uplift–Modernization–Diffusion Model

Very few contemporary communication researchers or policy makers, probably inclusive of the scholars who originally advanced these concepts,[36] would subscribe to the modernization–diffusion model of national and international communication development proposed in the 1950s and 1960s. Essentially, this model conceived of national sociocultural and economic development as the extension of the culture, technology, and social organization from the elite pole of a country or from the great world centers of culture and technology to the lower status population and rural hinterlands of a country or to less-developed countries. In these models, the task of communicating a "higher" culture, technology or other information was entrusted to the traditional, literate elites and/or to the entrepreneurs of a country, assuming that such individuals were motivated, at least by self-interest, to share their information with the less advantaged. The major obstacle to communication was assumed to be the attitudes of backward people—their traditionalism, bad taste, superstition, fatalism, etc. This theory placed a great deal of emphasis on the role of the mass media and central broadcasting bureaucracies in national life and development. It presupposed that, once the mass media channels between elites and lower status or rural populations were in place, information would flow out and trickle down through two-step flows and interpersonal networks. This theory was useful and was used simply because of the sheer rationality of what it proposed. It contained little or no analysis of the problems of structural rigidity or the lack of resources of lower status people in employing communication knowledge.[37] It took for granted that, if a market structure was established, enterprising and motivated people would be able to get the resources to use this information effectively.

Despite criticism of the failures of this model, it is still the dominant form of development communication in most countries. The logic of this model is embodied in broadcasting institutions whether these be commercial or state controlled.[38] The priority in the allocation of national budgets is the development of a technically advanced urban metropolis modeled after North Atlantic nations. The communication of information about agriculture, health or other needs is entrusted to bureaucracies staffed by people of an urban, middle-class background with little knowledge or sympathy with the lower status people they are to serve. Rarely are there attempts to adapt the technology or communication methods to the special conditions of groups such as small farmers. Rarely are grass roots organizations controlled by local people who have local interests at heart allowed to have a role in the diffusion of information.

Development bureaucracies continue to incorporate aspects of verticalism, centralization, and professional elitism that expose them to easy control by powerful elites and that present formidable barriers to public accountability and participation. This model also accentuates the formation of an urban-technical elite class which, in developing countries, is increasingly North oriented and increasingly separated culturally, socially, and politically from the people it is supposed to serve. There is a growing concentration of information power in these urban-technical elite sectors and an ever more rigid, less participatory communication systems.

The Race to Catch Up in Communication Technology

The development of recent information technology, especially the combination of computers based on microprocessors with satellites, has caught much of the world unprepared. This technology is so capital intensive and requires such an advanced technological base that information power is being concentrated in a few countries such as Japan and the United States.[39]

Leaders in many countries are aware that microprocessor technology is radically affecting the international division of labor as well as affecting comparative economic advantages. Formerly, many less developed countries, during early stages of industrialization, could expect to take advantage of a relatively cheap labor force to begin building competitive industrial bases. Now, however, industrialized countries facing economic problems, labor unrest, and political crises are pulling labor-intensive manufacturing processes back to the home country and replacing them with capital- and computer-intensive processes. The priority political–economic policy in many counties is now to catch up technologically with the North, even though even the most advanced countries of the South admit that this goal is almost hopeless.[40]

Much of the new computer and satellite technology is essentially intended to gain efficiencies by centralizing the storage and transmission of information. This is rapidly increasing centralization of information networks and is bringing information under the control of technological elites who would make public accountability ever more difficult. This centralization is occurring both at a national and international level, and, in the midst of a world-wide economic crisis, such efficiency has become regarded as essential to survival. For example, many Latin American countries find it quicker, more efficient, and less costly to work with databanks in the U.S. than to develop their own.[41]

One could imagine ways of adapting the technology of information storage, transmission, and display that would encourage greater public access and participation,[42] and would favour the interests of less advantaged sectors. But in the panic to catch up, it is argued that there simply isn't time to worry about its consequences. Even in countries which have had a tradition of public accountability, these considerations are being pushed aside and free rein is being given to whatever entrepreneur can come up with the quickest solution.

Much of this effort to catch up is justified in the name of a policy of national self-reliance and the protection of national political, economic and cultural autonomy. Policies of self-reliance, however, must be part of a long-term plan to cut old colonial linkages, to introduce internal democratization of communication and to establish regional solidarity with other nations. Otherwise, a headlong rush to introduce the latest technologies can mean an over-hasty commitment to transnational firms and greater dependence within the international system.[43] Some scholars would advise that it is virtually impossible for some developing nations to gain equality with large industrialized nations in every aspect of technological production and that it would be preferable to think in terms of an "alternative development" which implies less dependence on advanced technology. Unfortunately, most proposal for alternative development are still rather vague ideas.[44]

Democratization Through Technology Itself

Many policy makers, facing the political and economic resistance to the profound structural change that democratic communications may imply, turn to the prophets who hold out hope that the new technologies will automatically change the existing patterns of communication. Computers, for instance, offer new methods of vast information storage and instant retrieval so that a nation's individualized information needs can be responded to at the time, place, and manner that individuals prefer. The proliferation of channels through direct broadcast satellites, cable, and video cassettes means that every population segment—including lower status groups—can be served. New technology also offers enough interactive potential to enable everybody to put information into a communication system.

There is some reason to doubt, though, that the sheer abundance of information can automatically insure its wider distribution and availability. The high cost of new communication technology may restrict use to affluent sectors or to groups whose high level of productivity insures a return to society. It may not make more information generally available, but may make more intensive in-depth information available to highly selective, economically productive sectors. Even granting that more information will be available, key questions of information control and the redistribution of social power have not been addressed by this model.

One of the aforementioned problems of authoritarian patterns of communication is that, in asymmetrical power relations, rarely do more powerful parties give information which is relevant and significant from the perspective of the dependent party. In the process of democratization, one of the first steps of lower-status groups in establishing an alternative pattern of communication is to redefine in terms of their own perspective what is information and to reorganize this information around a new set of symbols so that it is relevant for them. Thus, unless more participatory controls are established to redefine the symbol systems that are coded into new communication technologies and redefine the social contexts in which technologies are typically used, there will not be more information but simply more noise. The result will be like two persons speaking two different languages and trying to communicate.

The research on "knowledge gaps" suggests reasons why this type of control may be especially important in information-rich societies. If more information is made available in social systems in which there are no changes in social structure or in which there are not better allocations of resources, then the increase becomes irrelevant for those people who lack the opportunity to use it, and the socioeconomic inequalities are increased by the new information.[45] One of the most pertinent examples of this problem is access to public decision-making processes. Much of the information made available in public communication systems deals with decisions at the level of a local community or a nation. Unless there are social structures that permit wide participatory decision making, then much of this information is irrelevant. For those people involved in decision making to some degree, information becomes a source of power and influence. Further, the more information that an individual receives, the greater the differentiation of meaning areas in his or her knowledge, and the more able he or she is to absorb additional information. One solution to this dilemma is to change social structures in order to afford more equal opportunities for the use of information. Another solution is to make available information more adapted to the capacities and actual needs of lower status people. This latter step implies that lower status people can attain some influence over the definition of information.

Even if information is relevant, the advent of an information-rich society makes control doubly important. As information becomes more important in every aspect of our lives, we become more attuned to and dependent on information. If an information control structure remains authoritarian, then we are likely to become increasingly dependent on, and more open to, manipulation by the people who control information. Given the rapid advances of information technology, a democratic control system becomes far more important for the direction of our personal lives and the development of society than other types of systems.

Democratic Access and Control in Local Media: Opening to the Future or Tokenism?

Although some of the objectives of democratic communication are directed at national systems, much of the research on access and participation describes experiences within local or community media.

The development of local, publically controlled media, or of local media that permit access to and control of local programming, is important, because such media indicate that there exists a need and a demand for public participation in the public media. The experiences of local, publically controlled media represent many degrees of participation, from simple phone-in programs to cases in which a medium has been a public facility directed by a community council, allowing free access and freedom in programming design.[47] This local, public media policy of expansive access and participation has been most significant when it offers a voice to ethnic or lower status groups or to other minorities. When a local medium is serving an oppressed and voiceless majority, such as the Radio Popular in Latin America, which offers access and participation to the population of landless and semisubsistence peasants, this medium can be an extremely significant political and sociocultural factor.

The experiences of local, publically controlled media demonstrate a wide variety of forms of participatory communication, which, in turn, indicate how a national system of democratic communication might develop. In communities where there is local access to radio, television, or cable, an increasing number of nonprofessionals are learning to use local media. The mass media are gradually being demystified.[48] There is also increasing experience with public, representative governance of local media, especially through community councils.

There is evidence that the movement toward public-service, democratically controlled local media is spreading in various parts of the world, and that this movement may well become an accepted and proven dimension of communication institutions. Further, there is a growing opinion that a democratic system of communication should include this form of local, participatory media.

However, at present, most of these experiences with local access and local control have been the exceptions to the rule of dominant, authoritarian communication. One might suspect that these experiences have been merely tolerated, token expressions of participatory communication which have been operationalized with the constraint of interests. In Canada and the United States, countries in which cable television operates on a commercial basis, for instance, cable companies have reluctantly accepted the regulation of providing public access channels and public access programming facilities. Usually these channels and facilities are poorly funded appendages with poor equipment and inadequate technical staff. When there is a regulation that local stations must have a local community broadcasting council, as in the case of the BBC local radio, the staff and manager have often resisted outside influence as much as possible. In other experiences, whenever there are budget cutbacks, whether in public or commercial systems, the first activities to suffer are often the public access and participation programs.[49]

As long as public access is merely tolerated and is certainly suspect by the public or commercial systems, any moves toward opening issues that are threatening to established interest, especially media interests, are discouraged. In Latin America the facilitators of Radio Popular have been lauded for their work in popular education and community development, but when these same communicators began to represent the interests of the peasant farmers, they were harassed and suffered the loss of their broadcast licenses. The development of local media with fully public ownership under representative governance has also been slow, and is exemplified by few successful cases. The problem of funding without cooption is one of the most serious ailments of local, publicly controlled media.

One the whole, it can be concluded that access and participation—even in a relatively benign, local form—is far from integral to the public philosophy of public communication in most countries and is even further from being an integral part of national communication policies.[50]

The Paradox of a Nondemocratic Process of Policy Making to Achieve a National Pattern of Democratic Communication

The discussion of the implementation of a New World Information and Communication Order, including the discussion of moves toward more democratic communication, has emphasized the formulation of national communication policies and plans. In practice, though, policy formulation is often conceived of as the work of a planning office in a ministry and of a small circle of associated experts. Policy implementation is expected to begin with governmental legislative debate and executive decision, and its implementation is considered an action of governmental bureaucracy.

Obviously, achieving the aforementioned objectives of democratic communication requires, at some point, a competent process of public planning and decision. The MacBride report, however, recommends that policy formulation should be a participatory process involving all social sectors of the nation;[51] planning alternatives must emerge out of the experiences and initiatives that are developing in a country.

The policies that appear to be most congruent with a particular culture and a particular process of sociopolitical development are likely to come out of the experiences of popular organizations and out of the conceptions of participatory communication embodied in popular movements. In reality, though, policies are often formed on the basis of a collection of untested high ideals rather than on democratic communication in the country. Also, in reality, policies are only nominally calculated to foster the beginnings of indigenous institutions of participatory communication already present in a country. As a result, the very groups that might be expected to give political support to a policy fail to see their aspirations reflected in it.

For media policies to reflect democratic communication, it is important, not simply to incorporate the ideas of groups working toward democratic communication, but, in so far as is practical, to also involve these groups in the policy formulation process. These groups are more likely to be the true protagonists of participatory communication than bureaucratic planners or media interests closely associated with governmental action. A participatory strategy may be slower and less brilliant, but, in the long run, it may be more solid.

Decentralization of Media Systems

Most countries considering a policy of democratization of communication start with a media organization of highly centralized public broadcasting systems or with commercial firms linked with powerful financial interests. Whether public or commercial, these broadcasting institutions and newspaper organizations are managed and staffed by media professionals whose identity is dependent upon their autonomy from any kind of direct public accountability. For various reasons, these organizations are often extremely resistant to proposals for public access or to proposals for representative public councils. They are beholden to the powerful public figures and bureaucracies or to large private firms from which they must get the information that constitutes news. It is difficult for the public to conceive of access and participation in these cases, because the greater public is so distant geographically, socially, and culturally from these organizations. These media organizations are located in large urban centers, and are greatly distanced from rural, lower status people in developing countries.

In some new nations it may be expedient to preserve a centralized media system, inherited from a colonial period, for reasons of economics, better use of professional trained persons, and to weld diverse tribal, ethnic, and linguistic groups into a single nation. Nevertheless, bringing these centralized media into some structure of public accountability is essential to any policy of democratic communications. It also seems important, especially in developing countries to encourage the development of a complementary and balancing decentralized media.[52]

Consider how geographical decentralization, in the form of local, market-town radio or the rural press, can bring the media close to local interests, issues and problems, cultures and ethnic identities. Local media can also incorporate elements of traditional communication and the formats of local folk media. One of the major problems of the centralized media in developing countries is that they usually borrow their formats from the international media culture and cast their entertainment and news in a "language" that is amenable primarily to their urban, middle-class audience. In centralized organizations, media professionals are, themselves, frequently drawn from an urban, middle class and have a more Westernized education than the great majority of people. They have few ties with the indigenous culture and find it difficult to express themselves in the language of the local culture. Local media are more likely to work with local people than centralized media, perhaps less professionally, but with greater capability of adapting local cultural expression which may later be usable in the national media. With the multiplication of local media there is also a greater possibility for access and participation, and, with the proper kind of public interest management, local media can include representative lower status groups.

A decentralization along the lines of major social sectors may also be advisable. A flexibility that permits and encourages minorities and lower status popular movements to develop media under their own control can be an important aspect of participatory communication. The development of the rural press in some countries of Africa, or of *radio popular* in Latin American countries, constitute examples.[53] Such local media allow these groups and movements to reorganize information around symbols that are meaningful to them and to adapt information to the specific needs they may have.

Research in Support of a Policy of Democratic Communication

Nearly all of the current proposals for a policy of democratic communication emphasize in some way that pervasive authoritarian power structures sustain a monopoly on communication. Democratization of communication is seen as part of a larger process of structural change and the redistribution of power in a society. If nations attempt short cuts for change, sooner or later the nations will be back where they started. Our questioning of the past proposals for the democratization of communication is, in great part, an identification of their superficial and partial solutions. We must acknowledge that many early theorists were aware that they were touching only part of the problem. Their short cuts usually boomeranged when their concepts were incorporated into practical policies that sought results too quickly.

We can observe simultaneous tendencies toward concentration and redistribution of social power in virtually all societies, and it is in the tension between these two tendencies that a process of structural change and democratization of communication appears. A policy of democratization builds out of these movements toward a redistribution of social power and attempts to foster the growth of new patterns of communication. If policy makers are to foster these more democratic forms of communication, they must first be able to detect them and to evaluate their significance. It is here that communication research may have a new and important role.

The term *new role* is used advisedly because of the recent growing awareness among communication researchers that much of the research tradition in the field of communication—concepts, methodology, and research designs—has been in the service of an authoritarian communication.

The starting point of most research in communication has rarely been from the perspective of people who are the protagonists of a new pattern of communication, and rarely has research gone behind a particular organization of media to analyze the sociopolitical movements that influenced it. Rather, the focus of most research has been on existing media organizations, on the content of their messages, on the significance of new media technology or other aspects of the self-contained subject of the media. The media are assumed to be the cause of whatever is to be explained. Most research is concerned with the influence of the media on society, but not with an explanation of how a society has produced a particular form of media, or with clarifying claims and responsibility for the media. Indirectly, communication research has supported the sense of absolute autonomy among media owners and professionals; it has been implicitly aiding media to be unaccountable to the public and to exercise an existence and authority not delegated by the public. The social responsibility concept of media ethics remains a vague ideal—in practice, media ethics is a list of prescriptions for how to stay out of trouble with the law.

The concern, in media research, for measuring effects assumes a powerful source directly imprinting its message on passive receivers. Terminology such as *a media-shaped society* common among communication specialists, indicates an acceptance of this depiction of the media's relationship to society. For instance, the purpose of effects research has been either to test the effectiveness of messages or to suggest ways of increasing the power of this effectiveness. If sources that have funded the research disagree with the kind of effects discovered by scholarship, the purpose of the research becomes to show the harmfulness of a message and to suggest a different message for a preferred effect. Despite this narrow research focus, the interest in effects continues.

A further consequence of this narrow focus on media and media effects is the use of a communication model in which communication is depicted as initiated by a source and in which the information of a media source is considered to be normative. For this model, the measure of successful communication is the degree to which the passive consumer accepts a message exactly as it is proposed by the source. If the receiver is not getting a message, then something is wrong with the receiver, and research is conducted either to increase the persuasiveness of a message or to explain the resistance to the rationality of a message in terms of the irrational attitudes of the receiver (traditionalism, fatalism, etc.). This research tendency to make a source normative has relegated many people to the category of *the information poor*, when in fact the information they received may simply not have been relevant for them.

This narrow emphasis on media and media effects has also led to a premise in communication research that media information is an all-powerful panacea for problems of human and socioeconomic development. The questioning of this premise began largely with Third World researchers who pointed out that more information was not necessarily a solution to human and socioeconomic issues in cases in which social structure, and the allocation of productive resources that this structure implies, make it impossible to use this media information. The exclusive emphasis on media information not only avoids the need of structural change, but also, because it exaggerates the role of centralized mass media, empowers elites who would use the media to inculcate an ideology of passive acceptance of inequities.

As a result of this questioning, new approaches in communication research which are more supportive of democratic communication are beginning to emerge, as well as a pattern of communication that expects a public to be active in seeking and using information, to be active in seeking access to information channels, and to be interested in participation. Central to these new approaches are concepts of communication that are user oriented rather than media source oriented.[54]

With this change of focus, researchers are discovering that the supposed passivity of media consumers and the knowledge gaps between source and receiver are, in part, constructs of a faulty, source-oriented concept of communication. Conventionally, communication models have reified and objectified information as if it existed apart from individuals and as if it could be transported from source to receiver. A message as held by the source was considered normative. New approaches are looking more closely at the activity of individuals in seeking information to make sense out of situations and to creatively construct meanings. In this alternative view, every message is the construction of some individual limited by time and space and can never completely fill the need of another individual who is also bound by time, space, or change. Communication occurs when at least some aspects of the meanings of communicating persons are shared and these aspects are integrated into individual meaning patterns. Such rethinking of the basic concepts of communication is important for research related to democratic communication, because this rethinking shifts the focus away from knowledge gaps between a dependent receiver and the unique powerful message holder to the most critical gaps in communication, "gaps that individuals see in their pictures in the world and [that individuals] sometimes try to fill with input from messages."[55]

However, to conceive of individuals as seeking bits of information in order to create personal meanings abstracts individuals from social reality. One may find that groups, or a whole society, try to make collective sense out of situations and try, collectively, to create new meanings and new patterns of communication. This collective process is more pertinent than the individualized one to the development of democratic communication when dependent, powerless sectors of society find dominant patterns of communication supported by powerful elites not only meaningless, but exploitative, and when dependent, powerless sectors of society seek new central symbols that can reorganize an entire subculture of meanings and values.

Communication research can be especially useful to the formulation of a policy of democratic communication if it can help detect alternative and more participatory patterns of communication emerging in a social process, new "languages" (patterns of meaning), new forms of media expression, new ways of using media that encourage more participatory communication, and new forms of accountability of the media to the local or national community. As critical researchers, we ought to avoid absolutizing the value of popular movements as if these values were the norm. Rather, in formulating policies, we ought to try to see how the state of the art of our public philosophy of communication is being realized within the historical process, and, as we examine this sociocultural process from its own perspective, strive to enrich our own conceptions of the public philosophy of communication.

ENDNOTES

[1]Michael Schudson, *Discovering the News: A Social History of American Newspapers* (New York: Basic Books, 1978) 20–21.

[2]Dan Schiller, *Objectivity and the News* (Philadelphia: Pennsylvania UP, 1981) 76–95.

[3]International Commission for the Study of Communication Problems, *Many Voices, One World* (London: Kogan Page, 1980) 166; and Juan Somavia, "The Democratization of Communications: From Minority Social Monopoly to Majority Social Representation," *Development Dialogue* 2 (1981) : 21.

[4]James D. Halloran, "The Context of Mass Communication Research," *Communication and Social Structure: Critical Studies in Mass Media Research*, eds. Emile G. McAnany, Jorge Schnitman, and Noreene Janus (New York: Praeger, 1981) 28.

[5]International Commission *Many Voices*, 166.

[6]Emile G. McAnany, ''The Role of Information in Communication With the Rural Poor: Some Reflections,'' *Communication in the Rural Third World,* ed. Emile G. McAnany (New York: Praeger, 1980) 3–18.

[7]Brenda Dervin, ''Communication Gaps and Inequities: Moving Toward a Reconceptualization,'' *Progress in Communication Sciences* Vol. II, eds. Brenda Dervin and Melvin J. Voight (Norwood, NJ: Ablex Publishing Corp, 1980) 73–112.

[8]International Commission, *Many Voices,* 167; and Fernando Reyes Matta, ''A Model for Democratic Communication,'' *Development Dialogue* 2 (1981) : 90.

[9]Frances J. Berrigan, ''Introduction,'' *Access: Some Western Models of Community Media,* ed. Frances J. Berrigan (Paris: UNESCO, 1977) 19.

[10]Matta, ''A Model,'' 86–87.

[11]International Commission, *Many Voices,* 169.

[12]Matta, ''A Model,'' 85–86.

[13]Somavia, ''The Democratization,'' 25–28; and Máximo Simpson Grinberg, ''Comunicación Alternativa: Dimensiones, Limites, Posibilidades,'' *Comunicación Alternativa y Cambio Social* (Mexico: U Autónoma de México, 1981), 109–129.

[14]International Commission, *Many Voices,* 172–173.

[15]International Commission, *Many Voices,* 203–212.

[16]Peter Golding and Graham Murdock, ''Theories of Communication and Theories of Society,'' *Communication Research* 5.3 (1978) : 353.

[17]Elizabeth Fox, ''Conclusions,'' *Media and Politics in Latin America: The Struggle for Democracy,* ed. Elizabeth Fox (Newbury Park, CA: Sage Publications, 1988) 178–179.

[18]Cees J. Hamelink, *Communication Research in Third World Realities.* Policy Workshop, Institute of Social Studies. The Hague, 1980, 2–26.

[19]International Commission, *Many Voices,* 166–168.

[20]Hamelink, *Communication Research,* 26–31; and Robert A. White and James M. McDonnell, ''Priorities for National Communication Policy in the Third Word,'' *The Information Society Journal* 2.1 (1980) : 5–13.

[21]Armand Mattelart, ''Introduction: A Class Analysis of Communication,'' *Communication and Class Struggles.* Vol. I, *Capitalism, Imperialism,* ed. Armand Mattelart and Seth Siegelaub (New York: International General, 1979) 46–53.

[22]Peter M. Blau, *Exchange and Power in Social Life* (New York: John Wiley and Sons, 1964) 121–123; and John Westergaard, ''Power, Class and the Media,''*Mass Communication and Society,* eds. James Curran, Michael Gurevitch and Janet Woollacott (London: Edward Arnold, 1977) 97–101.

[23]Mauk Mulder, ''The Power Variable in Communication,'' *Communication and Culture,* ed. Alfred G. Smith (New York: Holt, Rinehart and Winston, 1966) 259–274; and Frank W. Young, ''A Proposal for Cooperative Cross-Cultural Research on Intervillage Systems,'' *Human Organization* 25 (1966): 46–50.

[24]Stuart Hall, ''Culture, Media and the 'Ideological Effect','' *Mass Communication and Society,* eds. James Curran, Michael Gurevitch and Janet Woollacott (London: Edward Arnold, 1977) 327–331.

[25]Hall, ''Culture,'' 336–346.

[26]Glasgow Media Group, *Bad News* (London: Routledge & Kegan Paul, 1976); and Glasgow Media Group, *More Bad News* (London: Routledge & Kegan Paul, 1980).

[27]Jean-Francois Barbier-Bouvet, Paul Beaud, et Patrice Flichy, *Communication et Pouvoir: Mass Media et Media Communautaires au Québec* (Parks: Editions Anthropos, 1979).

[28]Willard D. Rowland, Jr., "The Illusion of Fulfillment: The Broadcast Reform Movement," *Journalism Monographs,* No. 79, College of Journalism, U of South Carolina. Dec. 1982, 34–36.

[29]Mattelart, "Introduction," 55–57.

[30]Robert A. White, "Structural Factors in Rural Development," diss., Cornell U 1977, 141–179.

[31]Robert A. White, "Communication Strategies for Social Change: National Television Versus Local Public Radio." In *World Communication: A Handbook,* George Gerbner and Marsha Siefert, eds. (New York: Longman, 1984), 279–293.

[32]White, "Structural Factors," 58–65; Peter Singelmann, "Campesino Movements and Class Conflict in Latin America: The Functions of Exchange and Power," *Journal of Interamerican Studies and World Affairs* 6 (Feb. 1974) : 59; and Joel Migdal, *Peasants, Politics, and Revolution* (Princeton, NJ: Princeton UP, 1974), 232.

[33]Robert A. White, "Comunicacion Popular': Language of Liberation," *Media Development* 27.3 (1980) : 79–97.

[34]Cees J. Hamelink, *Cultural Autonomy in Global Communication: Planning National Information Policy* (New York: Longman, 1983) 87–124.

[35]Gavriel Soloman emphasizes that a medium must be considered under four aspects: content, technology, symbol systems, and the typical social context in which it is used. However, the most important communicative aspect is precisely the symbol systems which encode meaning within the potential offered by a particular technology. *Interaction of Media, Cognition and Learning* (San Francisco: Jossey-Bass, 1979).

[36]Everett M. Rogers, *Communication and Development: Critical Perspectives* (Beverly Hills, CA: Sage, 1976).

[37]Larry Shore, "Mass Media for Development: A Reexamination of Access, Exposure, and Impact," Emile McAnany, ed., *Communications in the Rural Third World* 19–48.

[38]Elihu Katz and George Wedell, *Broadcasting in the Third World* (Cambridge, MA: Harvard UP, 1977).

[39]Juan F. Rada, "The Microelectronics Revolution: Implications for the Third World," *Development Dialogue* 2 (1981) : 57–60.

[40]Ibid., 49.

[41]Ibid., 56.

[42]Edmund F. M. Hogrebe, *Dangers and Opportunities of Digital Communication Media* (Mexico: Instituto Latinoamericano de Estudios Transnacionales, 1980).

[43]Hamelink, *Cultural Autonomy,* 87–124.

[44]Ashok Parthasarathi, "Technological Bridgeheads for Self-Reliant Development," *Development Dialogue* 1 (1979) : 33–39.

[45]Dervin, "Communication Gaps," 74.

[46]John M. Phelan, "Automating Authority," *Disenchantment: Meaning and Morality in the Media* (New York: Hastings House, 1980) 130–146.

[47]Frances J. Berrigan, *Access: Some Western Models of Community Media,* ed. Frances J. Berrigan (Paris: UNESCO, 1977).

[48]Ibid., 197.

[49]Ibid., 145–211.

[50]Jeremiah O'Sullivan and Mario Kaplun, "Communication Methods to Promote Grass Roots Participation for an Endogenous Development Process." Paris: UNESCO, 1979.

[51]International Commission, *Many Voices,* 258.

[52]Ibid., 170.

[53]S. Bashiruddin, *Rural Press in India* (Singapore: Asian Mass Communication Research and Information Centre, 1979; and Paul Ansah, Cerif Fall, Bernard Chindji Kouleu, and Peter Mwaura, *Rural Journalism in Africa* (Paris: UNESCO, 1981).

[54]Dervin, "Communication Gaps," 87–106.

[55]Ibid., 105.

9

The Rhetorical Situation and Situational Ethics in the Symbol of the *Refugee* in the Israeli–Palestinian Arab Conflict

Samuel M. Edelman

Professor of Rhetoric and Intercultural Communication
The California State University, Chico

The Middle East remains an area, for Westerners, in which reality and appearance are often both an appearance. Myths become reality and reality future's myths. Middle Eastern ethics, intercultural concerns, and rhetorical concerns are usually beyond the perspectives of Americans and Europeans. One example of how current Middle Eastern epistemology is mysterious to Westerners is the Palestinian refugee situation. The refugee has become a rhetorical pawn in a very real game of strategy and counterstrategy. In the following pages, the rhetorical uses of the *refugee*, as a symbol to overcome exigesis as presented from dialectical and rhetorical perspectives, is offered.

Rhetoric, in the modern age, has been defined by some thinkers as the reconcilation of individual and systemic goals and constraints, frequently with the purpose of overcoming an exigence.[1] In the case of the conflict between Israelis and Arabs in the Middle East, too often, this type of reconciliation takes a distant second place to violence. For instance, in the current situation in the

West Bank and Gaza, called the *intifada*, violence has supplanted rhetoric as a favored *modus operandi* from both parties. Without motivation for two-party dialogue between Israelis and Palestinians, the only choices left for resolving conflict are violence or rhetoric focused on a third party. The motivation for two-party dialogue is lacking because for too long now both parties have developed a long cultural history of mistrust of each other. The Israelis see the Palestinians as having the sole goal of the destruction of the Jewish State. The Palestinians see the resolution to their desires as being obtained only through third party intervention, because they see the Israelis as usurpers of their right to the land. When Israelis see Palestinians refuse to directly negotiate with them, they begin to see their visions of destruction reified. In this way the world is treated to an ongoing circle of violence and recrimination which feeds upon itself in a violent, self-perpetuating, machine-like fashion. Unfortunately for the Israelis, the Palestinians have somewhat successfully co-oped much of the third-party rhetoric, previously used by the Israelis, to create the world-wide sympathy for the Palestinian cause. Much of this rhetoric is similar to the rhetoric that ultimately led to the creation of Israel in 1948 out of the British Palestinian Mandate.

THE RHETORICAL SITUATION, THE ENTHYMEME, AND RHETORICAL ETHICS

Of crucial importance to the Israeli/Palestinian conflict are a number of rhetorical concerns, any of which may be understood as part of myth creation in both rhetorical and intercultural Middle Eastern communication. The first of these concerns is that of the rhetorical situation. The rhetorical situation may be defined as exigencies which may be overcome through rhetoric under certain conditions. The rhetorical situation is an expression of the conditions permitting words to overcome a blockage or difficulty or problem. The rhetorical situation is:

> a complex of persons, events, objects and relations presenting an actual or potential exigence which can be completely or partially removed if discourse, introduced into the situation, can so constrain human decision or action as to bring about the significant modification of that exigence. Prior to the creation and presentation of discourse, there are three constituents of any rhetorical situation: the first is the *exigence*; the second and third are elements of the complex, namely the *audience* to be constrained in decision and action, and the *constraints* which influence the rhetor and can be brought to bear upon the audience.[2]

The second concern is the idea that the enthymeme is not just a syllogism with one premise missing, but an argument so closely tied to the visions, conceptions, perceptions, and myths of an audience that it is accepted even as the argument's premises are being communicated. Not all enthymeme's work with all audiences.[3]

The third concern is that of situational ethics and the resultant manipulability of concerns for auditors and communicators. Simply defined, ethics represent the evaluative, judgemental, moral twists of human communicative behavior focusing on the right and wrong of human interaction. Situational ethics represents that arena of philosophy and theology which focuses on the changeability of ethics based upon the changing conditions and contexts surrounding human communicative behavior.

Of greatest utility for examining the rhetoric of the refugee is the concern voiced in the newer concept of situational ethics that "situational perspectives focus regularly and primarily on elements of *the specific communication situation at hand*."[4] In essence, situational ethics make allowances for special circumstances. For an extreme situational perspective, judgements are made in light of each different context.[5]

From 1945 until 1948, the image of Jewish refugees, many of whom had just been liberated from concentration camps, and the images of their desire to return to their ancestral homeland, became the most persuasive arguments for the world-wide support of the creation and acknowledgement of the State of Israel. The ability of the World Zionist Organization and the Jewish Agency of Palestine to manipulate world opinion in favor of their cause through the judicious use of these images was a public relations and argumentation success. The symbol of the refugee ship became the symbol of Jewish self-determination in the face of British military intransigence. Ragged, gaunt-looking men, women, and children on rusty, decrepit boats, facing neat and crisp British soldiers and sailors on shiny, large warships, when seen in the daily newsreels, created a strong and sympathetic image. The image created by those refugees, further, had an extensive half-life. The vision of the State of Israel as a haven for refugees lasted until the early 1980s. The activities of David Ben-Gurion, the first prime minister of Israel, and of the Jewish Agency of Palestine, the shadow government of Jewish Palestine, in bringing refugees out of Europe through what was called the *Berihah*,[6] or the Jewish underground rescue activites, gained European cooperation and sympathy.[7] Then, use of the refugee image, as manifest in depictions of British anti-Jewish immigration policy by boats such as the "Patria"[8] and the famous "Exodus,"[9] became telling rhetorical strategies in developing what would become grand enthymematic arguments in the United Nations and in the ears of the world as the for a vote on whether or not the United nations should partition Palestine into a Jewish and an Arab state grew nearer. In November of 1947, the Jewish rhetorical strategy paid off and the UN voted for partition. The general effect of the use of the refugee as a rhetorical strategy was extremely positive and very long lasting.[10]

The result of these images ultimately led to a perception of the British as the evil villian in the Middle East. That image alone created the rhetorical groundwork in the development of the the enthymeme that these men and women have suffered enough; now it is time to give them a place of their own in the world. The image was also pointed, not at the Arab world, but rather at the member nations of the United Nations, with particular focus on the United States. Ben-Gurion clearly understood that the center of world power had moved from Great Britian to the United States. It would be in the United States that the future of the new State of Israel would be decided.[11]

The image of the refugee created by the Israelis was the same image needed in 1988 by the Palestinian Arab cause. Thus from 1966 to the present a new argumentative strategy, based upon an old and successful one, of the downtrodden refugee and the brutal oppressor, was employed. In the media in 1988, the world again sees graphic images of young boys, their faces covered only with *kaffieyahs*, throwing rocks at armed, uniformed, helmeted soldiers. There could be no better enthymeme. Unfortunately with enthymematic argument, truth comes with only a small *t*. The crux of the difficulty with this shift in the hero of the refugee argument lies in the historical context of the conflict which can not easily be communicated in the confines and immediacy of enthymematic strategy.

By examining the exigence, the audience, and the constraints in the current Arab use of the refugee in the Palestinian Arab–Israeli conflict, we might begin to better understand that situation. Beginning with the exigences, we can readily see two that represent essentially the same perspective. For the Israelis in prestate Palestine, the refugee was a rhetorical symbol for their larger battle to create a Jewish state out of the British mandate. This symbol was manipulated to gain adherence for the Jewish perspective over that of the Arab perspective for the third-party audience of, mainly, Europe, the United States, and Canada and Latin America. For the Palestinians, on the other hand, the refugee was originally a symbol for Arab rejection of both the new State of Israel and any settlement except the removal of both the Jews and their nation from the area previously called Palestine. Initially, Arab vision was focused only cursorily on Europe and the United States. The symbol of the refugee was primarily a rhetorical strategem for use only to communicate to Arabs. *Refugee* was used as a badge of courage for the *martyrs of the Zionists*, the Palestinians. From 1948 until the later part of the 1970's, *refugee*, for the Arab world, symbolized the steadfast rejection of any settlement with Israel and the Jews. The refugee became the prod for Arab anti-Israel violence.

Ultimately, that Arab vision changed as Palestinian Arab concerns moved away from a sole vision of a return to all the lands lost to an interim vision of the creation of a Palestinian state made up of the West Bank and Gaza. It is this interim vision that changed the Palestinian discourse and that changed Arab perceptions on who the audience was.

Now Palestinian rhetoric focuses on the poverty, frustration, and national desires of the refugee in the camps and cities and villages of the West Bank and Gaza. These are singularly different images, and they are focused on a vastly different audience. This Arab rhetorical strategy is focused, not on intra-Arab audiences, but rather, like the Israeli strategy of 40 years ago, on world wide audiences. The Arabs point their rhetorical activities primarily at the United States, the Soviet Union, and, to a lesser extent, Europe.

The Israelis were successful in their rhetorical strategy of using the refugee as a symbol for the conflict, first with the British and later with the Arabs, over the creation of the Jewish State in 1948. There is a stark similarity between descriptions of the camps for Jewish refugees in 1948 and the description of the camps of Palestinian refugees 40 years later.[12] Both Palestinian spokespersons and the media in general have used this comparison as a rhetorical strategy focused on the audience of the western world.[13] Nevertheless, the significant difference that belies the comparison lies in the fact that, in Israel today, there are no more camps, and the new immigrants have with relative success been absorbed into Israeli culture. Forty years later, the Arab refugees from Israel to such areas as Lebanon, Syria, Jordan, the West Bank and Gaza, remain unabsorbed into their new culture and still call themselves refugees.

ISRAELI AND PALESTINIAN SHARED RHETORICAL USE OF THE SYMBOL OF THE REFUGEE

The literature represents the shift of perspectives caused in part by the shared rhetorical use of the symbol of the refugee.[14] The refugee, for the Israelis, was a clear representation of the attainment of the highest degree of the Zionist dream of recreating a Jewish national home and of the reacquisition of power and of the sense of self lost in the diaspora. The refugee, for the Palestinians, though, represented the loss of power and the separation of connectedness. The Arab nation's lack of desire, or their inability to absorb or assimilate the refugees from the war in 1948 ultimately became its tool for maintaining hatred and passion.

Hatred is one of the byproducts of the refugee from both the Israeli and Palestinian perspectives. One cannot be kept in squalor for 40 years with only the hope that, one day, another armed effort will kick the Jews from Palestine and things will return as they were before without taking some toll in the psyches of even the very young. This view of the refugee is an all-pervasive perception of most Israeli writers, thinkers, and politicians with regard to the Palestinians. The world, though, through a sympathetic media and a modestly skillful PLO public relations campaign, sees the refugee in a different light; as a disadvantaged, underpriviledged, economically downtrodden people.

The statistics of both standard of living and general healthcare of Palestinians in the occupied territories is in opposition to much of the perception of the world and underscores the success of the Palestinian rhetorical strategy. Under the occupation, according to UN and Israeli figures, the standard of living in the territories has almost tripled since 1967. In Gaza alone the unemployment rate in June of 1967 was 48% in the refugee camps and 40% in the villages and cities, dropping to 0.4% in 1983.[15] Exports from Gaza and Judea and Samaria improved dramatically because of the Israeli policy of open bridges: in 1968 the territories exported less than 50 million dollars of goods; today just under 500 million dollars in goods are exported.[16] Generally, the Arabs of all the territories have a higher standard of living than those living in Egypt, Syria, Lebanon, Iraq, Sudan, and Yemen. In general the territories saw a 10% growth rate per year from 1967 to 1983, when oil prices began to drop (Israel Information Centre document). Today the growth rate is around 4% to 5%.[17] In point of fact since 1967 the per capita rise in the standard of living has been exceptional.[18]

The Palestinian Arab childhood death rate has dropped too, and general healthcare has improved, with modern health facilities being built by the dozen in the last 10 years. According to UN statistics the Palestinian infant mortality rate in Gaza dropped from 87 per 1,000 in 1968 to 41 per thousand in 1983. Health care clinics and hospitals have more than doubled in number since 1967.[19] The adult life expectancy was 48 years in 1967 versus 62 years in 1983. This expectancy is higher than that of adults in Lebanon, Syria, Iraq, or Jordan.[20]

It becomes apparent that the image created in the media, in part stimulated by Palestinian rhetorical strategies, is at variance from the statistics Israeli and UN sources provide. It is also true that, when compared to other Arab nations surrounding Israel and the occupied territories, the Palestinians have achieved a far greater standard of living. Yet, when compared to both Jews and Arabs living in Israel proper, that standard of living is much lower. Thus we see even the image of the Palestinian as an underpriviledged and disadvantaged person contingent upon the context to which they are compared. This contextual or situational concern is not only expressed in rhetorical strategies but also in the ethical communication concerns with regard to the refugee.

SITUATIONAL ETHICAL CONCERNS IN THE SYMBOL OF THE REFUGEE

As indicated in the above discussion, in over 40 years' time the Palestinian refugee has become a symbol for resistance and intransigence in the conflict between Israel and the Arabs. Alinsky's proposition that "the less important the end desired, the more one can afford to engage in ethical evaluations of means . . . and in war the end justifies most any means"[21] becomes paramount in any attempt to understand the rhetorical implications of this conflict.

Thus, the world sees in the use of the refugee as a symbol, for Israelis, one that helped the Jews of Palestine to create a nation in 1948 and to gain time and sympathy for it. Questions of ends and means in this symbol were in complete harmony. Israel was created as a homeland for the Jewish refugees of the world following World War II. For them, Israel's existence meant sanctuary and a strong feeling of solidarity with the general goals of the state.

In contrast, for the Palestinians, no such means/ends harmony exists. The Arab goal for the eradication of Israel is antithetical to the refugee goal of resettling and starting a new life. Therefore, it is incumbent upon the refugee to act as the moral guardian of the rejection of a settlement between Israel and the Arabs. The Palestinian refugee became "the means to the end" of the destruction of Israel, the soldier in the war against Israel. All rhetorical strategies and rhetorical arguments therefore focused on promoting the refugee to the status of symbolic memorial to Arab failure to live up to the end goal promised in 1948 of the eradication of the Jewish State.

The Israelis have lost the moral high ground; they were too rhetorically effective in combining both the means and the ends in the settlement and assimilation of hundreds of thousands of Jewish refugees. Conversely, the Arabs have been able to take over the high ground by usurping the Israeli end goal of creating a state for the stateless through the means of confronting refugees with Israeli soldiers. This utilization of situation ethics is a testimony to the malleability of the Palestinian cause and media sympathetic to that cause, as well as to the world's extremely short memory of history. Situational ethics still remain strong in the conflict. At one moment the PLO representatives speak about their desire to resolve the plight of the Palestinian refugees, but in the next, they promise the refugees a return to all of the land, including today's Israel.

Situational ethics are not just limited to broad philosophical concerns of the PLO; they are also intimately tied to the very languages and audiences that the various spokespersons are attempting to persuade. In English, PLO spokespersons often sound reasonable and willing to negotiate; in Arabic, the opposite is true. For example, in Yasir Arafat's, Chairman of the PLO, speech to the United Nations in Geneva on December 13, 1988, he implied that the PLO eventually would recognize Israel's right to exist. In the third part of the Palestinian plan outlined by Arafat in his UN speech he said:

> Third: The P.L.O. will seek a comprehensive settlement among the parties concerned in the Arab-Israeli conflict, including the state of Palestine, Israel and other neighbors, within the framework of the international conference for peace in the Middle East on the basis of Resolution 242 and 338 and so as to guarantee equality and the balance of interests, especially our people's rights in freedom, national independence, and respect the right to exist in peace and security for all.[22]

The translation of the speech, originally delivered in Arabic, was provided by the PLO. The general problem of translation always is a concern. Nevertheless there was a telling difference between what Arafat said in his speech and the English translation released by the PLO. which led to the United States withholding a positive response for 24 hours, until Arafat could clarify further in his now famous press conference. In the Arabic, "Arafat used the Arabic word *Aish*, which means the physical existence (life) of individuals (i.e., Israelis) and not the Arabic word *Kiam*, which means national existence of the Israeli state."[23] By ambiguously wording a phrase in English which had unambiguous contexts in Arabic, the Palestinians intentionally or unintentionally hoped to continue to only imply recognition without fully granting it. But this semantic game playing is not the true concern in the ongoing rhetorical struggle between the Palestinians and the Israelis. For the Israelis consistent and unambiguous statements of the Palestinian desire for both peace and open negotiations are crucial. They are not concerned with implied recognition but with real recognition.

The problem of consistency and reality leading toward the development of mutual trust and respect between Israelis and Palestinians is evident in the press barrage in the Arabic papers following both the Palestinian National Council's meeting in Algiers in November of 1988 and Arafat's speech to the United Nations in Geneva in December of 1988. For example, Arafat said in his Geneva speech that:

> I come to you in the name of my people, offering my hand so that we can make true peace, peace based on justice. I ask the leaders of Israel to come here under sponsorship of the United Nations, so that, together, we can forge that peace . . . And here, I would address myself specifically to the Israeli people in all their parties and forces, and especially to the advocates of democracy and peace among them. I say to them: Come let us make peace. Cast away fear and intimidation. Leave behind the specter of the wars that have raged continuously for the past 40 years.[24]

Arafat's image in English is one of hope and an outstretched hand to the Israelis to make peace. Three days later Abu Iyad, second-in-command in the PLO, in an interview with the Qatar News Agency, on December 17, 1988 contradicted Arafat's vision of moderation by stating that Arafat's declaration at the UN on the abandonment of terror did not include military attacks. He said:

> If President Reagan thinks that we will cease our attacks against Israeli military targets, I'll tell him to halt the dialogue right now. Neither military attacks nor the heroic intifadah will cease. We will continue our struggle until the Palestinian flag waves over Jerusalem.[25]

This is not an isolated statement by Abu-Iyad: in an interview with the Kuwait Newspaper '*Al-Anbaa*', while Arafat was in Sweden conferring with a group of Jewish peace activists, he stated:

> We swore that we would liberate Palestine even before 1967 . . . The borders of our state as we declared it represent only part of our national aspirations. We will work to expand them in order to realize the aspirations for all the land of Palestine.[26]

Abu-Iyad is not the only Palestinian leader whose Arabic public statements are at odds with the PLO's English public statements. For example, Sheik Abd-el Hamid Sayekh, the Speaker of the Palestinian National Council, said in an interview with '*Al-Siasa*' (Kuwait, December 21, 1988):

> We are also striving for the same objective . . . The leaser of the Moslem Brotherhood in Egypt says that even if the PLO succeeds in establishing a state in the West Bank and the Gaza Strip, this would not prevent a continuation of the struggle until the liberation of all Palestine. I say that this is what must be the goal for us all . . . We must take, and continue to ask for more, yet, without offering concessions. We will not offer concessions. Nevertheless, we are working to achieve what is possible in the present phase, and next, we will demand more.[27]

George Habash, head of the Popular Front for the Liberation of Palestine and noted terrorist, told the Lebanese weekly, '*Sabah Al-Hir*', on December 31, 1988 that:

> We shall continue the struggle until the Zionists are removed from all the land of Palestine . . . After the Palestinian State will be established it will constitute the focus for continuing the struggle against the Zionist program.[28]

Habash is not out of the mainstream of Palestinian thought. Even a more mainstream Palestinian official, Rafik Al-Natshe, the PLO's representative to Saudi Arabia, said in an interview with the Saudi News Agency on January 2, 1989 that:

> Our return to Palestine and our victory will be possible only with Allah's help and with our return to Faluja, Jaffa, and Haifa.[29]

Even Arafat is not immune to uttering inflammatory oratory attacking Israel. In a radio broadcast from Baghdad on January 1, 1989 in his Fatah Day message, Arafat said:

> The heroes of the stones have exposed (Israel's) fake democracy, and how it is a robbing and conquering entity . . . Our people are determined to continue the popular revolution and uprising against the Israeli occupier, till a free and independent Palestinian state will be established on the soil of Palestine. The rule of the people shall impose the will of the masses, and I say to you that the hour of freedom will arrive and that we are very close to victory.[30]

This ethical duality of Palestinian moderation in English and extremism in Arabic is endemic to the Israel–Palestinian conflict. The problem may be as deep as the way in which Arabic is used to express a vision of the world. Arabic is a passionate language and as such tends toward emotionalism. Almaney and Alwan point out that:

> The emotionalism to which Arabic lends itself sometimes reduces the ability of the language users to think clearly and rationally. This may account for the empty arguments in which even those Arabs who are both intelligent and learned often

> engage. The interplay of the debators' mutual emotional effects leads to a vicious spiral of rising emotions which finally reduces reasoning to a minimum and contributes to controversy and quarreling.[31]

This duality is also an excellent example of the two audience concept of Palestinian Arab rhetoric. One audience remains essentially militant and needs frequent oratorical bursts to reify its visions. The other audience, the United States, Europe, and the other member nations of the United Nations, is plied with a different rhetorical strategy based on sympathy for the plight of the refugees and a seeming willingness to negotiate with anyone but the Israelis for an end to the conflict and a resolution of the problems facing the refugees.

CONCLUSION

Richard Weaver's final words in *The Ethics of Rhetoric* have a prophetic ring when viewed in terms of the rhetorical strategies of both sides in the Israel/ Palestinian conflict:

> Lastly, the student of rhetoric must realize that in the contemporary world he is confronted not only by evil practitioners, but also, and probably to an unprecedented degree, by men who are conditioned by the evil created by others. The machinery of propagation and inculcation is today so immense that no one avoids entirely the assimilation and use of some terms which have a downward tendency. It is especially easy to pick up a tone without realizing its trend. Perhaps the best that any of us can do is to hold a dialectic with himself to see what the wider circumferences of his terms of persuasion are. This process will not only improve the consistency of one's thinking but it will also, if the foregoing analysis is sound, prevent his becoming a creature of evil public forces and a victim of his own thoughtless rhetoric.[32]

Both parties in the conflict between Israel and the Arabs are in some fashion guilty of either becoming "creatures" of public forces or "victims" of their own thoughtless rhetoric. In the case of the Palestinian Arabs, they are both creature and victim of their own rhetoric. In forty years of conflict, time and again the Arabs have shown a singular ability to "snatch defeat from the jaws of victory". For 40 years, Arab rhetoric has created untenable positions which have led to greater suffering among the Palestinian refugees. For 40 years, the Arab Palestinians have become a creature of evil forces and have been blown by either Syrian, Egyptian or Jordanian winds in directions far from their own choice. Each time the Arab Palestinians have been made worse off than before in relation to Israel.

The Israelis, for the last 20 years, too, have gradually and inexorably become creatures of evil forces. Their occupation of the West Bank and the Gaza Strip has empowered the rise of political extremism embodied in such ideologues as Meir Kahane; it has split the state as it has never been split before, and furthermore, it has engendered a moral malaise that has weakened the very fiber of the state.

In the end, both the Israelis and the Palestinian Arabs have been caught in the whirlwind of their own rhetorical strategies and ethical imperatives. The Israelis had the images they used so effectively to create their nation in 1948 turned against them by a world whose memory was extremely short. The Israelis, through their very success in combining both ethical means and ends in the absorption of over two million refugees in 40 years, has lost the moral high ground in the conflict because the world stopped looking at them as the underdog but as the mighty conqueror.

The Palestinians, while achieving a sort of media success in turning Israeli images against the Israelis, have suffered under self imposed tortures because of their inability to come to terms with a Jewish nation in their midst. The Arab focus on duality of purpose, language and audience as well as situational ethics has created the problem of mixed and confusing messages. In attempting to remain vague, so as to wrest the greatest possible advantage from the public relations perspective, the Arabs have closed off most channels of direct communication with the Israelis. Therefore, in the case of the Palestinian Arab/Israeli conflict situational ethics has been the direct cause of a significant part of the mutual misunderstandings between the two groups. These misunderstandings have been a consistent block to a resolution of the conflicts in the area.

There is hope in the end. Given the Arab proclivity toward language as action, the recent statements by Yasir Arafat tacitly acknowledging the right of Israel to exist, if repeated unambiguously and consistently and tied to some lowering of the tensions in the West Bank and Gaza, may lead to a positive spiral effect where positive rhetoric fosters positive rhetoric. There is some very small suggestion of movement in this area, given the softening and modification of the position of the Israeli Prime Minister, Yitzhak Shamir, in showing greater flexibility in the positions his government has been taking vis-a-vis the Palestinians. The rhetorical situation confronting Palestinian and Israeli is changing and fluid. If all parties can adapt and be flexible in the coming months and years, and the rhetorical strategies of both groups can become more and more focused on problem resolution rather than rhetorical aggression, then there truly is hope.

After more then 70 years of mistrust and conflict the time has come for both ethics and rhetorical strategies to move more in line with each other in resolving what has been the unresolvable: The Israel/Palestinian conflict. We can only hope for a true dialogue to begin to develop the trust both sides need to have in each other for this conflict to end.

END NOTES

[1]Many thanks to Carroll Arnold and Gerald Phillips of Penn State, and Lloyd Bitzer of University of Wisconsin for that definition.

[2]Lloyd Bitzer, "The Rhetorical Situation," *Philosophy & Rhetoric*, 1 (Winter 1968):2.

[3]Lloyd Bitzer, "Aristotle's Enthymeme Revisited," *Quarterly Journal of Speech Communication*, (December 1959): 399.

[4]Richard L. Johannesen, *Ethics in Human Communication, 2nd ed.* (Prospect Heights, IL: Waveland Press) 67.

[5]Ibid., 71.

[6]The word *Berihah* mens *flight* in English.

[7]Yehuda Slutsky, and Yehuda Bauer. "Illegal Immigration and the Berihah," in *Immigration and Settlement* (Jerusalem: Keter Publishing House. Israel Pocket Library. 1973) 35–49.

[8]The Patria was sunk during World War II with two hundred Jews perishing in sight of Haifa. See Nora Levin, *The Holocaust* (New York: Schocken Books, 1973).

[9]The "Exodus 1947" reached the shores of Palestine with over 4,000 refugees. After a fight in which 28 refugees were injured and three killed, the British then placed them on three transports and attempted to return them to France. France refused to accept these refugees who in turn began a hunger strike. They were eventually interned in Hamburg, Germany but not before world opinion was significantly aroused. See Slutsky and Bauer, op. cit., 46.

[10]The PLO attempted to replicate the voyage of the Jewish refugee ships in the summer of 1988 thereby underscoring the the PLO's use of the older Jewish refugee strategy.

[11]This was the essence of David Ben Gurion's Biltmore Address in May of 1942.

[12]David Grossman, *The Yellow Wind* (New York: Farrar, Straus and Giroux. 1988) 5; Abba Eban, *My Country: The Story of Modern Israel* (New York: Random House, 1972) 80–82.

[13]Fawaz Turki, *The Disinherited: Journal of a Palestinian Exile* (New York: Monthly Review Press, 1972) 15–16.

[14]Amos Oz, In the Land Of Israel (New York: Vintage 1983) 79–82; Grossman, op. cit., 24–25; Michael Curtis, "Israel and the Territories," in *Middle East Review: Special Report* (New York: American Academic Association for Peace in the Middle East, 1988) 4.

[15]Shmuel Sandler, and Hillel Frisch. *Israel, the Palestinians, and the West Bank* (Lexington, MA: Lexington Books. 1984) 27–102.

[16]Curtis, op. cit., 3–5. Prior to the uprising the Israeli government, Jordanian government, a Consortiuum of European countries and the United States were setting up an Arab bank to fund industrial and computer-based industrial expansion in the territories. The PLO refused to commit to the project. The first casualty of the uprising was this bank, its assets, and its personnel *Jerusalem Post* (February 1988).

[17]Curtis, op. cit., 3–5.

[18]Only under Israel have colleges and universities been developed in the territories. Under Jordan, prior to 1967, only the university in Amman, set up in 1964, could educate Palestinians. Under Israeli rule, four universities servicing over 8,000 students, six colleges serving an additional 2,000 students and a number of teacher training schools serving another 2,000 students (Israel Information Centre; *Judea, Samaria, and the Gaza District since 1967* have been created. The Palestinians, rather than use these institutions of higher learning to train teachers and engineers, have used them as training grounds for political and terrorist action. See Moshe Aumann, *The Palestinian Labyrinth—A Way Out* (Jerusalem: Israeli academic Committee, 1985). Nevertheless, the Israelis have permitted the Palestinians to continue to use these resources until the early part of 1988 when many of these institutions of higher education were closed down during the *intifada*.

[19]Curtis, op. cit., 3; Aumann, op. cit.

[20]New roads, sewage treatment plants, electric lines and telephone facilities have been built in many cases over the objections of the PLO. Less than ten years ago the Israeli government attempted to build new housing with sewage treatment, running water and electricity in Gaza as a model for Arab development. The the PLO, the local Arabs, and the United Nations led a world wide outcry condemning Israel for forcibly evicting Palestinians. The Israelis soon after took down the apartments. A wonderful opportunity to change the squalid conditions of Gaza into something more comfortable was turned into a propaganda victory for the PLO. See Curtis, op. cit., 3; Aumann, op. cit.; Israel Information Centre, op. cit.

[21]Richard L. Johannesn, *Ethics in Human Communication 2nd ed.* (Prospect Heithts, IL: Waveland Press, 1983) 71.

[22]*New York Times*, December 13, 1988, A12.

[23]Harry Kney-Tal, *What the PLO Is Really Saying* (San Francisco: Israeli Consultate Publication, January 1989) 1.

[24]*New York Times*, December 13, 1988, A12.

[25]Harry Kney-Tal, *Words Are Not Enough* (San Francisco: Israeli Consulate Publication, December 16, 1988) 1.

[26]Harry Kney-Tal, *Quotes from the Arab Press* (San Francisco: Israeli Consulate Publication, January 1989) 2.

[27]Kney-Tal, *What the PLO*, 2.

[28]Ibid., 3.

[29]Kney-Tal, *Quotes*, 2.

[30] Ibid., 1.

[31]A.J. Almaney and A.J. Alwan, *Communicating with the Arabs* (Prospect Heights, IL: Waveland Press, 1982) 81.

[32]Richard Weaver, *The Ethics of Rhetoric* (Chicago: Henry Regnery, 1953) 232.

Author Index

H

I

J

K

L

M

Subject Index